Lost in France

Lost in France

The Story of England's 1998 World Cup

MARK PALMER

With best wishes,

Mark Palmer

FOURTH ESTATE · *London*

First published in Great Britain in 1998 by
Fourth Estate Limited
6 Salem Road
London W2 4BU

Copyright © 1998 Mark Palmer

10 9 8 7 6 5 4 3 2 1

The right of Mark Palmer to be identified as the author of this
work has been asserted by him in accordance with the Copyright,
Designs and Patents Act 1988.

A catalogue record for this book is available from the
British Library.

ISBN 1-85702-855-4

Typeset in Monotype Ehrhardt by
Rowland Phototypesetting Limited,
Bury St Edmunds, Suffolk
Printed and bound in Great Britain by Clays Ltd, St Ives plc

For Henry

Contents

List of Photographs   ix

Acknowledgements   x

Preface   1

1   Funeral Week   3

2   Who's Got the Key to the Changing Room?   11

3   XAIPEO   40

4   Me and the Gaffer Are Fine   52

5   Faith   72

6   Thirty Minus Eight   88

7   France at Last   111

8   You Could Have Walked Away   127

9   Scoring   142

10 Salsa in Toulouse   150

11 We're in the Race Now, Aren't We?   166

12 A Chance to Put Things Right   179

13 Bottle   187

14 Writing on the Wall   205

Photographs

Ronaldo, Brazil (© Sporting Pictures)
Paul Scholes scores for England against Tunisia, Toulouse
(© Allsport)
Glenn Hoddle, England Manager (© Allsport)
Pete and Mark in Marseille
Dan Petrescu, Romania and Graeme Le Saux, England
(© Allsport)
Darren Anderton in the England–Colombia game, Lens
(© Express Newspapers)
French police arrest an England fan, Lens (Albert Facelly, SIPA
Press, Rex Features)
Michael Owen scores at the Argentina match, Saint-Etienne
(© Thierry Gromik, D. Nivière, V. Sichov, SIPA Press, Rex
Features)
David Beckham kicks Diego Simeone, Saint-Etienne
Glenn Hoddle watches Beckham walk off the field (© Express
Newspapers)
David Batty misses his penalty (© Express Newspapers)
David Seaman comforts Paul Ince (© Thierry Gromik, D.
Nivière, V. Sichov, SIPA Press, Rex Features)
Brazil after being defeated by France in the final, St Denis
(© Sporting Pictures)
Zinedine Zidane holds aloft the World Cup, St Denis
(© Allsport)

Acknowledgements

This book could not have been completed without considerable help and encouragement from people within and without the world of football. Eileen Leahy provided both with extraordinary kindness, and I am deeply grateful to her. I also want to thank the following for their unending support, especially when my tangled life impinged on theirs: Richard Addis, Denys and Denny Blakeway, Bella Hadjaz, Chris and Catherine Haddon, Georgie Brewster, Tamsen Bunker, Eleanor Retallack, Tony Holden. I am indebted to David Davies at the Football Association and to the England players, coaches and backroom staff, past and present, who took time to see me. I know my presence was not always appreciated by fellow journalists, but many went out of their way to help: Matt Lawton, Henry Winter, Paul McCarthy, James Lawton, Charlie Sale, Robert Hardman, Jeff Powell. Denise Glynn played a blinder selecting photographs, and Nicholas Pearson, my editor at Fourth Estate, was a joy to work with. Many thanks, also, to Mike Graham, John Haydon, the late, great Tommy Zumbo and David Price, who came up with the name *Lost in France*. Finally, I would like to thank my mother and brother and, above all, Irene, Henry and Olivia.

Preface

Paul Ince was wearing a pair of plastic slippers.

'Let's sit in the car,' he said, pointing at a black Audi and pressing the remote control to unlock the doors. Liverpool's training ground is sealed off on all four sides by concrete walls topped with barbed wire. Rows of semi-detached houses and blocks of flats line the neighbouring roads. It was cold and windy and beginning to rain. A fug built up inside the car so that you could barely see through the windows. The World Cup was four months away.

'I've got to go off and see the house I'm having built,' he said. The house was costing him almost £1 million, roughly his salary for a year.

'At what point did you know you wanted to be a footballer?'

'I was about eleven or twelve. I had nothing else to do. I was no good at school. Football was the only way out. I would have got myself in big trouble if I hadn't been a footballer, so I concentrated extra hard on it, or at least a lot harder than other people.'

Ince seldom turned up for school in Ilford, and when he did it was more to join the fights than the lessons. He signed for West Ham as a YTS trainee at the age of fourteen.

'This World Cup is the pinnacle of my career. Looking back, I know I have achieved a lot. I have played for Manchester United and I have experienced football in Italy, but this is the biggest you can get. I just wish it had come earlier. I am very aware that for me and some of the others this is our first and last chance. I get pumped up for England matches without having to think about it.

1

Like the Italy game in Rome. It was incredible. I felt the whole nation behind us. I'm not saying I don't get fired up for Liverpool, but then it's just the Liverpool supporters hoping you do well, not the whole country. That's the difference. You should have seen David Seaman in Rome. He is usually unflappable. He never shows any nerves and then six minutes before the game he said to me: "I feel sick." That's how much it means.'

I asked him about penalties. People think he froze in Euro 96 against the Germans, that he couldn't face it, that he made himself scarce when the short straws were being handed out.

'It wasn't like that. We were all standing around in groups and before I knew it they had sorted out who the penalty-takers would be. I asked, what number am I? And someone told me I was number six or seven. I really didn't have a say in it. It wasn't that I didn't want to take one.'

'If it came to it in France would you want to take one?'

'If I have to take one . . .' He looked down at the steering-wheel and then at me and then his eyes began dancing about the dashboard. 'If it means going to take a penalty . . . then I will have to take one.'

'But you would rather not.'

'If it happens it happens. You have to have guts to take a penalty. You need a lot of bottle.'

'Do you think about it much?'

'No.'

'Why?'

'Because I would feel so awful if I missed.'

Chapter 1

Funeral Week

'ENGLAND DROP DRINK-DRIVER' ran the headline above a two-paragraph story on the front of the *Daily Telegraph*. 'Rio Ferdinand, the West Ham United footballer, was yesterday withdrawn from England's squad to face Moldova next week after being convicted of drink-driving. Glen Hoddle made the decision because of "sensitivity towards the offence following the death of Diana, Princess of Wales in a car driven by a man who had been drinking".'

It was a sound move by Hoddle, even though he had been put under pressure by Keith Wiseman, the Chairman of the Football Association. The country was in an alien emotional state. The funeral was about to take place in London amid scenes never witnessed before in the United Kingdom. For nearly a week, people queued patiently to sign books of condolence in memory of someone they had never met but felt they knew as if she was a member of their own family. On day two there were five books of condolence at St James's Palace; by day four there were forty-three. Flowers piled up outside buildings and in parks. Priests, politicians, analysts and all manner of 'royal experts' tried to make sense of it, but by the end of the week it was not always clear for whom people were grieving, or why. It was profoundly moving and it was deeply disturbing. The only certainty was that the country had surprised itself by the manner of its reaction.

I visited Kensington Gardens just after Diana's coffin had arrived from St James's Palace. The park was choked. There were businessmen carrying briefcases and mothers cradling babies; there were teenagers and pensioners, cynics and sentimentalists, the buttoned up and the washed out. There were Japanese students and American tourists. Every tree had been turned into a shrine and thousands of people were camped out along the funeral route to Westminster Abbey. Two billion people around the world would watch the procession on television.

Five days later, England were supposed to play a football match. An important football match. Losing would plunge the country into deeper despondency and ensure that for the second time in eight years the world's biggest sporting extravaganza would take place without England.

Meanwhile, the Scottish FA was sinking into a quagmire by insisting that their equally crucial game against Belarus would go ahead as planned at 3 pm on Saturday 7 September in Aberdeen, a little over thirty minutes before Diana was to reach her final resting-place at Althorp. True, football matches had been played on the day of Winston Churchill's state funeral, but this was a different matter altogether. Estonia failing to turn up twelve months previously for their game against Scotland had nothing on this. The Lord Provost of Aberdeen said that if Scotland was intent on playing she would stay away as guest of honour. Then Donald Dewar, the Scottish Secretary, made it clear that he was 'particularly concerned' about the decision 'in the light of tragic events'. Tony Blair disapproved as well. And then three senior players, Andy Goram, Gordon Durie and Ally McCoist, told their coach, Craig Brown, that they did not wish to be selected. Late on Wednesday, the Scottish FA ate humble haggis and moved the match to Sunday. Scotland 4 Belarus 1.

There was no such dilemma for the English FA, but 16 Lancaster Gate would have to tread carefully. The first David Davies, the FA's Director of Public Affairs, heard of Diana's death was at 5 am on the morning she died, when Sky Sports telephoned, wanting to know the FA's official position about that afternoon's game between Liverpool and Newcastle going ahead as planned. And if the Liverpool game was cancelled then the only other scheduled League match, Crewe v. Port Vale, would also have to be stopped.

Davies telephoned Jack Straw, the Home Secretary, at 8.30 am. He and Straw were friends from their respective university student days at Sheffield and Leeds. Wait and see was the agreed policy, but not for long. By 10 am, both games had been called off.

Rio Ferdinand was going to miss out on gaining his first cap and becoming, at eighteen, the youngest player to represent England since Duncan Edwards in 1955. Hoddle, already almost a year into the job, had been generous in offering players clemency for their untidy private lives. He had stuck by Paul Gascoigne after he admitted beating up his wife, and he had been prepared to give Ian Wright the benefit of the doubt on more than a couple of occasions. There were those who thought Hoddle was guilty of double standards, but the idea of allowing Ferdinand, a convicted drink-driver, to face the Royal Box and sing the National Anthem and then stand in silence to honour the 'People's Princess' so recently killed by a man three times over the limit would have been an absolution too far.

Instead, Hoddle suggested that Ferdinand might like to talk things over with Tony Adams, who had spent eight weeks in Chelmsford Jail for driving across a dual carriageway while almost four times over the limit. It was a sobering lesson for young Rio, not least because his timing and grace on the ball were being compared variously to Bobby Moore and Franz Beckenbauer. His mother went into the witness-box on his behalf. 'Rio's devastated,' she said. 'When he went out on Saturday to celebrate he went in a taxi and came home in a taxi. Then on Sunday he went out for a meal with friends and was dropping them off when he was stopped by the police. He was breathalysed and was just over the limit. We believe that that must have spilled over from the evening before. We are not drinkers in this house and none of us realised that was possible. At home he only ever drinks water and fresh juices. Rio has such a solid head on his shoulders. He has been very strong and positive about keeping away from temptation. He's really walked the straight line.' And what had he been drinking? Alcopops.

Hoddle told his squad to disperse on Friday for the funeral and meet up again on Sunday evening. The players had been affected by Diana's death. Hoddle had been discussing with Diana's office how his players could become involved in raising money for some of her charities. 'We were hopeful that it would be settled after we had qualified,' he said. 'Whether it would have been a match or something else had not been decided. It was just in the pipeline.'

There was never any doubt that the game would be played. And there was never any doubt that there would be a minute's silence and that the players would pin black ribbons to their shirts. But what else should happen? Elton John's 'Candle in the Wind' was going to be a poignant moment at the funeral, and several F A officials wanted to invite Elton to sing it live at Wembley. Davies was keen. Graham Kelly, the Chief Executive, was worried that it would put too much of a dampener on the occasion. He feared that the players and the crowd would lose their enthusiasm for what was a crunch game. But Davies pressed on, making contact with Elton's manager in New York. Elton, he was told, would not be available but was in favour of having the song before the kick-off. Hoddle then insisted that 'Candle in the Wind' should be played before the players emerged from the tunnel because 'the sadness and the emotion of 75,000 people at Wembley might be too much for some of them'.

England had no captain. Hoddle's potential leaders were all ruled out – Shearer injured, Adams injured, Ince suspended, Pearce injured, Sheringham injured, Platt not selected. That left a choice between Gareth Southgate and David Seaman – or Gascoigne as an outside bet. It went to David Seaman.

'Some people pick captains for their experience and the respect they've got from the players,' said the Arsenal keeper. 'Some people have captains like Tony Adams, who shouts here, there and everywhere. I have the respect and the experience to calm the youngsters down. It won't make me play any different. I won't be shouting any more than usual. Part of being a goalkeeper is that you've got to organise people. Hopefully, I won't have to do much shouting at all because everyone will be up the far end.'

Seaman had signed a book of condolence at Harrods and visited Kensington Gardens with his fiancée Debbie. 'It was strange,' he said. 'I went down to Kensington Palace and a lot of people recognised me but not one bothered me for an autograph.'

Moldova (population 4,335,000) were coming to Wembley with a short, unimpressive CV. They had lost each of their five previous qualifying games, conceding thirteen goals in the process. But they had only been playing professional football for five years. What they needed was a bit of confidence, a dollop of self-belief – something you tend to look to your coach to provide. But it was hardly forthcoming. Ion Caras didn't think they had a prayer and was quite happy to say so. 'We are well aware that we are not capable of playing on a par with England, and in many ways this is because our players lack confidence,' he said. 'Most of the squad is very down. We are sitting ducks.'

The England squad seemed subdued. And for the first time in years, Paul Gascoigne was not the centre of attention. Some saw it as a sign that Gascoigne had been eclipsed by the new intake. Hoddle put it down to his growing maturity. 'He's hit thirty and has had opportunities to learn lessons. Possibly he's learnt them. I have seen a mature Gazza around the hotel and in his training. It looks as if he's trying – no, that's not right, not even trying, it seems more natural than that. He is settling down, on the pitch and off it. He is less hyper, much calmer, much more assured within himself, and that's what everyone needs.'

'They're Yugoslavs, aren't they?' said a man on the Metropolitan Line on the way to Wembley.

'Nah,' said his friend, 'they're Czechs.' They are former Soviets actually, from the bottom end of the once mighty empire, sharing borders with Romania and the Ukraine.

'They've got to be crap,' said the first man.

On the brilliant-to-crap scale, FIFA ranked San Marino 164th in the world. Moldova were 122nd, tucked just behind Burma and Ethiopia but ahead of the Faroe Islands and St Kitts and Nevis.

There was much tension around the creaking stadium an hour before kick-off. The quality of the football would be crucial but the quality of the minute's silence was going to be important too. 'Candle in the Wind' worked. People stood with dewy eyes and candles held aloft.

The guest of honour was Tony Banks, the new Sports Minister, who, with immaculate timing, was quoted in the morning papers as saying that England were not good enough to win the World Cup. He was booed as he walked – hurried, rather – along the line of players, shaking hands as the crowd shook its fists. Since his appointment, Banks had been in spectacular form. At his swearing of the ministerial oath of allegiance to the Queen he had kept his fingers crossed and then suggested that one team should represent Britain in international competitions instead of the four separate home nations. He argued that foreigners who play for English clubs should be eligible to play for England, and that ballroom dancing should be made an Olympic sport.

It was strong, solid booing. Just what was needed – a reminder that the country had not entirely taken leave of its critical senses. And then 74,102 people stood for a minute's silence and you could hear a tear drop. It seemed fitting that the official period of grieving should culminate in a football match, and that a referee's whistle would mark the moment when life would return to normal.

Graeme Le Saux, David Batty, Robert Lee and David Beckham were all one yellow away from missing out on the Italian game in a month's time. You play your strongest side available because the cliché says there are 'no easy games at this level' was the general consensus. Then news came through that little Georgia had held Italy to a draw in Tbilisi. Hoddle rested Le Saux and there was no place for Robert Lee. But Beckham and Batty played. The team was: Seaman, G. Neville, P. Neville, Batty, Campbell, Southgate, Beckham, Gascoigne, Ferdinand, Wright, Scholes.

England began in lively fashion. In the third minute Gazza was tripped but got up and patted the culprit's head.

'Gascoigne looks relaxed,' I said to Brian Glanville, seated next to me.

'He's a busted flush,' said the sage who wrote for the *Sunday Times* for more than twenty years.

There was no score after twenty minutes, then Gazza cut a swathe through the Moldovan defence and tapped the ball to Ferdinand, who missed from four yards. Eight minutes later, Beckham took a corner which was punched straight back at him. He crossed again towards the head of Paul Scholes, who sent the ball flying into the top right-hand corner. 1–0.

The injured Shearer spent the game in the Sky TV glass box. A minute into the second half, he watched Wright score his first goal for England at Wembley after a clever interchange with the busted flush. Two up and time to take off Beckham. Stuart Ripley came on for eight minutes and pulled a hamstring. Gascoigne wanted to get on with the game. He wanted to score because so many other people had made statements during the week and he needed to make his. Gascoigne must have felt a degree of sympathy with Diana. She was troubled. She was forever being chased around by photographers. And she, like him, courted publicity – and then complained about it. Gazza wanted publicity now and time was running out. Then, in the eightieth minute, he found the ball at his feet just inside the Moldovan half, trundled past two defenders, gave it to Wright, got it back and steered it past the goalkeeper. Glanville hardly stirred.

Sitting ducks now. Wright scored just before the final whistle to make it 4–0, and the Wembley crowd that fell silent at 8 pm in memory of Diana was now on its feet in anticipation of the Battle of Rome on 11 October.

> 'Are you watching,
> Are you watching,
> Are you watching I-T-A-L-EEEEEEE,
> Are you watching Italee.'

The England fans were not the only ones who seemed happy with the result. The Moldovan manager was remarkably jolly as he sat in Wembley's gloomy interview room below the medical centre beside his interpreter. 'The result was never in doubt,' said Caras. 'I always expected an England victory. It was only a question of whether the floodgates would open. England have shown that they are one of the superpowers of world soccer.' After beating a team ranked 122nd in the world. 'I hope and pray you qualify,' he went on. 'You are a great footballing country.' After Caras had left the room, his interpreter rose to his feet. 'Off the record,' he said, 'I can tell you that Mr Caras is a great supporter of English football.'

Hoddle was pleased with the evening's work. 'Everything went to plan. I was delighted with Paul. On the ball he was as good as he has been for some time. But we know that in Rome we will face a battle.' What sort of battle? 'Titanic.'

Chapter 2

Who's Got the Key to the Changing Room?

It was entirely appropriate that five days before the England–Italy showdown I found myself heading for Wembley Arena to catch a glimpse of the man who only a few months earlier had been Knockin' on Heaven's Door following a contretemps with an infected chicken. For me, my teens *were* Bob Dylan and football.

Big week, even though at the end of it there was no guarantee we would be any clearer about England's summer plans. The hype began to percolate on Sunday, with papers producing mini-sections on what everyone agreed was a massive football match. There were the ubiquitous man-by-man assessments, and sermons galore from the experts. Patrick Barclay in the *Sunday Telegraph* had interviewed Paolo Maldini, the Italian captain and son of Cesare Maldini, the coach, and was impressed. 'His smile', wrote Barclay, 'greets a familiar list of additional endowments: talent and temperament in such measure that he is surely the finest left-back of all time.' High praise from Barclay. I played on the same side as him at Wembley during a media tournament when I was on his paper. It was a shock watching him – one of the fiercest critics of hustle-and-bustle-style English football – scampering back and forth on the wing with no compass whatsoever.

Reports elsewhere gave the impression that all was not well in the Italian camp. Maldini senior had been hailed as the saviour of Italian football when he took over at the beginning of the year from Arrigo Sacchi, but after the goalless draw in Georgia the knives were out. 'Maldini, what have you done?' screamed a headline in Rome's *Corriere dello Sport*, while *Gazzetta dello Sport* concluded that Maldini was 'living in the clouds'. Italy had never failed to qualify for the World Cup finals, but there is always a first time, and in Rome it might come down to who wanted it most. And England wanted it badly.

One intriguing development was the news that Roy Hodgson, the Blackburn Rovers manager, was acting as secret agent without portfolio. Hoddle, it was reported, had asked him to compile a special dossier, of which the *News of the World* had been given an 'exclusive' sneak preview. According to Hodgson, Maldini would play with a '3–5–1–1 system – three central defenders, two of them as markers, picking up the England forwards, the other playing as a spare man'. According to Hodgson, according to the *News of the World*, that is.

'There is no dossier. There never was. There never will be. I don't know where that idea came from,' David Davies told me, as the England squad assembled at Bisham Abbey, the national training centre near Marlow. Which is not to say that Hodgson wasn't to play a part. In fact he had been asked to act as interpreter to Hoddle. 'I know we could find thousands of people with better Italian than Roy, but the danger is that they translate everything too literally. Roy will make sure, from a footballing sense, that the Italians hear exactly what Glenn wants them to hear.'

I wondered what Hodgson would be paid for this little sideline. 'Absolutely nothing,' said Davies, 'but don't tell Roy that.'

It was a big week. Before the Dylan concert I told my ten–year–old son and seven–year–old daughter that it seemed inevitable we would sell the house and that his mother and I would buy two separate homes.

'Well, I imagined something like that would happen,' said the oldest.

We didn't speak again for fifteen minutes, and I feared what he was thinking. His world was falling apart and soon it would be Christmas. Then he piped up: 'Is the England–Italy game live on television?'

Dylan's gift had always been to remind you that however bad

you feel you could so easily feel a lot worse. And then you feel a lot better.

Bisham Abbey on Monday morning was England at its best. Slight crispness to the autumnal air, leaves gently on the turn, unblemished sky, warm sun. Officially regarded as an Ancient Monument, the house and grounds of the Abbey are now home to the National Sports Centre, which is run by the Sports Council. It is set back from the road on the Berkshire side of the Thames, in a village lined by beech woods and brick-and-timber cottages dating from the eighteenth century. Here we were in 1997 with half a dozen Italian camera crews parked on the lawns training their lenses on the silvery-grey building and speculating about whether England had the skill and discipline and desire to win a match in Rome for the first time. Or would Rome do for Hoddle what Rotterdam did for Graham Taylor in 93?

Gascoigne was doing sit-ups. Hoddle was walking around with his hands behind his back. Paul Ince was throwing water over David Beckham, and Steve McManaman and Robbie Fowler were lounging on plastic chairs on the touchline after being excused doing their prep because they had played a League match the day before and needed time to recover. Tony Adams, Graeme Le Saux and Gareth Southgate were also rested. The remainder of the crew looked sprightly but the first-time shooting was woeful. Each player pushed the ball up to either Hoddle or his assistant John Gorman and got it back – sometimes on the ground, sometimes on the bobble, sometimes on the full. Most shot high or wide or straight at Seaman. Except Ian Wright, who was deadly.

Davies worked for the BBC for twenty-three years before being recruited by the FA to sharpen up its public relations. He reminded me of a middle- to high-ranking police officer at the Met, a deputy commissioner perhaps. Neatly turned out in functional lightweight suits or blazer and beige trousers – and always wearing a huge gold ring inscribed with the initials DD – he was part minder to Hoddle, part spin doctor to the FA and full-time fixer to the media. The word was that he had eyes on Graham Kelly's job as chief executive.

That day there was the small matter of a Mini Cooper sitting on the lawn outside the house. Green Flag, England's main sponsors, brought it down from Leeds as a prop for photographers wanting to reconstruct a scene from *The Italian Job*. Fair enough, but then Rob Shepherd of the *Express*, the paper for which I was now working, began berating Davies on the telephone, claiming that the Mini Cooper idea was his and his alone and that he wanted three Mini Coopers to be brought down, and the picture was going to be exclusive to the *Express*. Hoddle wouldn't have been interested if there had been 33 Mini Coopers on the lawn. He wasn't going to pose. Why pretend you're in some half-forgotten movie when you're the star of a new one? 'He's not trying to be difficult or anything,' Davies explained to me, 'it's just that this is such a big, one–off match and he is so 100 per cent focused that the last thing on his mind is whether to lark about behind the wheel of a Mini. Frankly, he can see through all that kind of stuff. Thank God.'

That first training session at Bisham had to be stopped short fifteen minutes early because Hoddle felt it was too intense. 'My job', said Hoddle, at the first of his daily press conferences, 'is to make sure that when the team is waiting in the tunnel on Saturday every single one of them will go out believing they can win.' And he already knew who those eleven men would be. He picked the team on Sunday evening but would not make it public until an hour before kick–off. The guessing–game had begun.

'Was Paul Merson's call–up anything to do with giving Tony Adams moral support?' Hoddle was asked.

'No, it was entirely football-related.'

'But will they room together?'

'No, most of the guy's single–up nowadays.'

'But Adams was having counselling on the telephone before the Georgia match, wasn't he?'

'Yes, but he's better now. As an individual his character has changed a lot.'

Adams had been injured and had only played four or five games for Arsenal since the start of the season. Off the field, he was sorting out his addiction to alcohol, his impending divorce and what he described as 'the enemy within'.

An Italian moved the conversation away from Adams. 'Do you realise', said Giancarlo Gavarotti, *Gazzetta dello Sport*'s man in London, 'that there is a feeling in Italy that you could actually win this match?' What he meant – and what was clear from his tone – was something like: 'Some Italians may now see England as an efficient, hard-working unit, but they know nothing, poor things. Whereas I, Signor Giancarlo Gavarotti, still believe your team is heavy on perspiration and light on inspiration, big on graft but devoid of craft. And my job as the long-term London correspondent of Italy's premier sports newspaper is to remind everyone of that.' 'He hates us,' said the *Daily Star*'s Lee Clayton.

Interviews at Bisham Abbey take place in the wood-panelled Warwick Room, where varnished portraits of period women stare out from the walls. There is no furniture as such, just a room full of chairs and three tables with Formica tops. At one time, journalists could talk to whoever they pleased after training, but in the age of managed news in Blair's New Britain it is Hoddle who decides which of his squad should speak, and when, and to whom.

Today was the turn of Steve McManaman, Gary Neville and Ray Clemence, the goalkeeping coach. Clemence was singled out for this ritualistic chore because he had experience of playing Italy in Rome in 1976. They were not happy memories. Under the caretaker boss Ron Greenwood, England lost 2–0, the game effectively ending any chance of qualification for the 1978 World Cup.

'It could have been a lot worse than 2–0,' said Clemence. 'We had Stan Bowles making his début, and perhaps on reflection it was not the sort of game to have someone playing his first match. I think Glenn will go for experience, pure and simple.' Which was not what he did against Italy at Wembley a few months earlier when he gave Matt Le Tissier his first full cap – and paid the price.

How much of an influence would Clemence have on Hoddle's team choice? 'We have a meeting every evening and Glenn asks us for our views, but he makes all the decisions.'

On these occasions, the players, accompanied by an F A official, sit behind a table, with journalists seated around them. Because most of the people asking the questions know the players well after dealing with them day in and day out while covering the Premier League, the mood is friendly: less confrontational, more informal than I had expected.

McManaman, a back-to-front baseball cap man who had annoyed Hoddle by not making himself available for Le Tournoi in France during the summer, was omitted from the squad for the Moldova game, but had been on sparkling form for Liverpool. He was back.

'I don't need any kick up the backside,' said the twenty-five-year-old, who, with a little help, was writing a column in *The Times*. 'Of course I want to be in the team on Saturday. But, there again, so does everyone else.'

At the other table, Gary Neville, who had smelt Italian blood five days previously when Manchester United gave Juventus a spanking in the Champions League, was showing a healthy contempt for the reputation of Italian football. 'I don't think they are any better than us. We match them man to man. It's about time we went there and beat them. I don't think it will be a nice game, but the country senses that the England team is better than it has been for some time. The boss has brought in a club team spirit.'

Neville has bright brown eyes that enliven an otherwise solemn, drawn face. He was asked how he would feel standing in the tunnel waiting to walk out into the Olympic Stadium, and it never crossed his mind that he might not actually be picked.

'I love playing for England. There is no higher accolade. I play for Manchester United but there is nothing like walking out there for your country and standing for the National Anthem. To say you are an England international gives you so much confidence.'

Steve Double is Davies's number two. He had worked for the F A for two years after being on the staff of various tabloids. His last job was investigations editor for the *People*.

'I think we come from the same neck of the woods,' he said. 'We probably support the same team.' Which is Reading. There was never a lot of choice. Never is. My father worked for Huntley &

Palmers all his adult life, and Reading always used to be known as the Biscuit Men. The Huntley & Palmers name was painted on the roof of the century-old corrugated-iron main stand, and the firm used to provide the match ball most weeks. Huntley & Palmers weren't a bad side themselves. They were in the Spartan League when I was playing for their under-18 team, which led to a trial for Berkshire schoolboys. That was the summit. I was taken off after half an hour because, frankly, I wasn't good enough. And that was it. Now it's the occasional five-a-side game behind the Arndale Centre in Wandsworth.

I told Double all this and wondered why I had burdened him with such a doleful tale. I think it was because when you are somewhere like Bisham Abbey for the first time, with people around you who either play or write about football professionally, you need to justify yourself. But I was pleased he supported Reading. Double, never the most pro-active of press officers, was sorting out applications for tickets from 250 journalists. His Italian counterparts were not making his task easy. 'I won't bore you with the details,' he said. Which was a tactful way of saying what a hideous mess the Italians had got themselves into, and if they couldn't sort out seats for a couple of hundred journalists God knows what hope there was for the paying punter ending up in the right section of the ground. Double said there had never been so many applications for press tickets to an overseas game. The biggest turn-out before this was 180 for the crucial qualifier against Holland in Rotterdam, 13 October 1993, where, as now, all England needed was a draw. I was one of those 180. It was a brutally depressing evening, made worse by my afternoon encounter with a group of English supporters in the town centre.

'Are you following us?' the spotty one had asked me. 'You are, ain't you, scumface?'

'You're either a plain-clothes copper or a journalist, ain't yer?' said Spotty's mate, who had letters tattooed on his knuckles. I couldn't read what the letters spelt, but I'm sure he couldn't either.

Before I could answer, Knuckles screwed up his face and sneered:

'You're gonna have to wise up a bit, son. You don't go following us around if you want to stay out of trouble.'

They closed in and formed a tight circle around me. The brute with the spots raised his hand in the air and slapped me across the face so hard that just for a second I thought I was going to hit him back.

'Now get down and kneel, you bastard. And kiss the flag of England.' Spotty had unfolded a Union Jack and down I went.

'Kiss it, fuck-face.' And so I did. It was more of a peck, but good enough to earn a reprieve, albeit with a suspended sentence.

'Now get out of here before we do you some real damage,' said Knuckles as I made my excuses and ran.

I wondered if anything had changed in four years. No one seemed to believe that the hard-core, hard-drinking football hooligan had disappeared. Trouble was expected in Rome. Then, on the day that the National Criminal Intelligence Service football unit identified 670 known hooligans, almost all of whom had criminal records for violence, David Mellor, head of the Football Task Force, urged the Italians not to treat the English like animals, which must have gone down a treat in the Carabinieri's canteen. Of those 670, about 70 were thought to be category C, the worst of the worst.

The plan was to search all English fans three times at the stadium, and then inspect their tickets some 300 yards from the main entrance. No alcohol would be on sale anywhere near the ground. But none of this had impressed Pat Smith, the FA's deputy Chief Executive, who wrote to all corporate hospitality firms warning that the only segregated part of the stadium would be taken up by members of the England Travel Club. Since most of these companies had bought tickets to the match in Rome it was assumed that their clients would be sitting in comfortable seats in neutral areas. But Smith knew that anyone looking like an English supporter would be thrown into an unofficial English pen. The hospitality companies were taking it all in their financial stride. 'We realise the dangers of heavy drinking on an empty stomach,' said a spokesman for Flight Options, which was taking out 800 fans on a £349 day-return

18

package from Gatwick. 'So we always ensure there is a hot breakfast on our flights.' That would do the trick.

Behind the scenes, the position was far worse than anyone realised. The Italian Football Federation was refusing to answer letters from its English counterpart, the first of which was written by Smith on 26 September, after it became obvious that the Italian police intended to shovel English supporters into unreserved seats even if they were official members of the England Members Club. In other words, it mattered not one bit whether you were a member or not. You would sit where you were told.

With little more than a week to go, Smith fired off a stinging letter to Stephano Caira of the Italian Football Federation, demanding a reply by return to her earlier missives. 'You must understand the seriousness of this matter,' she wrote. 'We are very worried that you seem to have chosen to stop communicating directly with us about these extremely important matters.' No reply. Graham Kelly, the FA's Chief Executive, then wrote to Dr Giorgio Zappacosta, the Italian Federation's General Secretary, pleading for some kind of response. He sent a copy of his letter to FIFA – which seemed to put the wind up the Italians. The next day, a fax was winging its way from Rome to Smith – but the contents were far from reassuring.

'We apologise for not having informed you day by day about the situation,' it said, 'but our silence was due to the fact that no final decision was taken to solve the matter and all the suggestions and hypotheses were subject to frequent changes . . . we kindly ask you to communicate all the necessary information you have regarding the transfer of your supporters directly to the attention of Mr Francesco Tagliente.'

A fiasco was assured. The only question was whether it would be a bloody fiasco.

At Bisham, Hoddle was living up to his reputation as being expansive when he wanted to be and virtually monosyllabic when he didn't. 'Are you aware of this business involving Paul Gascoigne and an

Italian photographer?' was the opening gambit in the Warwick Room.

'That's private and I won't discuss it.'

What Hoddle wished not to discuss was the rumour that Paul Gascoigne would be served with a writ on landing in Italy. Lino Nanni, a photographer who Gazza had attacked in Rome on 27 January 1994, during his Lazio days, had instructed lawyers to seek compensation. Gascoigne was convicted in his absence and given a suspended jail sentence of three months, but Nanni, a well-known paparazzi snapper, wanted personal revenge.

Hoddle's plans for Gascoigne in Rome were simple. No one would talk to him before the match and he would only be seen in public during the team's one open training session twenty-four hours before the game. 'But will you take extra security for him?' Hoddle was asked.

'We will take security but not extra security.'

'He's going to get pretty hyped up, isn't he?'

'Actually,' said Hoddle, 'before the Moldova game he was far more mature. He wasn't getting carried away by all the hype. As a result I think he could be a better player now. He used to run a lot with the ball. Now he plays delicate one-twos. He's reaching that age, around twenty-nine or thirty, when there is a new set of curtains that opens for a footballer.'

Exit Hoddle, enter David Beckham and Graeme Le Saux, who took up their respective places behind the tables. I joined the Beckham huddle. You don't get a lot of circumspection from Becks, but he has a mischievous grin that frequently breaks into a huge smile. He had a reputation for petulance, but as he sat sheepishly at that table he came across as nothing other than Posh Spice's almond-eyed little lamb.

Beckham is the son of a kitchen maintenance man and a hairdresser. He left Chingford High at sixteen, having failed all his GCSEs, but he didn't care because he had known since the age of eight when he played for Ridgeway Rovers on Sunday mornings that he wanted to be a footballer. And here he was sitting in front of a dozen scribblers all hanging on his every word, every nuance.

Because, deep down, every man in the room would have given anything to be David Beckham.

'You've got a bit of a cold, David.'

'Nah, not really. Nothing serious. Bit bunged up.' He was asked to describe what it had been like in the last few months when his face had stared out from the back, front and middle pages of newspapers and magazines. When sponsors and ad-men had been queuing outside his gate. And when Bobby Charlton had called him a sensation.

'It's been incredible. People now expect a lot from me. When I don't score they say something is wrong with me, but I don't mind. I would rather people were talking about me than not talking about me at all. I haven't scored for England yet and I would love to grab one on Saturday. A long shot – something spectacular. As a young boy I had dreams of doing something like that. It would be amazing.'

That afternoon, some of the players went to see the film *Spawn*, a sci-fi romp about a government assistant who returns from hell half-man, half-demon. Gascoigne went fishing. Le Saux read his book. And Adams went further into himself. Hoddle could not wait to get his players out of the country and into their Italian camp forty-five minutes from Rome, where they would not read English newspapers, not be offered alcohol, and would eat only food prepared by the team chef, Roger Narbett, on loan from the Lygon Arms in the Cotswolds.

It was pouring at Luton Airport. The under-21 squad arrived first, greeted by about forty admirers, mostly schoolgirls and professional autograph-hunters. A man with a centurion hat was waiting in the rain to have his picture taken. Then an FA official swept up in a blue Rolls-Royce Corniche. Rio Ferdinand led a charge into the airport newsagents to begin a run on strawberry splits, while other members of the squad stocked up on reading material – *Loaded* and *FHM* and *Maxim*. Several of the schoolgirls followed the players into the terminal and no one turned down requests for autographs or refused to pose for photographs. All were unfailingly polite with the woman at the till. 'They always come in here on their way out to big games', she told me, 'but this time I didn't recognise any of them. Where was Gazza and that David Seaman?'

If you blinked you would have missed them. Hoddle was running the operation like some secret underground mission. He was about to take his men deep behind enemy lines, where they would be immunised from the outside world.

There was just enough time to raid the shop in the departures lounge, where Gascoigne, Ince and Merson headed for the pick'n mix sweet stand. Gazza began to pop sweets into his mouth, but spotted a security camera on the wall staring at him. He found it unbearably funny. Merson was into mags in a big way. *Hello!*, in which he had starred recently after being taken back by his wife following his drug, drinking and gambling rehabilitation course, was on top of his pile.

Hoddle and his backroom staff wore Paul Smith suits and gold ties – and obligatory World Cup 2006 badges pinned to their lapels. The players were allowed to wear tracksuit bottoms and sponsored jackets. David Seaman was taller than I had imagined, Ian Wright shorter. Walking across the wind-swept tarmac in driving rain to board Britannia Flight 808, I discussed the blustery weather with Seaman. When I told him it was close to 80 degrees in Rome, he seemed pleased. He climbed the steps at the front and I went up the ones at the back. That's the way it is. Players in the front, media at the back, and FA officials and assorted bottle-washers in the middle.

Shortly before landing, the captain gave his team-talk: 'I want to wish you the best of luck on Saturday,' he said, and then added, 'But it's not luck of course. It's skill. Thank you and goodbye.'

The Italian staff at Rome's Ciampino airport were pleased to see Gascoigne and Gascoigne seemed pleased to see them. He signed his name a few times and went merrily on his way. It could not have been more different to the only other time I had travelled on the same plane as Gascoigne. It was the summer of 1992 when, after recovering from his self-inflicted injury sustained in the Cup Final, he finally went out to join Lazio.

It was some arrival. The pandemonium began immediately on

landing at Leonardo da Vinci airport, where TV crews had been allowed into the arrivals area to film the man who was meant to lead Lazio to the top of Serie A. Once we had shown our passports it was like being sucked into one of those water flumes where you twist and turn out of control before being spat out at the bottom on your backside. There were at least a thousand fans waiting to hail Caesar, the most important of whom was a bearded giant called Augusto, who used to be a wrestler. He had been appointed Gazza's bodyguard. Augusto was no intellectual, but he didn't need to be to steer his charge through the crowd and into a waiting limo, which was then escorted by police outriders to the hotel near the Villa Borghese.

Gazza had brought his brother Carl and friend Jimmy 'Five Bellies' Gardner with him to help adjust to life as an employee of Lazio. You feared the worst, but as Carl and Jimmy cracked open the Peroni, Gazza sipped mineral water, and there was a steely determination about him. I had booked into the same hotel as them. His sense of humour had flair. Within hours of arriving, Gazza had made his brother ring the front desk to tell the concierge to get hold of Augusto because Lazio's star signing had gone missing. The words escape and kidnap were mentioned. Augusto raced up the stairs and into Gazza's room, where he found the window wide open and a pair of trainers sitting on the sill. Gascoigne was hiding in the cupboard.

There was no such messing about this time. Within ten minutes of setting foot on Italian soil, Gazza and the rest of the squad were on a coach heading for La Borghesiana hotel complex, on the outskirts of the city. Customs, passport control, baggage collection were all waived as Hoddle whisked his team into the night through a side-door. A getaway bus was waiting, watched over by security men with barking dogs. And there was no sign of Signor Nanni.

On the coach, I came across Charlie Sale, from the *Express*. He wasn't on the plane because he had spent a couple of days at the Italian FA's technical headquarters at Coverciano, near Florence, where Italy were staying in five-star comfort amid saunas, tennis courts and a fully equipped injury clinic. Charlie had turned native.

'They look remarkably confident and relaxed,' he said. 'I didn't detect any signs of pressure. They think they will win and I agree with them.' So I bet him £20 that England would beat Italy, with no bet if it ended in a draw. Charlie made much of the way Italy seemed so at ease with the press. Unlike England's, their training sessions were open to the media and reporters were allowed to collar anyone they wanted afterwards. This was a refrain that could be heard day in and day out among the English media pack, who resented the lack of access to players.

The England coach believed in control and secrecy and subterfuge. At the beginning of the week there was a danger of this strategy getting out of hand when an FA official telephoned the sports editors of every national newspaper asking them to resist speculating on what the England line-up might be ('Could you fray the edges a little, please,' were the exact words) in case it gave an advantage to the Italians. Speculation went ballistic.

England's hotel was out of bounds. The daily press conferences were held on neutral ground in a hotel roughly equidistant between the players' out-of-town resort and the media's accommodation near the main railway station. On Thursday morning, Hoddle brought along Tony Adams, Teddy Sheringham and David Seaman. There wasn't a lot to ask Sheringham, and Seaman found himself discussing the floodlights in the Olympic Stadium.

But Adams was a different matter altogether. He was an alcoholic. We knew that. He went regularly to Alcoholics Anonymous meetings, we knew that too. We knew he had done time in jail for drink-driving. We knew he was estranged from his wife, who was battling against a drug habit; that he had started reading books and was considering sitting for an exam; that he had shown an interest in the piano and that he was heavily involved in a course of psychotherapy. What we didn't know was how all these things had combined to affect the man.

'How is the mood in the camp, Tony?'

'The mood?' he said, rocking gently back and forth, staring at his audience without looking at anyone in particular. 'I would say it is . . . serene.'

Adams looked so calm, so detached, that I thought he must be on medication.

'You seem a different man, Tony.'

'Thank you,' replied Adams, after a long pause. 'What you are seeing is a released man. I am not being eaten up any more. And I have taken the good points from my professional life and brought them into my private life. I have a different type of addiction now – an addiction to life. An addiction that makes me want to get up every Monday morning to try to prove myself as a person and on the football field. You don't get many opportunities to play in World Cup finals, and I'm running out of time.'

'Did you in the past take your professional life for granted?'

He stared into the middle of the room and paused.

'It's not that I took things for granted. I always realised I was a lucky guy. It was just that I got lost along the way.'

'You used to be known for going round the dressing room banging your head against the walls. You don't do that any more, do you?'

'Banging on doors has never won football matches.'

Hoddle, with Hodgson seated next to him, then gave his version of events inside the England bunker. Beckham still had a heavy cold and was resting in bed, and Southgate was carrying an injury. Then Hodgson stood up and began rubbing his thigh as he translated Hoddle's words into Italian. Davies looked on benignly as the Italian journalists scribbled down details of Southgate's not very secret injury, which turned out not to be an injury at all.

Hoddle was expected to announce in the next twenty-four hours that Adams would captain the side. He seemed quite content with his frame of mind, revealing that he had written to him in prison but that Adams at the time was not ready to receive any advice. 'But he is now,' Hoddle said. Adams was reading *The Celestine Prophecy* during the Rome trip. So was Hoddle. They appeared to be on the same wavelength.

The Italians, led from the front by Gavarotti, wanted to know why Gascoigne was not allowed out to meet the gentlemen of the press, given his former connection with the Romans. The answer was implicit in the question. All it needed was Gazza to see a past enemy in the back row for all hell to be let loose.

'We are here to win a football match,' said Hoddle. 'I told Gascoigne he can't do a press conference and he accepts that.'

'But', said Gavarotti, 'if Gascoigne is, as you suggest, a changed man, showing a new maturity, why is it you think that he could not cope with answering a few questions?'

'That is what I have decided,' said Hoddle.

'You seem to be insisting on an old Soviet-style regime,' Gavarotti replied.

Afterwards, I sat next to Gavarotti on the coach back to the hotel and invited him to expand on his thoughts about Hoddle's England. He did so with relish.

'It has to be like this,' he said, 'because Britain is unlike any other country in Europe. How many drug-addicts, wife-beaters and alcoholics are there in any other team? There's your answer. I can understand Hoddle not wanting to let Gascoigne out of the camp. The man is a nutter. Gascoigne has been a nutter all his life and always will be a nutter. Did you see him at the airport last night? As soon as he saw a policeman he began shaking and acting like a madman. Hoddle knows that if he brought him here he would be a gibbering wreck and then would not be in any condition to play the match. That is the reality. Hoddle says he has matured, but he has obviously not matured enough to behave as a normal human being. We should not be surprised by this.

'I was talking to someone yesterday at the Italian embassy who was saying that Britain is ranked forty-fourth in the world when it comes to general standards of education. Italy is considerably higher than forty-fourth. So we should not be amazed that Italian football players are better-educated, better-mannered and generally more civilised than their English counterparts. It is one of the great myths of the modern world that England is a sophisticated country. It is a myth reinforced by other countries who still like to see England as it was in 1850, when it could genuinely claim to have international influence. The tabloid press is one such symptom of the breakdown within English society. We do not have a tabloid press, so the players can come to a press conference and say what they like without thinking that anyone will twist their words into something completely different. You could see what a helpless country Britain has become by the reaction to Princess Diana's death. People were lost. They did not even know what to do during the funeral. Should they clap or remain silent? People have been clapping at funerals in Italy for years and years.'

We were getting off the point.

'Well, in football terms England has taken great steps to improve. You have gone from thinking some years ago that you have nothing to learn from foreigners to thinking now that only foreigners are worth having in your teams.'

It was only when I asked him who he thought would prevail on Saturday evening that he clambered on to the fence. 'Pound for pound, Italy have more ability, more flexibility, more skill, but the difference now is not as great as it was. Anything could happen on Saturday night.'

That evening I had dinner with Jeff Powell, from the *Daily Mail*, David Miller, from the *Daily Telegraph*, Roy Collins from the *People* and James Lawton, from the *Express*. We all named the team we would like to play on Saturday and then we named the eleven we thought Hoddle would play. None of us got it right. Powell and Miller thought Hoddle might easily do something stupid, as he did for the home game against Italy when he picked Le Tissier. Powell went as far as saying that he thought Shearer might become to Hoddle what Lineker was to Graham Taylor, because the England coach 'doesn't want anyone to become too big a star while he's around'. There seemed little evidence of this, but whereas the majority of the main football writers – known as the Number Ones or The Groins, as in groin strains – had swung four-square behind Hoddle. Commentators like Powell, Miller, Collins and Lawton – the elder statesmen – were a long way from being convinced. They doubted he had the character for the job. They disliked his haughtiness, his lack of clubbability. 'We are not fans with typewriters,' said Powell.

*   *   *

Italians woke on Friday to discover that they were without a prime minister. Romano Prodi had resigned after his far-left Communist cohorts withdrew their support over the government's 1998 budget proposals. No one seemed overly concerned in the Stadio Olimpico when the Italians arrived for training. It was a glorious morning and an awe-inspiring sight as twenty-two footballers ambled around the pitch looking like lions on the prowl. The huge empty stands made these millionaires look even more impressive, more dangerous. They trained for ninety minutes, concluding with an eleven-a-side game using only half of the pitch. Afterwards, I wandered down the tunnel and waited for the players to emerge from their dressing room. They were polite and patient. Gianfranco Zola looked so at ease that you had to remind him that Italy could possibly fail to qualify for a World Cup for the first time in their history.

'I don't think so,' he said. 'Really, I don't think so.'

I began to see Charlie Sale's point. Then Lawton started reminiscing about the days when he used to give Bobby Charlton a lift home after training.

'Now no one trusts anyone,' he said. 'I live in Cheshire, just down the road from Liverpool's young sensation Michael Owen. The other day I was thinking how I would like to go and knock on his door and tell him we are neighbours, and that if he ever wanted to chat I was just up the road. I thought I could be a sort of uncle figure to the young boy, help him along, take an interest in his career. But of course he wouldn't dare talk to me. His agent will have told him not to open the door unless there was money up front. It's very sad and there is nothing we can do about it.'

Things changed shortly after the 1970 World Cup when newspapers began signing up footballers to write columns. The footballer talked on the telephone to a journalist and the journalist produced a few words consistent with the player's general train of thought. Tabloid circulation battles didn't help retain much trust, and then along came the agents, 15-percenters who rammed a wedge between the players and press. So who could really blame Hoddle for his obsessive secrecy and slavish cosseting of his team?

'Look,' said Davies later that day as England arrived at the stadium for a final kick-about, 'I know what people are saying. I know there are complaints about the way we have gone about this, and, who knows, we may do it differently in France if we qualify, but this was our plan all along. We just wanted the team to be completely shielded. Call it control if you like. We think it's what is needed at this particular time.'

By this stage, Jeff Powell was desperate to unburden himself. He had been grumbling all week. That morning he wrote in the *Daily Mail*: 'Get behind the lads, is the order of the day, issued by everyone from the national coach and the team captain to the sanitation consultant operative responsible for the lavatories at Lancaster Gate . . . Getting behind the lads obliges constant repetition of this mantra: We are the greatest. Never mind that Italy won at Wembley earlier this year. Never mind that their World Cup record makes "Football's Coming Home" sound more like a cracked old satire than the new anthem of our national game. Never mind that the last time England won in Italy the Sixties had only just started swinging. This is triumphalism gone mad.'

I didn't get it. I couldn't detect an abundance of triumphalism in the England camp, and there seemed to be a healthy dose of scepticism simmering through the press corps.

There was an intensity about England's training that made the Italian session look casual, complacent even. It was a muggy evening. And a muddled one, too. But that, it later transpired, had been the big idea all along. Hoddle had told his squad before leaving London what his team would be – but with twenty-four hours to go he was determined to keep the world guessing. You couldn't help thinking he was doing this more for his own sake than anyone else's. Would it really make a huge difference to the Italians if McManaman was to play instead of Beckham or if Gary Neville would play at the back instead of Southgate? Hoddle must have believed so, because as the rest of the squad divided up into teams to play a game of one-touch, Southgate sat forlornly by a corner flag with the physio doing some stretching exercises, and Beckham was asked to impersonate that man on the bus with a blocked-up nose who is in desperate need of a packet of Tunes.

The Number Ones were not sure what to make of it. Their respective sports desks were waiting for their copy to drop, in which they would announce the 'probable' team. At least they would get the name of the captain right. Hoddle had announced in the morning that contrary to what he had led everyone to believe, Adams – thirty-one that day – would not be in charge after all. Paul Ince was to have the job. 'Paul is coming back to Italy and that will give him a lift', said Hoddle. 'He's in the hub of the side and vital to the team. The Italians respect him and slightly fear him, so that was an important consideration in my decision. Tony's been out for a long time. He's done a lot of good work in a short period but I just don't want to put that extra responsibility on his shoulders. It simply comes down to the fact that I don't think Tony is quite mentally prepared to be captain on such an occasion.'

Beckham suddenly bent double and called out: 'I can't breathe.' He was escorted off.

The streets of Rome were filling up. I took an evening stroll to the main train station, where groups of English fans were gathering in bars and on street corners. The police looked nervous. They moved swiftly into a bar to break up a group of Englishmen who looked more menacing than they were. There was a scuffle. A few chairs were thrown across the bar and about six of them were marched off into police vans waiting outside. The huge crowd that had gathered on the opposite pavement to watch this showdown gave it an importance it never warranted, and the sight of police vans with their lights flashing added to the drama. But when I came across Ben Fenton, a *Daily Telegraph* news man who had been sent out on what the papers call 'hooli-watch', he had just got off the telephone to his news desk stressing that there had been nothing so far to warrant an 'English Hooligans Go On Rampage' headline.

Back in the media's billet, the hotel manager was pacing up and down. He was upset about an incident the previous night when someone urinated in the lift. John Warren, who was handling the media's travel arrangements on behalf of the FA, had been summoned to explain how such a thing could happen. A former policeman, Warren had his suspicions about the identity of the culprit but could never prove it. It might have been one of the Japanese tourists in the hotel, but somehow they didn't look the type to have come all the way to Rome to relieve themselves in a hotel lift.

By noon on the day of the match, there were estimated to be 12,000 English fans in Rome. Paul Shadbolt was there with his friends Andy and another Paul, all from Barnet and all members of the England Travel Club for nearly ten years. They had done St Peter's Square, Piazza Navona and the Colosseum. An Italian hospital was never on their itinerary. They were getting three nights in Rome, return flights and tickets to the game for £335. Paul had been in Italy with England during the 1990 World Cup for six weeks and in Sweden for the 1992 European Championships. He had travelled to Poland a couple of times, and Norway and Holland. He even followed England in the United States *after* they had failed to qualify for the last World Cup.

Bobby Robson was in town. He was reading a newspaper in a corner of the hotel foyer when I interrupted him to ask the question I had wanted to ask for seven years.

'Had you ever thought of taking off Peter Shilton and bringing on Chris Woods shortly before the end of extra time in the 1990 semi-final?'

Robson looked me up and down and stood up. He began pointing his finger. 'Now look here. I don't know who you are or what you are doing here but I want to tell you that if I had done that and Chris Woods had made a mistake – say he let a penalty roll under his body – people would have crucified me for taking Peter off. So there's your answer thank you very much.'

'But did you ever seriously consider it? Woods was taller than Shilton. He would have been fresh. He would have relished coming on with the chance of becoming an instant hero, glory at the eleventh hour. And the Germans would not have known what to make of it. They might have panicked. Wouldn't it have been worth a try?'

'Maybe,' said Robson, 'but Chris Woods would have been cold. He might not have been able to read the pace of the ball. But, yes, I did think about it – for a fraction of a second. It was an option

31

that went through my mind but I was not prepared to risk it. Is that good enough for you?'

Her Majesty's Ambassador to Italy, Thomas Richardson, hosted a large lunch party at his residence off the Via Conte Rosso to celebrate the sixtieth birthday of Sir Bobby Charlton, although the main object of the exercise was to drum up support for England's bid to stage the 2006 World Cup finals. What a house. It sits on a hill, surrounded by palm trees and lime bushes. An ancient ruin runs through the garden.

Tony Banks was there, presumably to support the rival German bid, and Alex Ferguson showed up too. On arrival, the ambassador introduced his guests to Sir Bobby while someone took a photograph. I was twelve years old in 1966. Roger Hunt was my favourite player because he played up front like me. At school, we always pretended we were various players. Some boys imagined they were Alan Ball or Geoff Hurst or Nobby Stiles. A few even called themselves Bobby Charlton. No one ever dared to be Bobby Moore.

I had met Bobby Charlton once before – in Qatar of all places, during the Asian group qualifying competition for the 1994 World Cup. At that time he was a paid-up member of the Japanese Football Association as they battled with South Korea to stage the 2002 finals. I had asked him if he would spare ten minutes for a piece I was doing about Japanese football.

'Only if you buy me a cup of coffee,' he said. We talked about Japanese football, but the only question on my mind was how I could persuade him to pose for a photograph with me once our coffee break was over, and how I could do it privately and not in front of dozens of journalists who might regard it as unprofessional. We drained our coffee.

'I wonder if you really know what it meant to a twelve-year-old boy when you scored those two goals against Portugal in the semi-finals,' I said. 'And I wonder if you wouldn't mind if I got someone to take a photograph of me with you outside.'

We went outside and I asked a swimming-pool attendant to take the picture. Charlton put an arm round me and said: 'Say cheese, it's getting hot out here. And, yes, I do understand what it meant.'

His speech at the Ambassador's lunch was short and simple. Only when he got on to the 2006 bid did he begin to sound a little shaky. 'We like a good fight, us English,' he said, referring to the battle to stop Germany gaining the nod in our place. Police sirens sounded in the distance.

Then Davies got up and gave a fifteen-minute précis of his early life, highlighting the moment when he was arrested for nothing in particular in some foreign land and was thrown into jail. In his cell he had asked one of the guards if he had ever heard the name, Bobby Charlton, at which – hey presto – the guards let him out and they all ended up sharing a few tinnies while basking in the genius of Charlton. No one believed him.

I arrived at the stadium two hours before kick-off. The eternal wait in that city was nearly over. I could feel my pulse quickening as I climbed the stairs. The stadium was throbbing. England supporters were mainly behind one of the corner flags next to the *Curva Sud* to the left of the main stand as you looked out from it. A live band was on stage, while two huge screens showed footage of Italian and English past football triumphs.

A woman in a red suit who showed me to my seat said something, but I could not hear her above the music. I felt a surge of adrenalin race through me and would have tested positive if I had had a drugs test. I left the stand and made another entrance just for the sheer thrill of it.

The Italian team walked out to inspect the pitch at 7.30 pm, dressed in blue suits and ties. The screens showed the goals from their victory against Spain in the 1982 finals.

England spilled on to the field ten minutes later in their tracksuit bottoms and Umbro bomber jackets. There was no Paul Gascoigne. They walked off but reappeared shortly afterwards in their football kit. Le Saux waved to the crowd and clenched his fist. Then Gazza came out and the England supporters to my left erupted. The sound rose and reverberated back off the inside of the Bedouin-style roof like a clap of thunder.

The team was: Seaman, Campbell, Adams, Southgate, Le Saux, Beckham, Ince, Gascoigne, Batty, Sheringham, Wright – although that was not how the Italians spelt their names. England's walking injured had either made miraculous recoveries or Hoddle had been telling porkies all week.

At 8.40 pm, as the players gathered under the running track before emerging like frogmen from the depths of the stadium, the Italians behind both goals suddenly flicked over square cards to display the colours of their national flag. Ince led his side out and both teams lined up in front of the main stand. Adams was on the end, staring into the ground. You couldn't hear anything the announcer said, but presumably he ran through the two teams. No one knows if the national anthems were played or not. A banner next to the part of the ground where most of the England supporters were seated read: 'Fuck Off England'. Another, 'Good Evening Bastards'.

Italy kicked off and within a few seconds Wright gave the ball away. Italy broke down the left but their attack was snuffed out by Serenity Adams showing impeccable timing. After eleven minutes, Ince was involved in a clash with Albertini and reeled away holding his head in his hands. There was blood pouring from the wound and he had to go off. Cesare Maldini was on his feet, barking orders. A FIFA official told him to get back in his kennel. Gary Lewin, one of the physios, rushed up to the bench and told Hoddle something. I imagined he was saying that Ince could play no further part, but later it transpired that he was shouting: 'Who's got the key to the changing room?'

Then Sol Campbell went in hard, again, and was booked. If England qualified he would not be allowed to play in the opening game unless FIFA agreed to a general yellow card amnesty. Ince suddenly reappeared and went up to Albertini and gave him a pat. He had been out of the game for eight minutes. Wright wasn't getting a look-in and his first touch had deserted him. He won nothing in the air until the thirty-fifth minute. Paolo Maldini collided with Ince and went down holding his calf. His dad strutted up and down the touchline. An electrically-powered stretcher buggy came on to the pitch and removed the Italian captain. A few seconds later, Ince fired in a low shot straight at Peruzzi's body. Maldini came back but not for long. The Italians were in trouble. Di Livio fouled Le Saux and was booked. I hoped Gavarotti was enjoying it.

The English and Italian fans were throwing bottles of San Benedetto water at each other. On the pitch, the Italians were running out of space in midfield, where Beckham, Batty, Gascoigne, Ince and Le Saux formed a five-man barricade. Zola drifted further and further to the left to find a way round it. The tackling was hard. The police started wielding their batons. It was getting nasty. People were hurt. A policeman was rushed out of the stadium on the same stretcher as the one that had carried off Maldini. Gascoigne got himself booked, but England were in control. The Italians looked ragged, unimaginative, flustered. Wright began to come into it more. Batty was running himself into the ground. The three-man back line – Southgate, Adams and Campbell – was solid. The referee added on *seven* minutes.

Early in the second half Italy had England pinned down. It was going to be a long forty-five minutes. Zola was looking increasingly comfortable, and I assumed there was no way we could keep them out. And then Maldini took off Zola. On came Alessandro del Piero. For the next fifteen minutes England looked in danger, and Maldini seemed to take heart, waving his arms in the air and gesticulating at his players. The FIFA man tried to calm him down. Remember the pitiful sight of Graham Taylor in the dying minutes of that game in Rotterdam? It was Maldini's turn to suffer now.

Blood was spilling from Ince's face, and he left the field for a second time to have a bandanna wrapped round his head. There were twenty-five minutes to go. Del Piero went down in the England penalty area. It was a penalty. It couldn't be a penalty. Del Piero was booked for diving.

It was still unpleasant in the stand to my right. On the pitch, Di Livio chopped down Campbell and was sent off. I remembered when Italy had ten men against Nigeria in the USA and came back from a goal down to win 2–1. Then Beckham took a corner. It came out to Ince who rifled a shot into the keeper's body. Confidence soared.

Into the last ten minutes, and Italians on the far side began throwing debris on to the pitch. Small holes appeared in the crowd where Italians were leaving early. In the eighty-fourth minute, Nicky Butt came on for Gascoigne. Hoddle was being told to sit down by the FIFA official. John Gorman, Hoddle's assistant, was looking at his watch every three seconds and the English fans let out a long shrill whistle. But the Dutch referee just would not blow. In my row, we were all on our feet. Some lads from *Four Four Two* magazine were standing on their seats. The *Daily Star*'s Lee Clayton had fleas in his pants. At one point he almost disappeared under his desk.

England were going to qualify for the World Cup, and yet I couldn't prevent myself from thinking something terrible was about to happen. I looked at the referee and saw in him all the vindictive authority figures I had ever come across. He still wouldn't blow the whistle. We were into extra-extra injury time when Wright was put through. He rounded the keeper. The goal was empty but the angle impossibly acute. When he hit the post the Italians were still in it. It was their turn for a final hurrah. Del Piero attacked down England's right flank and crossed to Vieri. As Vieri rose it was like watching a cowboy slowly take his gun from his holster. Seaman just stood there and stared. Vieri missed. 'I knew it was going wide as soon as he headed it,' Seaman said afterwards. No one else did. The referee looked long and hard at his watch for the last time. When he finally blew, Wright went down on his knees and cried. Clemence embraced Hoddle, who embraced Gorman, who hugged Ince, who fell into the arms of each player in turn. Gascoigne went to the English fans and shook his fists and they went crazy.

David Miller sat down in the press conference room and said: 'It was a penalty, no question about it.' And Jeff Powell agreed with him. I went down to what's called the 'mixed zone', where you can talk to players as they emerge from the dressing room. Ince explained how the team doctor, John Crane, had given him six stitches and then smeared a blob of grease on his cut, like they do with boxers, but that the blood began to ooze out. The only answer had been a swathe of bandages. 'But I don't care,' he said. 'We played so hard and in the end we deserved it. The last ten minutes were a bit panicky, they had ten men and maybe we let go of it a bit, but we dug in there and we had enough chances to do it. I think over the campaign we haven't conceded a goal away from home, and that says a lot. We were fully focused, nothing was going to take our attention away. The fans have been fantastic. This is a great day for the team, a great day for the fans and a great day for English football. There is a feeling now that we can go on and actually win something.'

Hoddle looked relieved. 'We deserved it. We passed the ball well and we kept our heads. It's great for the nation. It's eight years since we qualified and now the hard work starts.' Wright had to be restrained when he was interviewed in the tunnel. He was delirious. 'We knew we had to dig in and we did. I'm going to the World Cup hopefully – please pick me Glenn Hoddle.'

Adams was one of the first out of the dressing room. He walked with his head down and boarded the bus without a word to anyone. There was no sign of Southgate or Sheringham. They had both been selected for a drugs test, but neither of them could produce a sample for two hours after the final whistle.

It was already 1 am, but the police were refusing to let many of the England supporters leave the stadium. Hundreds were going to miss their flights home. Those staying in Rome would have to walk back into town. Paul Shadbolt and his two friends were finally allowed to leave at 1.30 am.

'Once we got out of the ground there was no one around. It was as if the police had done their shift and gone home. We didn't know where to go, so we just started walking towards the centre. We had hoped to find a bar where we could get a drink but everything was either closed or chocker so we decided to go back to the hotel. Once we got close to the train station we knew where we were. We were walking along quite slowly and were just about to cross a road when I felt a burning sensation in my back, like a red-hot poker going into me. I fell face-down into the street. There were about eight or ten of them. As soon as I hit the floor I felt a knife go in me again and then a third time. I got it twice in the back and once in the side. The only thing I remember thinking was: I have got to get fucking out of here. I have got to get off the floor or I'm dead. I started running. There was a bus coming and I got round it just in time. I saw a Sky TV van coming round the corner. My breathing was getting worse and worse. I thought one of my lungs had been punctured. Andy stopped the van by standing in front of it and banging on the bonnet. We got in and quickly came across a police car, which took Andy and me to hospital. We had lost Paul by this stage. I knew I was dying because when I got to the hospital I had no blood pressure and my pulse was racing. I have learnt quite a lot about it all now. The thing was that my heart was pumping away like crazy but there wasn't any blood to pump. One of the stabbings had gone through my spleen – and the one in my side had a rounded wound to it, as if they'd used some kind of screwdriver.

'I came round on Sunday afternoon, and the first thing I saw was a great big cross with Jesus Christ on it. I thought, bloody hell, I'm in heaven. Then I saw Andy and realised I was still in this world.'

I left the stadium shortly before 2 am and met up with Helen Willis, from the FA, outside the main entrance. The coach had left without us. We tried to find a taxi or a bus going into the centre of Rome. We tried to think what we should do next. Suddenly, a police car came screeching round the corner, its blue light flashing, siren wailing. It stopped abruptly. Sitting in the back were Graham Kelly and Pat Smith. We explained our predicament. Helen suggested we both jump in, but the two policemen in the front said there was only room for one. Helen said I should go. I think she was looking forward to an extra night in Rome.

It was a record run. Once we got on the motorway the speedometer never dropped below 150 kph. 'I don't think the plane will leave without the chief executive and his deputy,' said Smith.

'You wouldn't bet on it,' said Kelly, who was sitting with a football on his lap.

'Is that the match ball?' I asked him.

'No, it's one the players signed for me after I scored a hat-trick this week,' he said. I had never met Kelly before, and here we were squeezed into the back of a souped-up Fiat at 2.30 am on an Italian motorway being driven at breakneck speed by a policeman who looked fourteen.

'It's kind of you to give me a lift,' I said. 'How come you left so late?'

'I wanted to watch exactly what they did to our supporters – and I am not best pleased. The only reason I was given for why they kept them in the stadium half the night was because they feared for their safety if they let them out any earlier. That's a good one.'

'What did you think of the organisation generally on the Italian side?' I asked.

'What organisation?' said Kelly. 'But it was a great night. I am so pleased for Glenn. I think when we look back on Saturday, 11 October 1997, we may just remember it as the night that changed English football forever.'

By the time we boarded Britannia flight 809B, most of the drink had been consumed. But there was not a party atmosphere, more a sense of mission accomplished. And overwhelming fatigue. Ince wandered down to the back of the plane. Everyone liked Ince and I could understand why. Gascoigne chatted away amiably. He was asked what it had been like in the dressing room.

'The players came in one at a time and we enjoyed the moment. Even the lads who didn't play got involved. It was great. Now we are just tired, just drained.'

There was a crowd of more than a hundred people to meet the plane when it landed at 4.40 am. As I collected my luggage I looked across at Hoddle. I assumed he was going back to his house in Ascot, where he would be greeted by his wife and children and bathe in the restorative powers of family life. He seemed a supremely fortunate man.

Chapter 3

XAIPEO

Three days later, Hoddle was on the front page of every newspaper. 'Hod Divorce Shock'.

It was totally unexpected. The first the FA knew about it was when Hoddle walked into Davies's office on Tuesday morning and said: 'I have something to tell you.' Not even John Gorman was aware of exactly what was going on inside the head and heart of his great friend as they went about their business in Rome – but he had his suspicions. On several occasions, Hoddle had said to Gorman, 'I want to get something off my chest,' and Gorman had said: 'Go on, then, you will feel better for it.' But he never did.

Davies put out an FA statement at 6 pm on Tuesday evening. 'This is a personal and private matter. It is unconnected to his football responsibilities. Nobody else is involved. Both Anne and Glenn would request that the privacy of themselves and their three children is respected at this very difficult and painful time.'

The timing of the announcement was impressive, coming so soon after the Italy triumph but more than a month before England's next game – a friendly against Cameroon. The beauty of Hoddle as a player was the way he would take a difficult ball on his chest and kill it dead, letting it drop quietly at his feet before moving effortlessly forward.

The Hoddles had been married for eighteen years, having met while they were both still at school. They had three children, Zoë, Zara and Jamie, who was only five when the separation was announced. In the current Shredded Wheat advertisement, the Hoddles were depicted as the happiest of happy families, sitting around the breakfast table wearing contented smiles. The ad was immediately pulled.

The next day, Hoddle's R-reg BMW 735i was seen parked on the driveway of a house in Wokingham owned by Eileen Drewery, a fifty-seven-year-old faith-healer. It was to become his home for the next twelve months. They had first met when he used to go out with her daughter Michelle during his playing days with Spurs. On one occasion he had hobbled into the Drewerys' house complaining of a torn muscle. When Eileen offered healing Hoddle turned it down, but she went ahead and performed 'absent healing', and the next day his muscle was dramatically improved. Two decades later, Mrs Drewery was to become the Mother Superior of the England football team.

Hoddle said nothing for the next three days before breaking his silence in a TV interview shown on Grandstand at lunchtime on Saturday. He was sparing with the details. 'It has been a very difficult week for me,' he said. 'Obviously there have been some ups and downs, but I have had to detach certain things and put them away and it's all been a bit stressful.'

England's plucky performance on the pitch in Rome was nothing to the bulldog spirit deployed at home by the FA, high on the adrenalin of victory, or perhaps just basking in the relief of qualifying for a World Cup for the first time in eight years. The Italians were given no quarter. Davies led the charge. After touching down at Luton airport, he was driven straight to Burnham Beeches Hotel, where he had a shower, glanced at the Sunday papers, picked up his car and headed for the BBC to tell David Frost all about it. David Mellor, the newly appointed chairman of the Football Task Force, was also in the studio and quickly teamed up with Davies to deliver a scathing attack on the Italian security operation. Mellor raised his truncheon with additional venom because his seventeen-year-old son, Anthony, had been at the game and had given his father a first-hand account, which Mellor Junior followed up in a letter to *The Times*. It was precisely the sort of testimony the FA were keen to encourage:

Sir, Along with a few thousand other England fans, I arrived at the Olympic Stadium in Rome at about 6.15 pm on Saturday and was subjected to a rigorous search, with everything from belts to keys to coins to lighters being confiscated. Inside was chaos. We had tickets for the 'official' section but were sent to an area for which these were not valid, so the police (there were no stewards) told us to sit wherever we wished . . . Forty seconds after kick-off the Italians started to throw full water bottles, coins and other objects into our stand. The English could not have thrown anything back – everything had been confiscated. The Italian police did not react to the missiles being lobbed into our area, yet when the English started to return the rubbish thrown at them, the police started a baton charge . . . The behaviour of both the Italian fans and the police was disgraceful. The latter seemed to bear a grudge against every English fan – their attacks on us were both bizarre and terrifying. English fans certainly retaliated and some threw seats at the police in the stadium; but rather than instilling fear and anger, surely the police should have protected and helped innocent fans in such a situation.

Yours faithfully,
Anthony Mellor

The Times printed a second, shorter, letter just beneath it which made a different but equally valid point:

Sir, As an Irish resident in Rome for the past three years, I am surprised by how press reaction to Saturday's match has concentrated on the heavy-handedness of the Italian police. From Friday night until kick-off I saw many groups of English fans parading around the centre of Rome, shouting abuse at locals, especially women, and in some cases throwing bottles and other implements at mopeds, cars, police and in one case smashing the window of a bar. All this in the capital city of the country which was the main victim of the Heysel disaster in 1985.

I have never seen anything like this behaviour in Rome, even though many European teams play here on a regular basis. When will the F A learn that the root of the problem still lies with their fans and not the authorities of the other countries? I believe that the French authorities will react in the same way at the World Cup finals next year unless the English fans can prove that they can act in a civilised manner.

Yours etc,
Ronan Donoghue

For the next two weeks you could hardly turn on the television without seeing a clip of English fans being bashed by Italian riot police. It was either that or the trial of teenager Louise Woodward, both cases in which objectivity got lost in the swelter of debate. The F A's hastily drafted report returned a guilty verdict on all counts, concluding that the police had been variously inefficient, provocative and brutal.

The Italians struck back – none more so than dear old, roly-poly Giancarlo Gavarotti who, in a *Gazetta dello Sport* editorial, described English supporters as 'vomit on the beautiful face of Rome'. Verbal warfare continued until FIFA eventually came out with its own inconclusive but predictable conclusion: both sides were to blame. As a result, England and Italy would each be fined for contributing to what FIFA described as the 'deplorable' events in Rome. It was a vintage example of fence-sitting, complete with the tamest of warnings that a repeat of such behaviour, either by England fans or Italian police, would result in 'a lot stiffer punishments'.

Sepp Blatter, the FIFA General Secretary, who did not wish to fall out with England or Italy since he was hoping to win their vote as successor to Joao Havelange, the FIFA President, made things charmingly clear. 'While FIFA did not have authority over the police forces, the methods used by the police should be better adapted to the specific requirements of football,' he said, scrubbing the whitewash from his suit as he spoke.

*   *   *

Woodward was freed on the day Hoddle's England players volun-
tarily put themselves under lock and key at the team hotel in Berkshire in preparation for the Cameroon game, the first of a series of
friendlies during which the players would strut their stuff in front
of the coach in the hope of securing a place in the final squad of
twenty-two, to be announced on 2 June. It was to be a long and
tense and at times tedious beauty contest, with some contestants
dropping out of the reckoning and one refusing to take part
altogether. Others were to claw their way on to the catwalk at the
last minute.

This is what Phil Neville had to say about it: 'There are only
four players that you can look at and safely say that only injuries
could keep them out of the final squad, and they are David Seaman,
Paul Gascoigne, Paul Ince and Alan Shearer. For the rest of us, the
fight is on. We've qualified for the finals but this is where the
pressure really starts. I think we're all worried about whether we
will make it to France. I'm thinking about it every time I go on to
the training field with England and it's going to get worse.

'You look at every training session as a step nearer the World
Cup, and if you play and perform well you think of that as another
step forward. At the moment I'd say my main rivals for the wing-
back places are Graeme Le Saux and Andy Hinchcliffe. Then there's
David Beckham if I'm pushing for a place on the right.'

The last time Cameroon came to London, in 1991, the so-called
Lions of Africa refused to leave their hotel until they were paid
£2,000 each in cash. On this occasion, the FA guaranteed around
£150,000 to the Cameroon FA, plus a share of the TV rights. The
lions were tamed in an instant.

Hoddle's squad included the rehabilitated Rio Ferdinand and
Chris Sutton, Blackburn's top scorer. Both had been called up for
the first time. A seventeen-year-old called Michael Owen was also
there – on work experience from Liverpool FC, where he was taking
the Kop by storm. I had seen him on the first day of the season
when Liverpool played Crystal Palace at Selhurst Park, and I noticed
before the kick-off that Hoddle was sitting a couple of rows behind
me. Halfway through the second half, Owen was fouled in the

penalty area and the referee pointed to the spot. Owen didn't bother to look across to the bench or consult his captain. He simply picked up the ball, placed it on the small white circle and whacked it past the goalkeeper.

After the first day's training session at Bisham Abbey, someone thoughtfully passed Rio Ferdinand a glass of orange juice, and he managed a knowing smile. 'You can't call me an alcoholic. I don't need counselling or anything,' said Ferdinand, who had just turned nineteen. 'Glenn told me I would get another chance. He stood by me. He's an honest person and I have to be honest with him now. Everything he has said to me has made a difference. He has told me how to conduct myself off the pitch and what he's told me has stayed in. What happened with Tony Adams was more of a conversation really. I just found that I was sitting next to him on the bus and we started talking. He simply told me what had happened to him. The truth is that I don't really drink.'

I asked him if he had ever seen a video of Bobby Moore, and how it felt to be compared, however obliquely, to such a master craftsman. 'He was probably the greatest centre-back in the world, so it's a bit over the top to compare me with him. I try to do my own thing. I like to pass the ball and I like to have it at my feet. It's flattering the things people have been saying, but I have to make sure I don't get big-headed.'

Hoddle already had the spine of a team in his mind, and was looking at about thirty or thirty-five players who had a chance of making it by June. Rio Ferdinand's recall raised the question of whether Hoddle still hoped to play a sweeper system or if he would stick to his three central defenders and two wing-back formation. Much to Adams's displeasure, England had abandoned the flat back four. 'If I had fourteen games in which to experiment it might be different, but I don't,' Hoddle said. 'You can play with a sweeper in training and think to yourself, this is fine, but then you try doing it at Wembley in front of 75,000 people or during a World Cup and it can all go horribly wrong. I don't think we've got the players at the moment to do it – although Rio might do it in the future.'

45

Not one question was asked about Hoddle's personal life, and how the break-up of his marriage might affect his work.

It was an uninspiring game on a damp, uninspiring North London evening. The lions failed to roar. England won 2–0, with well-taken goals shortly before the end of the first half by Paul Scholes and Robbie Fowler. For Fowler it was particularly important to make an impression and move up a notch in the striker's stakes, especially with Shearer still injured and Wright suddenly finding it impossible to score for Arsenal.

But it's all so unfair. Chris Sutton came on with just over ten minutes of the match left, and could so easily have walked into the departure lounge for France if a cross from Fowler had been a few inches more accurate.

Hoddle gave Nigel Martyn an outing in goal, but he hardly got a touch. As it happened, his only real contribution was when he went down on one knee to stop an innocuous shot and let the ball roll out of his arms. He grabbed it again and managed a rueful grin.

There was one significant moment in the thirty-ninth minute when Rio Ferdinand trotted on to replace the injured Southgate. Suddenly there was a buzz about the place. Hinchcliffe shook his hand and then immediately passed him the ball. Ferdinand's international career was effortlessly into its stride.

England were now ranked sixth in the world – 100 places higher than Italy – and FIFA said they would take that into consideration when deciding which countries would be given one of the eight seeded places. Past World Cup performances were going to come into the equation, which meant England's failure to qualify last time round could cost them dear. The ghost of Graham Taylor was about to haunt Hoddle as the FIFA suits deliberated in Zurich. Everyone put a brave face on it. Sir Bert Millichip, the FA's former Chairman who now sat on the all-important FIFA committee, was banging the drum for England. Hoddle appeared unfazed, even suggesting that if England were not seeded it might be an advantage to be in the same group as Brazil – which was tempting fate, especially if that group was also to include countries such as Nigeria and Croatia. In the end it was a choice between Holland, Romania and England for the two last seeded places.

Holland and Romania got the nod. 'A shade disappointed' was Hoddle's immediate response, before taking solace in the traditional chirpy get-out that 'Come what may you have to go out there and beat whoever you come up against.' Manager and captain stood shoulder to shoulder. Shearer, who dropped into Marseille for twenty-four hours shortly before the draw to sign the world's second biggest boot deal – £15 million with Umbro until the year 2000 – played Hoddle's parrot. 'You have to meet the best in the end anyway, so it doesn't really matter which group you are in,' he said.

Meanwhile, Graham Taylor, now back where he belonged as manager of Watford, emerged from his vegetable patch to defend himself. 'I'm used to getting blamed for many things, but it is not my fault this time. If people think England have been left out of the seeding because of what happened in 1994 they should look at the rules. It's not just about non-qualification in 94. You have to take friendly games since then into account, because every international match counts.'

For the French, the *Tirage au Sort de la Compétition Finale* – The Final Draw – was a chance to road-test their organisational machinery. The media centre at the Stade Vélodrome was big, but not nearly big enough to accommodate the 1,200 visiting journalists. There were smiling girls with badges pinned to their chests, and goodie bags stuffed with watches, calculators, pens and key-rings – stocking-fillers galore. There was red carpet everywhere. The woolly baseball cap with flaps to cover the ears came in handy during the exhibition match between Europe and the Rest of the World before the draw, when the temperature at the top of the arched main stand plummeted. Europe scored within the first minute to begin a goal-fest. Gabriel Batistuta scored a couple, as did Ronaldo, who looked awesome. The 38,000-odd crowd seemed to enjoy it, but they could have done without the French cheer-leader who only highlighted the lack of competitive edge by urging spectators to join him in an inane chant for one side or the other.

It felt more like the opening ceremony than the draw, with a big blue stage at one end where glass pots into which the names of the competing countries would be poured were installed in front of an oversized football. Thousands of schoolchildren sporting different coloured T-shirts filled one stand, VIPs and the media in the other, and the rest sat behind the goal opposite the stage. There was a reproduction of an ancient mosaic in one corner, with XAIPEO in Greek lettering written on it. Greetings.

More than 1,500 people from the worlds of football, politics and show business were invited. Many of them had been in Marseille most of the week, being wined and dined by the sponsors who make sure FIFA's cup is always full to overflowing. During the second half I wandered through the sponsor's village just outside the stadium and was handed a Snickers bar and a Coke. And then another Snickers bar and another Coke. A man at the Adidas stand with an American accent was longing to talk to someone. He told me that most of the matches would be broadcast to more than 120 countries and that some games would be seen by 500 million people worldwide. I told him that only that week I had read somewhere that Nike was willing to spend £20 million – almost exactly what Adidas was paying to be an official sponsor – in an attempt to steal the limelight from their rivals. 'That's none of my business,' he said. 'What I know is that this is going to be far bigger than any Olympics, and with the extra teams in the final this will be the biggest sporting event the world has ever known. No one really knows exactly what it's costing us but I know it's worth it. Do you want a sticker?'

At the end of the match, there was a pitch invasion. Sepp Blatter would not have been pleased, since only twenty-four hours earlier he had called for all perimeter fences to be taken down by June because, he said, 'prisoners and wild animals should be behind bars, not football supporters.'

It took the stewards more than fifteen minutes to clear the pitch. One boy came on with his football and dribbled the length of the field until he got to the penalty spot in front of the empty goal. This was his moment. He missed, shooting high and wide into the stand, and no one would give his ball back. Others performed cartwheels and danced around in the centre circle until the stewards were told to show some muscle. France's superstar Zinedine Zidane had his shirt ripped from his back and had to be escorted off the field by police. And all of this from a hand-picked crowd, made up mainly of schoolchildren.

In the official programme, Michel Santini and Fernand Sastre, the joint tournament chiefs, made much of the decision to hold the draw outdoors in front of such a large crowd, but I am not sure the plan had been for Blatter and the Chairman of the French FA to be roundly booed whenever they appeared on stage. There was already a hostile atmosphere brewing in Marseille.

Dividing the thirty-two countries into eight groups of four could be done in a matter of minutes, but that would spoil Blatter's fun. A short, tubby man with a round, jovial face, Blatter was on course to succeed Havelange. He slowly unscrewed the little balls and pulled out small strips of paper bearing each of the countries' names. England had missed Brazil, Italy, France, Spain and Holland. That left groups headed by Germany, Argentina and Romania. It was Romania we wanted and it was Romania we got, along with Tunisia and Colombia. No one was complaining.

Immediately after the draw I made my way towards the VIP section, where I flashed my AA membership card and walked into the lobby. I found Graham Kelly and Pat Smith trying hard to disguise their relief at what was a kind draw. And it helped that they were going to be in Marseille for another twenty-four hours, where England were to play their opening game against Tunisia. It would give them an opportunity to count the number of glass-fronted bars around the Vieux Port where thousands of England supporters would gather for refreshment six months later.

'Where do you expect the English fans to stay?' I asked Smith.

'Well, the French like camping, don't they?' she said.

Hoddle was doing his best to make the group look tougher than it was. 'It could have been a lot easier,' he said.

Anything would have been easier for the Scots, drawn with Brazil, who they would meet at the opening match of the tournament, and Morocco and Norway. Craig Brown, the coach, didn't seem to mind much. He told reporters: 'It is real Roy of the Rovers stuff for us to be involved in the first match and at a new stadium which has an 80,000 capacity and on a day that will be a festival of football throughout the world. We have played them eight times and never won, so I obviously wanted to avoid them. But I always love facing the Brazilians and we will certainly be well prepared. There are often upsets in the opening games of World Cups.'

Outside the VIP area, I saw Geoff Hurst drifting behind a pillar. 'We're very fortunate,' he told me, 'but if we were really feeling greedy we might want to have swapped Iran for Colombia.' Then Bobby Charlton appeared out of nowhere wearing his England 2006 badge. 'You have to say it's an ideal group for us,' he said. 'Not that I know a lot about Tunisia.'

For the next couple of hours, clusters of TV cameras gathered around various coaches. Steve Sampson, the American national coach, was upbeat about the prospect of America playing Iran, with whom his country had severed diplomatic contact in 1979, when Iranian terrorists stormed the US embassy in Tehran and held 52 Americans hostage for 444 days. 'We will try not to allow the political ramifications to influence our preparation,' he said, fashioning a career in the diplomatic corps once he got sacked from his present job. 'I hope we can use the game to bring the two countries closer together.'

Even the French Prime Minister, Lionel Jospin, had a view. He described Denmark, who were drawn with France, as 'no longer the team they were', and expressed a not altogether surprising hope that the French would lift the trophy on 12 July. Havelange issued a personal statement, of course, though it was strangely defensive. 'Judging by the reaction of the public to the draw,' he said, 'they were delighted and happy, which shows just how much they appreciate the work done by FIFA.'

Late that night, I had dinner in a restaurant off the Quai des Belges and tried to envisage the scene in June. It didn't require a massive leap of the imagination.

The next morning I went and saw Marseille's head of police, Monsieur Jacques Guida, in his office in the Prefecture off the Rue de Rome. He was unimpressed with the stewarding the previous evening, and smiled wryly when I reminded him that England were on their way to his city.

'It will not be a problem,' he said. 'You should remember that here in Marseille we have some of the toughest football supporters in France. We will be prepared.'

Where, I asked him, did he think the English supporters would sleep, given that Marseille was not overly provided with hotel accommodation? 'Officials from the English Football Association are hoping there will be plenty of places to camp,' I informed him. He shrugged his shoulders.

'Where?' he said.

'On the beach, perhaps.'

'It's forbidden.'

Another person disturbed by the post-match entertainment in the Vélodrome was the woman responsible for security nationwide during the finals, Dominique Spinosi. She was quick to make sure the English did not get the wrong impression. 'Let me warn them that if they set one single foot on the grass they will be dealt with by our riot force. And anyone who breaks our strict rules about taking banned objects like bottles, knives, fireworks, flags or guns into the stadium will face immediate arrest, imprisonment for up to three years, a fine of £1,000, a ban from the stadium for life, and even a ban from France for life.' Greetings.

A more immediate concern was the ticket allocation. Only 5,000 tickets were to be made available to members of the FA's England Travel Club, of which there were already 30,000 members. This was because the French had awarded themselves 60 per cent of the total 2.5 million tickets to the 64 games. A further 12 per cent were going to sponsors, and 8 per cent to the seventeen tour operators licensed to run World Cup packages. It was perfectly obvious that thousands of French people with little interest in football but a huge appetite for making a quick franc would soon be selling their tickets on the black market.

'I wouldn't be surprised', said Monsieur Guida, 'if most of the stadium is filled with English people. But it won't be a problem. I look forward to welcoming you in the summer.'

Chapter 4

Me and the Gaffer Are Fine

Alan Shearer took off his tracksuit, stretched and returned to professional football for the first time in four months on 17 January, coming on as a late substitute for Newcastle against Bolton. Both sets of supporters and several Bolton players applauded respectfully as he sauntered towards the centre circle. His side were 1–0 down at the time but quickly drew level.

'He's back', was the agreed headline in most papers the next morning. He was back again four days later when Newcastle played Liverpool at Anfield. He was given thirty minutes, but it was young Michael Owen who caught the eye, scoring his twelfth goal of the season in spectacular fashion.

'He had no right to finish like that,' said Kenny Dalglish afterwards.

Hoddle was at Anfield ten days later, just before announcing his squad for a friendly against Chile, who it was thought would play in similar style to Colombia. Liverpool were playing Blackburn, and both sides came away with a point. Hoddle came away with pointers aplenty. There was Tim Flowers in one goal and David James in the other, competing for a place in the final twenty-two. Sutton, Fowler and Owen were also on the catwalk, as was McManaman. Jamie Redknapp, another man Hoddle was considering for the possible sweeper role, was out injured.

James saved well in the opening minutes. Then Flowers planted himself at Fowler's feet, and followed that with a fine stop from Ince and then a towering leap to deny Fowler from a free kick. Everyone wanted to play, but the more Fowler huffed and puffed the less he brought the house down. By the end he was snatching at the ball in frustration. Football, it is said, is all about angles and percentages – hence that old chestnut about the sliderule pass splitting a defence. On this occasion, Fowler was in need of an extra algebra lesson.

But then it's not every day that you come up against a full-back such as Colin Hendry, who ruined Fowler's afternoon with a sublime block tackle in the second half which Alan Hansen later described on Match of the Day as 'totally and utterly out of this world'. Fowler had a clear sight of goal. The ball was virtually over the line when Hendry covered five yards in half a second, stretched his left leg and stretched it some more until he made contact. Fowler seemed to lose heart. The sticky plaster on his nose began looking more and more silly. He was preoccupied, as if all the gossip about him insisting on £45,000 a week had got to him. Owen's matinee performance, meanwhile, was flawless.

Elsewhere, Rio Ferdinand made a couple of howlers against Everton and Paul Merson had an uncomfortable afternoon for Middlesbrough at Stoke. Dion Dublin scored twice for Coventry. Oh, and a linesman was knocked unconscious during Portsmouth's First Division match with Sheffield United.

There was a bigger turn-out than normal at London's Park Royal hotel when Hoddle announced his twenty-two-man squad. No fewer than ten television cameras were camped on the hotel doorstep. Hoddle and Gorman had been in Tunis the previous week on a spying mission. They had watched Tunisia lose 3–0 to Yugoslavia. Hoddle concluded that Tunisia tried to play like Poland and that he knew quite a lot about Poland.

The coach looked his dapper self as he strode into the hotel, the hair more coiffed than usual. I thought about Hoddle the player, his shirt always outside his shorts, hanging like a skirt. I don't know if you have to be vain to be a good coach, but I suspected it was helping Glenda. He was worshipped as a player, but not by everyone. There were those who thought he drifted in and out of a game, that he seldom tackled back, that he was prone to idleness. He still had a lot to prove.

Robbie Fowler's name was missing from the squad. So was that of Ian Wright, now a Friday evening talk-show host. And there was no Rio Ferdinand, no Chris Sutton, no Gary Pallister, Stuart Pearce, Stan Collymore. But Michael Owen and Dion Dublin were both included. And Shearer was there of course. Hoddle said he had spoken on Sunday night to Roy Evans and they had agreed that Fowler had gone off the boil but that Owen was sizzling. Hoddle said he thought Fowler would be back in contention as long as he got his work-rate up. Hold on. This was Glenn Hoddle getting exercised about work-rate, the same Glenn Hoddle who was persistently accused of not working hard enough when he wore an England shirt. Hoddle was always his own man when he played for England, and yet he seemed to have taken against Fowler and McManaman because they were not sufficiently compliant.

A barrage of questions was hurled at the England manager. He was prodded so persistently that in the end he simply said: 'I want to see if Michael Owen is a better player than Robbie Fowler.'

You could tell straight away how much Hoddle wanted to take Owen, but he didn't want to feel he was being swept along by the tide of public opinion.

'He will be a great player in five years' time, but the question for me at the end of the day is, can he do it in five *months*' time?'

Hoddle is very much an 'end of the day' and 'at this particular point in time' man, and it was beginning to grate.

'It's easier for me at the end of the day to take a risk with an attacker than a defender,' he said, 'but I have been impressed with the way Michael has never looked out of place against any opposition. At this particular point in time, I am the one who must decide if he is good enough to do the job. His age does not come into it.'

His age, however, would very soon get him into the record books. At eighteen years and fifty-nine days old he was about to become the youngest-ever player to represent England at senior level. It was worth a thought that the last time England qualified for a World Cup, Owen was only ten years old. He must have had pictures of

Paul Gascoigne on his wall above his bed, and now he was about to line up with him at Wembley.

Hoddle went out of his way to retract his comment of four weeks earlier when he suggested that Owen needed to clean up his off-the-pitch life, which was perceived as a rash remark at the time and one made on the basis of flimsy evidence. 'I did not say that specifically about Michael,' said Hoddle, bristling a little. 'I was talking about any of five young players. I never said he had a problem.'

Apparently Gorman had found him, Fowler and McManaman playing cards one night at 3 am in the team hotel. Alcohol had been consumed. Allegedly.

The day Owen heard he had been picked for England, he swapped his Rover for a brand-new metallic blue 3-series BMW – which would sit nicely beside Fowler's £100,000 Porsche and McManaman's Aston Martin in the Liverpool car park. But he was still living at home, and nothing about his personality gave a hint that he was anything but responsible and focused.

Dion Dublin was the other talking-point. Hoddle said he had almost picked him against Cameroon as a defender, 'but then I saw him one weekend and it was the best performance as a target player I had come across all season. The other thing that impresses me about him at the end of the day is that he seems a very level-headed boy.' He had needed to be. Ten years Owen's senior, he had seen the highs and lows of life as a professional footballer. He scored on his début for Manchester United but then fractured a leg two days later and Ferguson bought Eric Cantona as a replacement. End of story. For the last four years he had kept Coventry in the Premier League, and this was his big break. Coventry's chairman must have been pleased, too. Any club wishing to buy him now would have to add on an extra £500,000 to the price. But there was no way, surely, that Dion Dublin was going to France.

The next morning, a slightly different version of events emerged over the Fowler business. Hoddle had indeed spoken to Roy Evans, but contrary to what we had been led to believe twenty-four hours earlier, the Liverpool manager had given his striker a good report, not exactly glowing but favourable enough. Evans said he was amazed to discover Fowler had been dropped. 'Robbie hasn't been having the best of times lately, but I would have stuck with him,' said the Liverpool manager.

But it was Chris Sutton who got himself into a complete state over his selection in the B squad. He telephoned the boss and told him to stuff it. 'I am well aware of the implications of what I have done, but in my opinion you are on a hiding to nothing playing for the B team,' he said.

The normal platitude is that playing for your country is the highest honour and that when you pull on that England shirt – at whatever level – you feel a rush of pride rippling through you. Sutton was having none of that. All he felt was rage and indignation. 'If you play well in the B team, people say you still need to prove yourself at the higher level. If you play badly you are immediately discarded.' To which his old striking partner, Shearer, with whom Sutton never particularly got on at Blackburn, gently raised two fingers. 'I just can't understand it. I would have said: "Thanks for putting me in the B squad and I will show you what I can do." But I can't tell him what to do. It's his decision.'

The lease ran out on the house I was renting around the corner from my wife and children. I moved into the spare room of a friend and I wondered if it was bigger or smaller than the room Hoddle was staying in with Mrs Drewery. My solicitor's first bill arrived. She had written a few letters and I had had one or two telephone conversations with her, for which she charged me nearly £2,000. Hoddle was coping better than me, I suspected. Then, five days before the Chile game, a property tycoon called Jeffrey Shean accused him of sleeping with his wife and was naming him in a divorce petition. In a statement released through his solicitors, Shean, a Tottenham supporter who used to dote on Hoddle as a player, said: 'The reason our marriage has ended is that Vanessa has gone off with another man and that man is Hoddle.'

Hoddle disputed the charge in a short statement put out by the FA. 'The allegation of adultery involving myself is entirely untrue,' he said. But the story was up and running. The *Sunday Mirror* the next day ran a headline proclaiming 'Hoddle And His Vanessa: The First Photo'. It showed the two of them leaving the Ivy restaurant in London, and according to the caption, 'Vanessa, 39, a former air hostess, was wearing a sensual new look,' whatever that meant. The exclusive interview the paper had acquired with Jeff Shean amounted to all of three sentences. 'I was a friend of Hoddle's. Hoddle has been seen out with his mate's wife. Is that the way for a spiritual Christian man to carry on?'

Would any of the Number Ones breach the unwritten rule and ask Hoddle about his domestic difficulties? This was strictly a news job now, but the news reporters had not been allowed into the training ground. Davies primed Hoddle, telling him that John Gorman had been widely quoted as saying that the coach was in good spirits. A couple of hacks had reminded Davies that Hoddle seldom shrank from commenting on his players' difficulties, and therefore some people might expect him to say something on this occasion. Vanessa Shean, who separated from her husband towards the end of 1997, was expected to go flat-out to get the divorce through before the World Cup. That was certainly the hope within the FA, which was trembling at the possibility of lurid tales emanating from a courtroom just as England were about to set off for France.

Gorman was right. Hoddle looked a model of composure as he stood in the middle of the training pitch in his red, white and blue tracksuit top. As ever, he let Gorman do most of the shouting. Afterwards, he came into the Warwick Room with Michael Owen and sat down in front of about fifty scribblers. Hoddle put his arm around the back of Owen's chair and leant forward.

'This must be quite an amazing experience, Michael. How are you coping with it all?' Owen was asked.

'I never expected it to come so quick. The attention comes with the job. I just try to be as normal as possible and I don't really think my age is an issue. My dad has been a great help to me. He knows the game and he's there for me all the time. I feel ready. I'm confident of my ability. I don't feel a lot of pressure on me. I have got nothing to lose.'

He sat looking straight ahead of him, like a flyweight boxer at a pre-fight weigh-in.

'Football is a cut-throat business,' said Steve Howard, of the *Sun*. 'You must be aware that you have made it into the squad at a time when Robbie Fowler has been left . . .'

Hoddle pounced. 'Michael's here to talk about himself and his inclusion in the squad, no one else's.'

After Owen left the room, the pens shuffled forward towards Hoddle. He was asked the usual questions and gave the usual answers. Did he still have the spine of his team sorted? How serious was the injury to David Beckham? It was the dullest session that I had witnessed so far – until Paul McCarthy of the *Express* asked sheepishly: 'You have had to deal with other players when they have suffered adverse publicity off the pitch. How is it affecting you at this time?'

'I'm here to talk about the World Cup game against Chile and I'm getting on with it,' Hoddle said, quietly. I noticed he was still wearing his wedding ring.

'I'm not asking you to go into details,' said McCarthy.

'I'm getting on with it,' he replied. 'Okay?'

England lost 2–0 – and everyone seemed pleased. Marcelo Salas's first goal – when he took the ball on his thigh at pace before whacking it in from just outside the penalty area – was one of the best ever to be scored at Wembley, and when he calmly put away the penalty for Chile's second, a national sigh of relief went out round Wembley. By next morning, the phrase 'brought down to earth' sat comfortably on most people's lips. England might have swallowed the hype about their new-found greatness – and now they were choking on it. Hoddle was very quick to call it an 'experimental team', and went on to describe the limp and lustreless performance as a 'possible blessing in disguise'. But how could he really know if Dion Dublin – who played up front from the start because of an injury to Andy Cole – was viable as an international centre-forward while the men behind him had dried up? It desperately needed someone to turn on the creative tap, which was why Paul Gascoigne emerged as a curious sort of Man of the Match without having to set foot on the pitch, his absence visible.

The Michael Owen show kept on rolling. It was his first full game for England and he buzzed about all evening. He was easily the most effective and dangerous player in a white shirt. Dublin didn't do much wrong, while Sol Campbell didn't do much right. Hoddle said he learnt things from the game and that he would continue to experiment during the remaining five friendlies, which were to include two matches in Morocco at the end of May. He also reminded everyone that Brazil had been defeated by the United States a few days earlier and that there was no need to panic. Others thought the defeat should not be so easily dismissed. Roy Hodgson, who was in charge of Switzerland during the last World Cup, said: 'The top countries don't lose in their own temple. For years, England never lost at Wembley. We should never accept it.'

Hoddle said of Owen: 'It was the best international début by an eighteen-year-old I have ever seen.'

There was one problem for me. I wasn't there. Not even close. In fact, as Salas was taunting Campbell, I was 33,000 feet up in the sky on my way to the Gulf to report on an entirely different confrontation, one where the game of diplomacy between America and Iraq over Saddam Hussein's weapons of mass destruction had broken down to such an extent that the Americans, with the help of the British, were about to go to war. I landed in Dubai at four in the morning and rang London to get the result before heading off to HMS *Invincible*, which had come into port to fix its radar. The officers on board looked immaculate in their all-white strip, their shorts and shirts beautifully pressed, like Leeds United footballers from the 1950s.

From Dubai I moved to Kuwait just as the air-raid sirens were being tested and gas-masks handed out in case the madman over the border decided to unleash some lethal missiles. I was taken to the British airbase about thirty miles from the Iraqi border where eight Tornados from 14 Squadron had set up a temporary home. The surrounding desert looked like a giant slab of pitta bread, and the base itself was little more than a bombsite. In fact it *was* a bombsite – destroyed, ironically, by the RAF seven years earlier when they liberated it from the Iraqis. I told one of the ground-crew about the dramatic sacking of the Chelsea manager Ruud Gullit. 'I suppose he'll end up at Kilmarnock,' he said, but I have no idea why.

Thanks to Kofi Annan, the United Nations Secretary-General, I found myself en route to Liverpool and not Baghdad on Monday morning. When I arrived at Melwood, the Liverpool training ground, I saw McManaman, who I had arranged to interview, driving off in his Aston Martin. It was cold and wet but a crowd of at least thirty or forty schoolchildren were outside the red gates playing truant. The girls were in uniform: tight tops that did not quite cover their tummies, short skirts, big heels and big lipstick. There was something strangely romantic about the scene, helped, perhaps, by the sheer ugliness of the place.

I asked Roy Evans about Michael Owen and how he thought he had done against Chile. He said he was 'pleased for the lad' and that 'no one should worry about him getting above his station.'

Paul Ince came out in his blue plastic slippers. We went and sat in the front of his car and he put the heater on. I asked him if he thought the salaries in football were getting silly.

'I don't think it's fair to say they're silly. They've been getting that sort of money in Italy and Spain for years, and they don't pay taxes over there like we do. The way I look at it is that it's about time players made some money from the clubs. It's not a long career – about fifteen years at the most – and then when you're thirty-five or thirty-six and out of the game, no one will worry about you. Even if you get a bad injury the club won't bother with you. Once your time's up they don't want to know you no more. You're just a piece of meat.'

Paul Ince's father was a railwayman who had an affair with Paul's mother, Peggy, when she was a lodger in his house. After she became pregnant with Paul, she moved out, but continued to see his father, who was married at the time, until Paul was three. Then she went to work as a dancer and waitress in Germany, leaving Paul to live with an aunt in Dagenham. His father later did time in Pentonville after beating up his wife for sleeping with another man.

'I reckon I've got another four years at the top level and then I'll have to start thinking hard about what I'm going to do,' Paul told me. 'Management is a possibility. I can't think of anything else. Football has given me a good life. I have a wife and two boys. I think I'll either become a manager or spend the rest of my life on the golf course.'

'Scoring goals isn't really what you are about, is it?'

'I don't get that far forward very often, but the strange thing is that I have always taken Bryan Robson as my model player, and he scored goals. That was his great skill – arriving late in the box when you needed him. It's amazing to think that I took Robbo as my role-model and then I ended up playing alongside him at Manchester United. But I found a different role for myself. I was always the holding player and Robbo used to go forward. I do the same for England. Robbo was my hero but I'm more skilful than him now. Definitely.'

'Is there one player who has it all?'

'Not in England. No one.'

'What about Owen?'

'Well, put it like this. You need more experience than you do youth in a World Cup, but having said that I hope Michael goes. He's amazing.'

'How do you get on with Hoddle, and how is the atmosphere different under him compared to Terry Venables?'

'I got on really well with Terry. Hoddle's different. Terry was boisterous. Hoddle's quieter but I think he's got many of the same ideas as Terry about football. They're on the same level. If you ask me I would say the Holland game in Euro 96 was the turning-point for English football. We started passing the ball and keeping it on the floor. Terry gave us a different dimension and Hoddle has taken it on. I think they are both good managers. The important thing is that I understand what Hoddle wants us to do. He explains himself. He doesn't just shout and scream.'

*   *   *

61

Back at Euston Station, my mobile rang. It was Steve McManaman.

'What's going on with you and Hoddle?' I asked.

'Me and the gaffer are fine. We talk all the time,' he said, unconvincingly. 'If there is a problem I get it out with him. I know it all stems from Le Tournoi – or, at least, that's how people think it began. And there's no clique involving me and Robbie. He's my best mate. We do things together. There's nothing wrong with that. The fact is that I live a boring life, honest. After training I go home. I may play a bit of golf. The only thing is that I like to feel I am still an individual.'

I went back up to Liverpool a week later for the derby against Everton and watched as Robbie Fowler went to head a ball and landed nastily. He tried to stand up but only managed to get as far as his knees. He was staring into the ground looking as if he had been shot by a sniper's gun. He knew that all the fuss about whether or not Hoddle really rated him, all the talk about whether he would or would not be a bad influence on Owen, all the questions about his character, lifestyle and general demeanour, were now entirely academic. And with that he rolled gently over and waited for a stretcher to remove him once and for all from Hoddle's World Cup squad.

A strong whiff of foreboding hung in the spring air. Everywhere you looked things were creaking. Towards the end of March more than half the players Hoddle would have liked to pick for the friendly against Switzerland were injured, including his goalkeeper David Seaman, who was in danger of being upstaged by his Arsenal replacement Alex Manninger. The Manchester United injured contingent – David Beckham, Nicky Butt, the Neville brothers, Paul Scholes – were not just limping physically but struggling mentally to keep their spirits up after being dumped out of the European Champions League by an efficient but hardly breath-taking Monaco side. Adams, who was due to win his fiftieth cap, was ruled out by an ankle injury, while Graeme Le Saux, Andy Hinchcliffe and the newly elevated Ray Parlour were also on the casualty list. Gascoigne, meanwhile, was at the centre of frenzied transfer speculation that eventually saw him move from Glasgow Rangers to Middlesbrough just in time to make a brief appearance at Wembley in the Coca-Cola Cup Final. He failed to make Hoddle's squad because he wasn't remotely fit. Even Shearer seemed out of sorts as Newcastle slid further towards the relegation zone amid disapproving stories involving two prominent members of the club's board and a house of prostitution in Marbella.

They eventually resigned, but this didn't seem to cheer up Shearer, who hadn't taken kindly to remarks by one Premier League manager about how referees were 'letting him get away with murder' in opposition penalty areas. To add to the gloom, Shearer simply wasn't scoring.

It was looking grim on the hooligan front as well. A man called Matthew Fox, a Fulham supporter who either 'wouldn't hurt a fly' or who 'was first to get stuck in when things got nasty' – depending on who you talked to – was stabbed to death outside Gillingham's stadium, and there were pitch invasions at two Premiership grounds. Police sources were conceding that some of the worst offenders of a few years ago appeared to be back in business and raring to go.

John Gorman ushered me into a tiny room in the FA's Lancaster Gate offices, where I asked him if the keel was cracking on the good ship England. I suggested that for all the hype, England were nothing without Gascoigne, that it needed someone to control the game in midfield, to make things happen.

'Paul Merson can pass the ball better than Gazza in many ways,' he said. 'I know we've got the players. Forget the Chile game. We are on course and it will come down to the last month when we have the players with us all the time. Glenn is a good listener and he has built a good spirit. We know each other very well. We are on the same wavelength when it comes to football. We speak to each other for hours every day, and we have spent a lot of time editing videos of our opponents to show the lads. I have a romantic belief about the way the game should be played. You play from the back and you encourage every member of the team to be comfortable with the ball. I can see it happening, even with Tony Adams and Martin Keown. They don't just hit long balls any more. We start every training session using a small ball to help with their touch and control.'

Gorman was a full-back who moved from Celtic to Carlisle before arriving at Tottenham, where his friendship with Hoddle blossomed. He became Hoddle's assistant at Swindon and took over briefly when Hoddle got the manager's job at Chelsea. He has the weathered, suntanned face of a Scottish farm labourer. He is unfailingly friendly, greeting even total strangers with 'Good to see you again.' During his time at Hoddle's elbow he had won people over with his enthusiasm and attention to detail.

'People say I haven't played at the highest level, but nor has Alex Ferguson. My strength is on the training ground, getting the players going, keeping up their spirits. Sometimes I'm like a social worker to them, but there's nothing wrong with that. They can talk to me at any time and they do. I think they know what I feel about it all, that it's more than a game, it's a shared passion. I was brought up to worship football in West Lothian and to dream about it. It's an art in every sense of the word. I often get the players to paint a picture of a certain move in their minds and then do it. Belief is a big thing but there is always an element of fate at work as well. A Tunisian might do something extraordinary and we could be on our way out. I know that. It's always in my mind but I don't dwell on it. I think about what we are going to do to Tunisia. And I think we are going to take them apart.'

By the beginning of April, there was already World Cup overload. Even those who loathed football recognised that there would be little escape come June. The television schedules were filled with football dramas, football documentaries and visits down football's Memory Lane. Every other commercial had a football theme. Travel companies were having a torrid time trying to sell packages abroad for late June and early July; film distributors began frantically changing their release dates to avoid a clash with the football, and promoters of live events were either cancelling shows or busy installing television screens. Record companies were also holding back, aware that during the last World Cup in America, when England weren't even there, album sales in Britain fell by 5.5 per cent.

The ticket disgruntlement rumbled on. Most of those planning to be in France still had no idea if they were going to get a ticket and were showing signs of frustration. The protestations of the FA, supported by the British government, had led to a slight increase in the number of tickets available to England supporters, but still nowhere near the number called for. Then the European Union got involved. Karel Van Miert, the Competition Commissioner, decreed that the French Organising Committee's ticket policy was in clear breach of regulations, and was planning to begin legal proceedings. This didn't seem to bother the French. They were still refusing to release the remaining 110,000 tickets to nationalities other than their own.

Michel Platini, joint President of the France 98 Organising Committee, thought it was all splendid. 'We had 20 million applications for 2.5 million tickets, so naturally a lot of people are disappointed,' he said from the safety of his desk in Paris. 'And if everyone wants to have tickets, it shows that they're selling at a very good price. We wanted a World Cup for the people and the inconvenience with that is that everybody wants tickets. Many of them want tickets to sell on at a higher price.'

Like Mike Burton Sports Travel, one of two British companies licensed to sell World Cup packages. Burton, the former British Lions forward, was expecting to turn over £16 million by the end of the year, an increase of nearly 50 per cent on the previous twelve months.

'We paid £500,000 to get the licence,' he told me when I called at his office in Gloucester. 'Excuse me a minute.' His mobile rang. 'Excuse me,' he said again a couple of minutes later, as one of the two landline telephones on his mahogany desk trilled. Then his secretary dropped in with some new information. 'Excuse me, won't be a minute.'

Burton was one of the first rugby players to cash in on sponsorship, when he agreed to wear Adidas boots for £50 a game. That was in 1974. 'I got criticised at the time but I realised that I had an instinct for the commercial side of things and here I am a few years later with 16,800 World Cup tickets.'

Burton sent his son Andrew and his financial director Ian Edwards to Paris to retrieve the tickets. They were accompanied by three armed guards, and even their respective families had no idea where they were going when they left home one April morning. 'They had to be picked up from a French address between 8 and 11 am. Andrew and Ian stuffed them into two large cricket bags. I had set up an operations room to oversee the whole operation. They got back to London and the bags were immediately taken to a vault in the bank.'

It would cost £600 to get hold of one of Burton's tickets. Flights, fancy meal on arrival, fine wines, transfer to and from the stadium, good seats. And all in a day. The fax machines were purring, and by Christmas the company was to spill over into the next door building which it had acquired on the back of the World Cup.

The vast majority of English supporters would be travelling to France without tickets. As a result, the government spent £1 million on a campaign called 'Get The Facts', whose chief objective was to stress that all tickets bought in France on the black market would bear the name of a French resident, and that the identity of the person with the ticket would be checked at the turnstiles. But no sooner had the first ad gone out than the French police said 'The Facts' were nonsense. Monsieur Querry, the French police's top security man, turned Home Secretary Jack Straw inside out. 'There will be no identity checks when entering the stadium,' he said. 'It would be totally unmanageable to do so.'

Meanwhile, a summit of police officers from all fifteen European competing countries was gathering in Paris. In Lens, where England would play their last and potentially crucial first-round game against Colombia, plans to show the game on a giant screen in the main square were abandoned, and there were calls for the sale of alcohol to be banned in all cities where England were playing.

There were no such fears in La Baule, the genteel Breton resort where Hoddle's squad would base themselves. At the team hotel, the du Golf International, in the tiny village of St André des Eaux, about two miles from La Baule, the Three Lions crest was on display during Easter at the reception desk, with a signed England shirt to the right of it, inscribed during the team's stay twelve months earlier for the Tournoi. Locals were being encouraged to buy flags of St George and were hoping that English journalists would throw caution to the wind on the expenses front. The town's director of communications, Fabrice Jobard, went overboard. 'We want England to win it,' he said. 'We don't care about France.' In fact much of France didn't seem to care about France either. With ten weeks to go before the off, you would have been hard-pressed to realise that the world's biggest sports event was about to open for business – save for the cheery Footix mascots on sale at news-stands, in train stations and at airports.

Hoddle looked miserable when he arrived in Berne for a friendly against Switzerland. Whereas a week earlier John Gorman had been telling me that it was still only March and that there was plenty of time for the likes of Seaman and Wright to overcome their injuries and get back to their best, Hoddle was saying the opposite. 'I am at the stage where I have not got any more time. Compared to Brazil, England are a motorway behind.' Brazil had managed to squeeze in more than twenty international friendlies in the last two years. England were about to embark on only their third since qualifying nearly six months ago.

Hoddle's mood, which was not helped by a mild dose of flu, became ever more morose as he sat in his hotel room watching the England Under-21 side crumble before their Swiss counterparts. The 2–0 result was bad enough, but worse was the failed experiment of playing Jamie Redknapp as a sweeper. It was back to the drawing-board, even though Redknapp insisted that he could still fulfil Hoddle's dream role if given another chance.

Then there was the spin put on Hoddle's casual remark that Michael Owen was not a natural-born goalscorer. Owen had smashed goal records at every level for England right up to his elevation to the senior side. He had been tipped to become a greater goalscorer than Jimmy Greaves. But Hoddle saw fit to describe Owen's role as a 'very good sub'.

Not for the first time, Hoddle's attempts to ease the pressure on one of his players had backfired badly. The truth was that Owen was feeling very little pressure. It was Hoddle who was beginning to show signs of strain. Since the second week of October he had been living in a small room in the home of his faith-healer friend. The Shredded Wheat ad was a long time ago. Around the same time, Anne Hoddle was doorstepped by a newspaper and said she and her husband were beyond reconciliation.

It would require something special against the Swiss to lift his morale. Switzerland 1 England 1. The result was better than the performance. Towards the end of the first half, with the Swiss in the lead and looking comfortable, you could have been forgiven for thinking that this was 1992 and that Graham Taylor rather than Glenn Hoddle was sitting on the bench. You almost expected Tony Daley to be thrown on as a last resort. Owen played alongside Shearer, but his first touch deserted him and he came off in the second half to be replaced by Sheringham. Rio Ferdinand, who began and finished the match, played competently alongside Martin Keown. But there was nothing happening in midfield. There was no creativity. No spark. No Gascoigne.

Hoddle lost control, briefly, at the post-match interview. After getting unnecessarily defensive when asked to comment on the game, he abruptly cut off the interview, saying he wanted to be in the dressing room with his players. When he eventually came back out he had recovered some of his sang-froid but still said nothing. Later, while talking to the Sunday papers, his growing irritation with the press led to a telling outburst. 'To be frank,' he said, 'I couldn't care two monkeys what you think.'

Immediately after the Switzerland game, Hoddle headed off for a restorative cruise in the West Indies with Vanessa Shean. It did not go unnoticed, and within days the *Sun* saw fit to report that the bill for the two-week jaunt came to more than £10,000. Photographers snapped the couple strolling along the beach, hand in hand like, as the *Mirror* put it, 'teenage sweethearts'. Mrs Shean was 'stunning' in a white bikini.

'Not only do the pictures show a couple deeply in love,' gushed the copy, 'but they reveal what a striking figure Hoddle's 34-year-old love has despite having had three children. The images will be 40-year-old Anne's worst nightmare. She has also had three children but has been unable to hide the passage of time as well as Vanessa.'

The *News of the World* also ran the pictures, and launched a caption competition to go with a picture showing Hoddle rubbing suncream on his chest. The £100 winner suggested the following riveting exchange: 'I wonder how the others are relaxing,' says Vanessa, to which Hoddle replies, 'If I know Gazza he'll be doing the same as me – getting well-oiled.'

Hoddle's tan was still in evidence when he announced his squads for the full international against Portugal and the B game against Russia. He named thirty-four players in his first-team squad and twenty-five in the B squad, including Matt Le Tissier and Darren Anderton, whose injuries had prevented him from taking part in any England get-togethers under Hoddle's tutelage. He said everyone on his list had to turn up. 'Unless they are in hospital, unless they are in plaster, unless they can't travel because they are ill – and I'm talking about a serious injury, a serious reason why they could not get a plane or a train or a car – I expect them to be there. A letter has been sent to the players, and their clubs, saying unless there is an extreme situation with a player in plaster they are expected to be there. It is two months before a World Cup and I don't think I am asking too much to get thirty-odd players together to have a talk and run some tests. The tournament is round the corner and it's coming pretty quick.'

It was coming quick for the Reggae Boyz too, but they didn't have anything like the pressure. Jamaica, on their never-ending pre-World Cup world tour – with games against Iran, Saudi Arabia, South Korea and Santos – were drumming up wild and enthusiastic support wherever they went. They were in London to play QPR in a testimonial game for the club's veteran midfielder, Simon Barker.

So clogged were the streets of West London that kick-off had to be delayed fifteen minutes to cram everyone in safely. It's not often that you find ticket touts doing brisk business on a Sunday afternoon before a testimonial game, but then it's not every day that a football match becomes a carnival, or rather that a carnival includes a football match. The QPR official who presided over the pre-match formalities said over the Tannoy: 'I only wish we could get this sort of crowd at all our matches.'

You would have to reinforce the steel girders holding up the stands if this lot showed up every other week. Warren Barrett, the twenty-six-year-old captain and goalkeeper, led his team out for their first ever game in Britain to a deafening din. Like most of the Jamaica-based players in Brazilian coach Rene Simoes's squad, Barrett grew up in abject poverty. He did not own a pair of boots until he was picked to play for Jamaica schoolboys at the age of fifteen. He was earning crumbs as a regular in the Violet Kickers side back home, compared to his Jamaican colleagues in the Premier League.

Jamaica started as they meant to go on, winning the ball from the kick-off and then stringing together a sequence of twenty-two passes. Some had red boots, some green, a couple chose white. Several wore black gloves on a day when the sun shone permanently and the temperature climbed close to the 60-degree mark. The whiff of marijuana hung gently in the air. When Ricardo Gardner, Jamaica's nineteen-year-old left-back, crossed the ball for Theodore Whitmore to score in the thirty-fourth minute it was glorious pandemonium time, with women waving their arms in the air and looking skyward.

At the post-match press conference, Rene Simoes moved swiftly into fairytale mode. 'In Jamaica, the Reggae Boyz represent a Cinderella dream. You can be in rags and with no hopes, but you know your football team is doing great things around the world. We are hoping to postpone midnight and stop everything turning to pumpkin.'

I had dinner with Simoes that evening at the Meridien hotel in Piccadilly. He had done the rounds as a coach, including spells in

Qatar and Portugal. 'Football is the perfect example of how democracy should work,' he said, his accent showing signs of a Jamaican lilt. 'Unlike tennis, where the best player will almost always win, in football the little man has a chance. So many things can happen. I believe in luck and it could be that we will surprise the world in France.'

He also believed in his computer. 'I will show you my laptop. You will be amazed. I put in there every piece of information I need. I will be able to tell you exactly how many passes we made in our last match and how many of those went to a Jamaican player. For me there are two important things to consider. One is how well we pass to each other and the other is how well we get on with each other. And the question of how we get on with each other is going to be very important. There is a difference in thinking between the English-based players and those who still live in Jamaica. At the moment we are getting on fine, but I am going to have to keep an eye on it all the time.'

A fly-on-the-wall TV crew commissioned by Channel 4 was keeping its eye on it as well – and the Jamaicans were going to pay dearly for it.

Chapter 5

Faith

On 20 April, two days before the friendly against Portugal, Hoddle had some important news to impart. Eileen Drewery was now working with the England team in an official capacity. She had moved into the squad's hotel at Burnham Beeches and was busy working with the injured players. It was a clearing of the air for Hoddle. He had often been called a born-again Christian, but despite an affirming religious experience in Jerusalem while on tour as a player with England, he had never signed up with the happy-clappies. Born-again Christians don't believe in reincarnation. Born-again Christians are wary of anything not rooted in their particular interpretation of Scripture. Hoddle's spirituality was of the à la carte variety, and Eileen Drewery a vital ingredient.

'Three-quarters of the lads have seen her over the last eighteen months. It's nothing new. We're saving on expenses her coming to us. What she does is private. She's a healer, physically, and mentally, she can help out.'

There was the suggestion that some players might feel under pressure to see her so as to gain favour with the manager, and that it could be divisive to have such a person working so closely with a bunch of footballers. Route one to a place in the squad could be a series of appointments with Mrs D.

'Many players have seen her off their own backs between internationals. I want to explain that I have never made a player see her, only suggested it. It is difficult to talk about success rates because there is no set record, but no player has ever refused to go to see

72

her. Her approach and a scientific approach are very different but they can work hand in hand.

'Look, if you cut your finger today, in four or five days what happens to it? It heals. So there is a mechanism in your body, a natural mechanism that heals. She can trigger that off – it's as simple as that. You're asking the wrong person how she does it. Better ask somebody up there.' Hoddle pointed to the sky.

The sniggers began. The *Daily Mail*, which was emerging as Hoddle and the FA's fiercest critic among the tabloids, took a dim view of it all and posed the question: 'Has Glenn Lost The Plot?' The *Sun*'s headline was 'Come All Ye Faithful'. The *Express* 'Come On Eileen'.

'I'm not at all worried about ridicule,' said Hoddle. 'If you ridicule it you've got closed minds. I don't know what you would call her. What does it matter? Some call me a manager, some call me a coach, some call me a lot worse. Call her a healer if you like. I have more of an understanding of what she does now. I didn't when I first went. I was seventeen when I had the experience of healing. I didn't have any religious beliefs or anything like that, so it is nothing to do with religion. It's an individual mind-set. It's not just about footballers either. It's of benefit to all people. I have sent my own family. There's been a lot of good work from it.'

Support was immediately on hand from Ian Wright. 'I think she is blessed,' he said. 'It has helped me a lot seeing her over the last eight or nine months. This is not difficult to talk about as such, it is just that the work means a lot to me and she means a lot to me. I feel very close to her. It is very important and people can just take the mickey out of it. If I phone her up she knows it is important. She is very good, very wise. I just like being around her. Some people can take it on board and be quite interested about it but some will just call it rubbish. For me, it was easy because I have been God-fearing and spiritual all my life and my family are very much that way. The boss explained to us that we were under no pressure – if you want to go, you go. I wouldn't preach to anyone because that is not my place. I just say to someone, if they ask me, go and make your own mind up. It might enlighten you.'

Uri Geller, meanwhile, was getting in on the act, telling anyone who would listen that he had produced tiny booklets to send to all the England players, full of uplifting stories and mind-bending lessons. He was hoping they would pop them behind their shin-pads during games. He said that he had secretly taken the World Cup to his house in February and 'positively energised' it on behalf of England. He had been to Marseille and had sneaked into the Vélodrome stadium, where he had planted energy crystals in the pitch. Which was fine except that I couldn't help thinking how nearer to home his team, and mine, Reading, were rooted to the bottom of Division One and were about to drop another league just as the final touches were being made to our new £25 million stadium next to junction 11 on the M4.

The *News of the World* splashed a story alleging that Hoddle had performed a 'bizarre mystic ritual' on Geller during a visit with Eileen and the former Chelsea defender Paul Elliott to his Berkshire home. Hoddle said he had never been inside Geller's house and that he was instigating legal action. The *News of the World* wheeled out the Reverend Tony Higton, an Essex rector and member of the General Synod of the Church of England, to tell Hoddle to 'stop meddling with the forces of darkness'. I used to ring Higton almost every Friday afternoon when I was covering religious affairs for the *Sunday Telegraph*. Whatever the issue – women priests, sex before marriage, homosexuality – Higton never failed to produce a quote to enliven the flimsiest of stories.

The *News of the World* also lifted liberally from a book about Hoddle by someone called Phil Shirley, who claimed to be a black magic expert. He concluded that Eileen Drewery's methods were linked to the voodoo of witch-doctors in Haiti, whose rituals involved the sacrifice of dolls and chickens. That wasn't how Hoddle explained it to Brian Alexander on Radio Five Live.

'My faith in God is at a spirit level. We are here to learn spiritually and that's the reason we're on the planet,' he said.

'Will God decide whether you win the World Cup?' asked Alexander.

'It doesn't work like that. I believe in the power of prayer and prayer is a powerful tool. If you have a selfish thought it brings out a low vibration. A prayer is a high vibration. It's a thought you are giving out to the creator. If you don't believe he's there and don't have a one on one then you won't be able to be helped. It's like if I want to make a call to Australia I have to get up and physically dial the number. God is there. He's not going anywhere. He's been there for eternity. The problem is that we've blocked ourselves off from him. The thing we have to do is say to him, "Come into our lives, let's share." And you'll be amazed what can happen in your life. My life has changed. I've still got problems just like everyone else but I've got something that helps me during the hard times. I don't preach to anyone. Things happen at certain times in your life because we've been here before. The spirit comes back. This physical body is just an overcoat. Take it away and your spirit goes into another life in the spirit dimension.'

In the same interview, he was asked about discipline on the pitch. 'Some players are capable of getting themselves into silly situations when there's no need for it,' he said. Asked to name names, he paused before saying: 'Well, David Beckham has a few things to learn about that.'

Eileen Drewery, who shared the same agent as Hoddle, remained taciturn about her role, save for an appearance on the Richard and Judy programme, where she said she had asked God to stop Ian Wright from scoring in the dying minutes of the Italy game because she feared Rome would erupt in violence. She also said she didn't know till lately that teams change ends at half-time.

'It's with God's power that I work. I have always believed in God. I loved the story of Jesus when I was a little girl. I can halve the time it takes an injury to heal, but I can't take the credit. I give that to God. I don't want people to think I'm a mumbo-jumbo.'

Steve McManaman, who was thought to be in the anti-Eileen camp, used his column in *The Times* to say he had no objections to her involvement and echoed Hoddle's call for people to have an open mind about it. Another unnamed member of the squad likened England duty to 'joining up with the flippin' Moonies'.

* * *

The 22nd of April began with the sound of telephones being slammed down across the country with ever-increasing frustration. France Telecom registered 20 million calls during the day as the last 110,000 tickets went on sale amid farcical scenes that led to the intervention of the British prime minister, who promised to do his bit. There was nothing he could do.

A group of sixty operators were on hand in an office in Paris to cope with the calls from fans in eighteen European countries. By some strange chance a further thirty salespeople were manning telephones exclusively for the benefit of French nationals. Your chances of getting through from the United Kingdom were put at one in two million. Those who did defy the odds and found themselves talking to a human being after three hours of dialling, hanging up and redialling were not altogether placated when they were offered tickets to the Saudi Arabia–Denmark game rather than England–Tunisia. Others who got through found that they did not have the right credit cards. Then the whole telephone system crashed.

BT weren't complaining, taking a slice of the charge for each call, of which there were more than 250,000 within the first five minutes, four million within the hour. 'It is not abnormal that callers have to wait or that some calls don't get through,' said an unrepentant French official.

Maria-Pia Brown, a seventy-six-year-old woman from Southend, had an interesting morning. Her telephone number was the same as the first six digits of the French ticket hotline if you omit the 00 for an international call. She received her first breathless request for tickets at 7.01 am, and they kept on coming for nearly two hours until Mrs Brown dialled BT and begged for her telephone to be taken out of service.

Finding tickets to the England–Portugal friendly was an easier proposition, and by 7.55 pm on 22 April Wembley Stadium was pretty much stacked to the rafters. The official World Cup song, 'On Top of the World', written by Echo and the Bunnymen's Ian McCulloch and the former Smiths guitarist, Johnny Marr (but featuring all and sundry, including the Spice Girls, who just happened to be doing their own thing that night across the car park in the

Wembley Arena), was played in full for the first time just before kick-off. It reminded me of some ghastly New Labour jingle. When it ended the unofficial Three Lions mantra filled the stadium as the dignitaries were introduced to the players.

The experimentation was over. Hoddle had to play his strongest team. A failure now would unleash a barrage of criticism that would send Eileen Drewery reeling back to her Wokingham sanctuary. Many of the Number Ones thought the damage had already been done, that Hoddle was 'off his rocker' and had set himself up for a national lampooning. He had invited ridicule, but there was a feeling that he was perfectly capable of taking it. Even so, what was needed was a spirited rather than spiritual performance against the Portuguese, who were unlucky not to be going to France after losing only one game, to Ukraine, in the qualifiers. As expected Hoddle played pretty much the same side as the one in Rome six months earlier, except with Shearer in for Wright and Scholes replacing Gascoigne. Gary Neville was preferred to Gareth Southgate.

During the singing of the Portuguese national anthem a section of the crowd booed throughout, but when some Portuguese were heard chatting as the rest of the stadium observed a minute's silence in honour of Dennis Howell, the former Labour MP who was Minister of Sport when England beat the world in '66, an English voice shouted: 'Fuck off, scum.'

Portugal hadn't lost at Wembley in their last five visits. In fact you had to go back to 1969 to find an England victory, when Jack Charlton scored the winner. But now Portugal were one down after four minutes, Shearer steering the ball into the net with his head from close range. You could feel the tension around Hoddle's shoulders loosen.

There was little else to get excited about in the first half. Not a lot was going on in midfield, little creativity as ever. Hoddle brought Merson on for Beckham at half-time, which seemed bizarre. Why didn't he go for Ray Parlour? And then just as heads were being scratched, Sheringham scored virtually from the kick-off. Shearer let fly with a cracker in the sixty-fifth minute to make it 3–0. Owen replaced Sheringham with fifteen minutes to go and came within inches of scoring with his first sniff. Everyone wanted him to score and *everyone* – apart from Hoddle perhaps – realised that the Owen–Shearer partnership had far more potential than Sheringham–Shearer.

At the other end, Seaman was having a great night, which silenced the Doubting Thomases like me who suspected he had lost his edge and confidence. Adams scored in the eighty-sixth minute but the referee didn't give it. And then Owen was brought down by the keeper in the penalty area and that wasn't given either. After the game, the Portuguese coach, Humberto Coelho, was asked if England could win the Tournament. 'I think,' he said, before pausing to reflect on the question. 'I think . . . maybe.'

There was a buzz in the Wembley Banqueting Suite that evening. It had been a torrid few weeks. Hoddle had been tetchy and the players had struggled with end-of-season injuries. Now there was a sense that the show was back on the road. The players were in good spirits, patiently signing their names on anything from footballs to tight white T-shirts stretched across the chests of young women. The Banqueting Suite, with its wooden floor and tatty screens that divide up groups of sponsors, has a bar at one end and football memorabilia screwed into the walls. FA blazers were everywhere as many of the ninety-five-strong council that governs football in Britain shuffled about the room. A lot of people despised them, but at least they purported to represent the game from top to bottom. They were regarded as fuddy-duddies – for good reason, since only six of them were in their forties and only two in their thirties – but who wouldn't prefer them to be in charge than a committee made up of Premier League chairmen planning to bunk off to Monte Carlo once they cashed in their share options?

There was a bad guy waiting outside for Paul Ince. 'Judas, Judas,' he shouted before swinging a punch at the Liverpool captain, cutting his lip. The thirty-three-year-old man who was arrested claimed it was a case of mistaken identity. Ince had often faced 'Judas' taunts from West Ham supporters, the team he left for Manchester United seven years ago, but this was the first time it had ended in fisticuffs. It seemed a harsh penalty to pay.

* * *

With a month to go before the end of the season, Arsenal had barged their way ahead of Manchester United, and the Championship – and the double with it – was theirs for the taking. The mood at Highbury was, as Dennis Bergkamp put it, 'inspiring', and even those who hated Arsenal were having difficulty not conceding that the Gunners were exuding skill and sophistication. Arsène Wenger had built a unit made up of outstanding individual talent, with a level of intensity about their play that was awesome at times. English experience at the back, French dash in the middle and Dutch pace and guile up front.

From Hoddle's point of view it was a shame Ian Wright wasn't part of the race to the tape, because it was obvious he wanted him in his squad. Wright's ability to keep everyone amused and his general influence in the dressing room counted for a lot, and it helped that he was such a devotee of Eileen Drewery. Hoddle had always said that he would only pick players if they were 100 per cent match-fit, and there was no way Wright was ever going to be that. But Hoddle was not averse to making exceptions to the rule. 'One way of looking at it,' he said in a nifty move of rational gymnastics, 'is that it could be an advantage to have a fresh Ian Wright with us rather than an Ian Wright who has just finished a gruelling season.'

On 17 April, I went up to Arsenal's training session before their game with Wimbledon. The players change, eat and generally luxuriate at the Sopwell House hotel, near St Albans, where dozens of teams have pitched camp over the years – so many, in fact, that one corridor has been turned into what the hotel grandly calls a Hall of Fame.

'Some of the world's finest footballers and teams have stayed here before performing their magic at the famous Wembley and other football venues,' says a plaque. Signed team shirts in glass cases hang from the walls. There was a healthy bundle of supporters waiting to greet the players off the bus. Bergkamp walked across the hotel car park carrying his dirty football boots. No one rushed forward. No one shouted out a name. It was like watching a procession of priests file out of church after Holy Communion. I wanted to speak to the Reverend Ray Parlour, but the Arsenal press officer said it wouldn't be possible because his agent believed he was 'over-exposed at the moment'.

So I sat down with Martin Keown, who, barring injury, was certain to make it into the final twenty-two. He had had a superb season since coming back from a sickening shoulder injury suffered while playing for England against Brazil during the Tournoi. At the time, the doctors wouldn't tell him about the severity of the injury, but there was no way to disguise the pain. He was even given a special pump to administer his own levels of pain-killer. Initially he was told he would be out for two or three months. In fact it was more like five. He had not just broken his shoulder, but sheared it so badly that for a long time he could not lift his arm at all.

His rehabilitation included falling on mats over and over again to see how much pressure the shoulder could take. Finally, he was allowed to play in a reserve game and was sent head over heels.

'I remember just before hitting the ground thinking: Here we go again. But as I crashed down on the same place on the same shoulder it held perfectly.'

Now, at the age of thirty-two, he was about to take part in his first and last World Cup. 'Sometimes I find myself thinking back to the 1974 World Cup. I remember going to a swimming pool with some friends and it was empty. I became aware that something big was going on and that feeling of wanting to be involved in it. I remember that Cruyff drag-back and thinking how did he do that?'

Keown's forehead looks like it's had a tractor driven across it, and his nose belongs to a professional boxer. He has small, piercing eyes, and when he wants to say something important he leans forward and squints. 'I am very competitive and I have a lot of drive, don't give up. I drive and drive. I think that was what my parents noticed about me and they encouraged it. They wanted me to be good at something. My father was in construction and he hoped I would do something different. He kept emphasising what a chance it was if I became a footballer, and I suppose I never had much doubt about it. When my careers officer at school asked me what I was going to do and I said, "Play football," he said, "Don't be stupid, that's not a proper career."'

I asked him about the future. 'I got bitten by the bug to be a player but I don't think I want to be a coach. I want to do *something* with my life once the football is all finished. There are players at Arsenal who might not have to work properly again, but I am not one of them. Honestly, I think I might go and run a charity or something.'

I was back to the Sopwell House hotel two weeks later for a meeting with David Platt, who was already eyeing up Hoddle's job. Remember those impeccable driving runs from midfield, those sudden bursts into the penalty area. That is exactly how Platt intends to play it in the managerial game. That's why he didn't sign a four-year contract with Middlesbrough at the beginning of the season. It would have interfered with his career path.

'I have already started writing down the names of players I want to work with, and I spend a lot of time at the Subbuteo board working on tactics. I am good at making decisions. There are so many things in my head and I want to get out and see if they work. I just want to succeed, but physically I can't do the things that I could before. When I was twenty-three I wanted to be the best, but now that I'm thirty-two I realise I can't be the best, so it's the right time to go into something different.'

Platt's footballing life changed totally as the result of one touch of the ball in a World Cup. It came in the dying minutes of England's last-sixteen game against Belgium in Bologna in 1990. Penalties beckoned when Gascoigne took a free kick not far from the halfway line. Platt, who had only come on as a substitute in the seventy-first minute, turned, swivelled, jack-knifed and lashed the ball into the net. '*Ma che bravo ragazzo, questo Platt,*' the watching Gianni Agnelli, owner of Juventus, is reported to have said, getting out his chequebook.

'I'm not stupid,' said Platt. 'I know that the Belgium goal was the most important of my life. It changed everything for me. It was entirely instinctive. Nine times out of ten on the training pitch I would not even have hit the target. When it went in I knew immediately how important it was. I went down on my knees, which I normally never do. It was never part of my celebration routine. I was out of myself.'

He remained out of himself for the next twelve months, to the point where he sought professional help. 'Suddenly I was recognised wherever I went, and I was the man to stop on the pitch. I was finding it hard to get David Platt back into David Platt's body. I went and saw a psychologist, someone who wasn't biased, someone to talk to. It was good to pour everything out. I gave him the full truth and it helped enormously.'

I asked him if there was anyone in the present England set-up who might have a similar experience in France.

'There is only one person I could think of,' he said. 'Michael Owen.'

Football managers come and go, and so do newspaper editors. Towards the end of April, Lord Hollick called me and four other members of the *Express* boot room into his office, and within days we had either been sacked or forced to resign because our jobs had been given to other people.

What sort of football Hollick wanted us to play was never clear, but like many rich businessmen he liked being in charge of a club. I couldn't altogether concentrate on what he was saying because I needed to exchange contracts on a house by noon. And there was another important piece of paper waiting for me downstairs – confirmation that my official accreditation for the World Cup had been approved by FIFA. I was with England now – full-time.

Hoddle picked a thirty-man squad for the friendly against Saudi Arabia, the last game in England before heading off to a special training camp in Spain, from where they would pop over to Casablanca for a couple of warm-up games against Morocco and Belgium. If you weren't in that thirty you stood no chance of making the final twenty-two. That meant that Matt Le Tissier, despite a hat-trick a couple of weeks earlier for an England B side against Russia, would miss out. So would Andy Cole and Stuart Pearce. Paul Merson was preferred to Ray Parlour, which raised eyebrows. And Darren Anderton, who had played only three games all season, was on the list. So were Rio Ferdinand, Ian Wright and Dion Dublin. And so was Michael Owen.

'Some people might be surprised about you taking Darren Anderton,' said one of the Groins. 'He has only played eleven full games since Euro 96.'

'Well, he'll be nice and fresh won't he?' replied Hoddle.

There were two other matters on the agenda that morning at the Park Royal hotel, both of which were to get short shrift from Hoddle. First, there was the apparent row between the players and the FA about how the sponsorship cake was to be divided during the finals. Of particular concern was the way in which the FA had cut them out of a kit deal worth £28 million. A players' council of war had been convened, which included Alan Shearer, Tony Adams and David Seaman, and there were threats about taking the case to the European Court of Human Rights if the FA didn't back down. Most estimates agreed that each member of the squad would receive between £100,000 and £150,000 for getting through to the second round, but what would happen if they were to win the whole thing? The players wanted to be free to endorse products of their choosing while still wearing the Three Lions. The FA wanted to clear any such deals first. It was difficult to know who to support. When a player pulls on the England strip, does he become the shirt or does the shirt become him?

'It's got nothing to do with me,' said Hoddle, looking at Davies. 'The reality is that progress is being made,' said Davies.

The England players earned £60 a match in 1966. They received a bonus of £22,000 for winning it, and Bobby Moore insisted that it was shared out equally, £1,000 a man. Almost every member of the 1998 squad had set up a business in his name as a conduit for surplus funds – from Paul Scholes Ltd, which had as its company secretary Clare-Louise Froggatt, Scholes's girlfriend, to Shearer Promotions Ltd, which was already running its own pension scheme.

And then there was the question of Gascoigne's smoking. A piece in the *Independent on Sunday* had suggested that Gazza's fight for World Cup fitness included a packet of ciggies a day. 'I'm not here to talk about smoking. If you want to write about it that's up to you.' And with that he stood up, put on his jacket and walked off.

The nicotine fantasy team: Bruce Grobbelaar in goal, Jack Charlton at the back, Socrates and Ossie Ardiles in midfield, and one's spoilt for choice up front with Platini, Cruyff, Best, Law and Greaves all vying for places. I've got a picture of Bobby Charlton in the bottom drawer of my desk, sitting in an England dressing room enjoying a post-match smoke. And yet Gazza the Smoker was still a bit of a revelation. Twenty a day seemed a lot for someone struggling for full fitness after injury.

There was a third question, but it never got asked because no one knew about it at the time. It was to do with the FA's secret disciplinary hearing that was going on that very same day in Sheffield to decide whether Shearer should be punished for kicking the Leicester midfielder Neil Lennon in the head. Not Guilty was the result, leaving Shearer free to play in the Cup-Final on Saturday and roll on to France without the charge hanging over him. In fact the original decision was 'not proven', a verdict only normally permissible under Scottish law. The decision to let Shearer off met with little comment. Perhaps the FA's invitation to sports editors to play golf with Hoddle that week to discuss the sort of coverage expected during the World Cup had done the trick.

I was due to meet David Davies the next morning at Lancaster Gate, but when I got there his secretary said that all was not well. He had got a fishbone stuck in his throat the night before and was feeling a little delicate. I would find him at White's hotel across the road.

'I genuinely expected the hearing to be next week,' said Davies, triumphantly. 'But then Graham Taylor, chairman of the Professional Footballers Association, approached Graham Kelly and asked if we would get it over before the Cup-Final, and within twelve hours it was decided to hold it in Sheffield. We were amazed the story did not come out.'

But it must have helped that one half of the football media was listening to Hoddle in London while the other half was in Stuttgart for Chelsea's Cup-Winners' Cup-Final.

'Let's just say that the timing was good in that respect,' said Davies.

I asked Davies if Hoddle would talk to me. He said he wasn't talking to anyone but that he would be happy to discuss everything at the end.

Gazza went drinking. Escorted by his friends Chris Evans, Rod Stewart and Jimmy 'Five Bellies' Gardner, England's midfield supremo headed for The Pharmacy, a swish new London restaurant which you would avoid if you didn't want to be recognised. At around midnight, Gazza, Gardner and Stewart fell into a chauffeur-driven Bentley and made their way to Evans's flat, but not before a sequence of photographs had been taken showing Gazza in various states of drunkenness. Evans had nothing to lose and much to gain from the excursion, especially when he persuaded Gazza to turn up next morning on his Virgin Radio breakfast show. It was a pity Evans couldn't have got him to show up as promised that Sunday to a charity penalty shoot-out at Millwall.

'Tomorrow I'll knuckle down. I've had a seven-day break, so what. I've got nearly a month to get fit. If I'm good, I'm in the squad for the World Cup. It's as simple as that,' said Gazza, who was due to report for England duty in three days' time.

But in the early hours of Sunday morning, he was again out and about in Soho with Evans, Gardner and TFI producer Will McDonald, in search of a kebab and onions. This time, the *Mirror* had the photographic evidence, courtesy of a passer-by called James Eisen, who was quoted as saying: 'I asked Chris if I could take his picture and he nodded. I asked Gazza and he sort of mumbled, so I took the shot. I asked Gazza to move closer to Chris but one of his group stopped me taking any more pictures. One of Gazza's mates grabbed the camera and then it went flying. It ended up under a car but I was able to retrieve it. After that I decided it was best to leave them to it.'

The *Mirror* gave the impression that Eisen was minding his own business and just happened to take the pictures after asking politely if he might do so, and that the pictures just happened to end up at the paper's picture desk. But that was not quite how Eisen later explained it.

'Looking at Paul "Gazza" Gascoigne, I didn't see England's so-called ace midfielder or allegedly the finest British footballer since George Best, or soccer's equivalent of Tony Hancock. I saw lucre. Dough. Dosh. I saw a Canary Isles holiday (Fuertaventura and not Lanzagrotty!), a much-needed service and change of the bald tyre for the Metro, the nullifying of my student loan and the chance to ask my dentist next time to insert a white filling.'

By the time the squad had assembled at Bisham Abbey, Gazza's face was parked like a ton of lard on the inside pages of every newspaper, alongside learned words from doctors and nutritionists. No one seemed prepared to defend him. A poll of readers in one paper showed that 74 per cent thought Hoddle should dump him there and then. But Hoddle had always gone out of his way to defend Gascoigne, and since no one could think of anyone better to replace him in the centre of midfield, it seemed the manager would stick with him, kebabs and all. But it was grating, especially when Hoddle had invited Dr Yann Rougier, the biologist that Arsène Wenger employed at Arsenal, to give the players a talk about the importance of diet.

When I arrived at Bisham, there were two ginger-tops running around the pitch. One was Paul Durkin, the English referee selected for duty at the World Cup, the other was Paul Gascoigne, whose face had turned as red as Durkin's hair. It was the hottest day of the year, but Gazza was wearing a long-sleeved tracksuit top. You could almost see steam rising from the back of his neck.

'Why do these things keep happening to Paul?' Hoddle was asked.

'I don't know. Paul will be here in a minute. You ask him.'

Hoddle said Gascoigne was only 60 per cent fit, and made it clear that this was his last chance. 'There are a set of guidelines and anybody who steps over them will be dealt with. If he had behaved like that while under my control with England he wouldn't be with us now. He would have been hammered long ago. I've had a long

Previous page:
Brazil's fate rested at
the feet of Ronaldo,
billed as the greatest
player in the world.

Above: With a
spectacular goal
against Tunisia, Paul
Scholes confirms
England as one of the
strongest teams in the
tournament.

Right: Hoddle's
controversial line-up
worked in Marseille,
but sterner tests were
still to come.

Left: Pete (left) and Mark get dressed for a night on the town.

Left: Romania proves Graeme Le Saux and England's back line are fallible after all.

Above: Colombia couldn't cope with Darren Anderton's volley in Lens…

Below: …but the French police managed to contain the England fans.

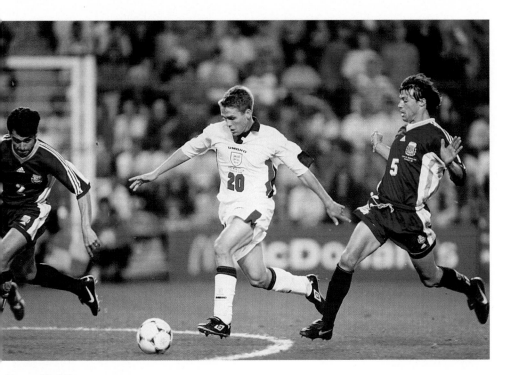

Above: Hoddle described him as 'not a natural goal scorer', but Owen cuts through Argentina with the goal of the tournament.

Below: The kick that went round the world. Beckham lashes out and leaves England to survive with ten men.

Opposite: The wrath of Hod.

Above: David Batty has still never scored for England…

Left: …and Paul Ince wonders why he volunteered to take a penalty.

Above: How did it all
go so wrong?

Below: France realises
that football isn't such
a bad game after all.

chat with Paul but I can't control what he does when he's not under my wing.'

'Did you have to tell him forcefully or did he get the message from the start?'

'Forcefully.'

The worry for Hoddle was how to keep the peace during the four or five days between returning from La Manga and gathering at Heathrow for the flight to France. Although the players would be allowed home they would still be under England rules. 'I don't want to see them on the front pages of newspapers inside some nightclub. If I do, that will be it', he said.

Gascoigne didn't walk into the room after Hoddle left. He swaggered, and you could tell from the moment he sat down that nothing his manager had said had made any impression.

'I'm not far from being fully fit,' he said. Hoddle said he was 40 per cent short of full fitness. 'Before every tournament starts there's flak flying around. I get most of the stick, but in fact I've had two nights out in sixteen days and got slaughtered for it. Had a kebab and been pictured eating it. It was nowhere near 2 am. How can you not be fit for having a kebab? The gaffer has talked to me about it and you don't know what he told me, do you? Every England player goes out for a night with his mates, but then perhaps they don't have a camera up their arse. Two nights out don't make you a bad footballer. Okay, I had a couple of beers with the guys. It was just unfortunate it was in the papers. During my time off after Spain and before France I'll see the kids. But no doubt you'll find out if I do anything else. I'll train as well and get myself ready. I can't believe the fuss over one night out, doctors coming on television to talk about it. It really pisses me off.'

And then Gascoigne was asked if he felt old. 'No', he said, 'I feel like having a nice kebab with onions on it.' Not even the most sycophantic scribe could raise a smile.

Chapter 6

Thirty Minus Eight

It was a gloomy flight to La Manga on the morning of Monday 25 May. A 0–0 draw at home to the Saudis, probably the weakest side to have qualified for the finals, was hardly the dream send-off. I had bought my son the new England strip before the game and the World Cup wall chart was already tacked to his wall – and mine. We were sitting behind a pillar at Wembley but it didn't blind us to gaping holes on the pitch. Anderton was so out of it in the second half that he looked like he needed a respirator. Shearer was miserable and Sheringham did nothing. Southgate and Adams were like cardboard cut-outs whenever the Saudis dared to run at them. Gazza was playing brilliantly by sitting on the bench and occasionally trotting up and down the running track. Then, shortly after half-time, the clamour began. 'If you want Gascoigne stand up . . . if you want Gascoigne stand up . . . if you want Gascoigne stand up.' And almost to a man, the stadium rose.

The crowd's desperation to see an unfit Gazza in action may have highlighted the paucity of talent on offer, but it also spoke volumes about the symbolism of England's most famous footballer. Paul Gascoigne was a self-confessed wife-beater who couldn't make it to the birth of his son because he was away with the lads, a joker, a smoker, a boozer who blamed the media for his troubles but who if the price was right would do an interview with *Hello!* in which he would admit to bouts of 'manic depression' on his way to the bank to cash the cheque.

'Take 'em on, Gazza, you fat bastard,' shouted a man behind us with genuine affection.

Hoddle had told the team to go on a lap of honour whatever the result, but when it came to it the boos rang out so loudly that no one dared. The sound system cranked up 'On Top of the World'. Gary Neville said the crowd was an 'absolute disgrace'.

La Manga is a golfing paradise, which to some of us means purgatory. Nigel Mansell and Kenny Dalglish have villas there. It's a purpose-built, artificially green and pleasant land where you wake up in the morning thinking for a second that the hissing sound is some rare indigenous insect before you realise that it's the computerised hose system. The wheelie-bins outside the villas have the La Manga logo on them, and there are club buses that shuttle guests around the 1,400 acres.

Hoddle is a regular. He brought along his Swindon players for some pre-season bonhomie a few years ago and had taken part in a celebrity golf tournament here. The football centre, with its grand gates and four almost full-size pitches, was a joint venture with the Norwegian Football Association, but there wasn't a Scandinavian to be seen when the England bus swept into the resort, escorted by a Spanish police car. Flags of St George hung from every lamp-post leading to the five-star Hyatt Regency. A regal entry.

It was half-term week, good news for British holidaymakers who had a chance to sit in on England training sessions and fill their autograph books. Shortly before the players arrived at the training ground, the small stand on the east side of the ground was almost full. The first face the crowd recognised was that of Chris Eubank, but only just. Wearing a floppy hat and dungarees, he looked like a groundsman at the Sabina Park cricket ground in Jamaica.

'I'm here to say hello to the team,' he said, when asked to account for himself. Eubank's big mate is Ian Wright. Wright gave him tickets to the Arsenal–Newcastle Cup-Final, but Eubank didn't use them because they were in the middle of nowhere. 'I would have been murdered. Michael Watson was very much an Arsenal man and a friend of Arsenal – of course he was a friend of mine, still is a friend of mine – but in light of what happened it would have been awkward.' He gave Ince and Wright a bear-hug and wandered off. We didn't see him again.

The crowd had eyes mainly for Gazza. They always do. He was wearing his long-sleeved training top and getting pucer by the minute, and while every other member of the squad went about his business with due reverence it was Gazza who played to the gallery, picking up a plastic cone and putting it on his head to show everyone he was the dunce. The troubled soul of the clown.

Teddy Sheringham was given clearance to speak afterwards. He is known as the thinking man's footballer, a label he doesn't care for. Presumably it means he should be able to explain the things he does on the pitch, but that might suggest he is not such a great player, because the great players are meant to know not what they do. They just do it. When Ronaldo was asked to describe what he does, he simply shrugged and said: 'I do what comes to me. Dare something, risk something, show the people something special. Apart from that I don't think about it.'

Sheringham acknowledged that there was a lot of apprehension around. 'You just don't know if you're going to be in it, but there is not a lot you can do. Some of the older players talk about who we think has made it and who is still on the border-line, but you know it's on everyone's mind all the time.'

He was asked, in the most tactful of ways, if he thought his own form had dipped in recent weeks and how much of a blow it was to have been left out of the Manchester United team towards the end of the season, and whether he accepted that Owen was threatening his place in the team. He killed it dead.

'There is always room for improvement.'

And Owen? 'I am in the team at the moment. I am not looking over my shoulder at him.'

Then John Gorman came in to report on the state of Hoddle's health.

'He's not tensing up at all. Honestly, that's a fact. He's fine.' He talked about the terrible deed that would have to be performed before next Monday, when seven players would be discarded from the squad. 'It's going to be horrible and I shall feel very upset for the players. There will be tears. I think Glenn will want to tell them first and then I will try to help them. We will have to be right on top of it because it can damage a player very badly, but I believe most of them are professional enough to take it.'

The neighbourhoods surrounding the vast concrete bowl that is Casablanca's Mohammed V Stadium have nothing in common with the celluloid charm of Rick's Bar. Rows of peeling apartment buildings, many under construction, others in the throes of demolition, line the main roads leading to the vast open-air amphitheatre. Children stand at traffic lights selling sweets, key-rings, newspapers. One boy, no more than ten years old, was holding a set of knives and forks, but did not seem to care if he made a sale.

It was odd that the streets were so empty. I couldn't understand why the pavements weren't spilling over with merry Moroccans on their way to the game. More than 85,000 were expected officially and another 15,000 would get in without tickets because they were friends of the stewards or the police. It was only on entering the main gates that it became clear. Everyone was already inside – and going loco.

I went to pick up my pass from a baking room underneath the main stand and marvelled at the audacity of the Moroccans for their daring bid to stage the 1998 World Cup finals. There was a long table at one end with four people seated behind it waving their arms in the air. In front of them, 150 journalists, VIPs, television commentators, radio men and satellite technicians tried to see if their name was on a list or if there was a list on which to put their names. Alex Ferguson, who was in town taking part in a documentary about the Scottish national side, took one look at the inside of the oven and walked off. Even the Crystal Palace defence was more organised than this.

The passes were there. No, sorry, they weren't there. No, they were on their way. New forms had to be filled in. No forms were needed. Curiously there was no sign of Steve Double, who had been out a few months earlier on a recce to satisfy himself that everything would be all right on the night. While his charges were locked inside the Moroccan sauna he was prancing around the stadium in his FA blazer, marvelling at the spectacle of it all.

Then a man in a blue suit and yellow shirt came along and introduced himself as Aziz.

'You all come with me,' he said, and off we went, passing baffled doormen in dark glasses who, after a wink from Aziz, began letting in anyone who had no badge attached to him. In fact, the only way of entering was to have nothing official on you at all. If you had shown a legitimate document you would have been detained under the Don't Confuse Me rule.

The teams walked out to a piercing shrill whistle. Leading the white shirts was Paul Ince. Yesterday he was withdrawn from training and looked to be in considerable discomfort, today he's captain of the team. You never knew with Hoddle. The English bench were wearing blue and white hooped polo shirts. From a distance they looked as if they'd just escaped from prison – which was one way to describe La Manga.

Tim Flowers was in goal, out to confirm his position as England's number 2. Either Ian Walker or Nigel Martyn would be left out on Monday. Keown, Southgate and Campbell were the three central defenders, with Le Saux and Anderton as the wing-backs. McManaman, Gascoigne and Ince were in midfield and Dublin and Wright, competing for a striker's place, were up front.

The Moroccan National Anthem is a real barnstormer. It ends with an almighty left and a right which sent the crowd into a frenzy. The England players lined up in anticipation for 'God Save the Queen', but an entirely different tune boomed out across the stadium. No one had a clue what it was. McManaman began scratching his groin. Ince kept picking up the ball and putting it down again.

It was Gascoigne's thirty-first birthday. Just seeing him survive a full ninety minutes of football was good enough reason to bake a cake, but it was still a shock watching him give the ball to the opposition every time he touched it. On several occasions a Moroccan just came up to him and removed it, almost pausing to say thank you. For the first thirty minutes, England failed to put together three consecutive passes of any significance. In the press seats, journalists kept turning round to each other in disbelief. 'Is it just me,' asked one, 'or is this total shite?' To which the reply was, 'No, it's not just you, it's 100 per cent total, fucking bollocks.'

Then Wright went down, clutching his left hamstring. On came

92

Owen, but ten minutes later he was out like a light, after clashing with the goalkeeper at a combined speed of close to 25 mph. The Moroccan players immediately waved to the bench, and Dublin rushed up to Owen and turned him on his side. Dr Crane was escorting Wright off the pitch when he realised what had happened. He jumped over the advertising hoardings behind the goal and ran into the middle. He was fast for a sixty-nine-year-old. Owen was just recovering consciousness and being helped to his feet. Dr Crane made him close his eyes to see how much control he had over his body. He was allowed to continue. It was the turning-point of the game. In the second half, McManaman, sensing he had only forty-five minutes left to set out his stall, started to play, and it was his pass that led to Owen scoring his first England goal and becoming the youngest-ever scorer for his country, beating Tommy Lawton's fifty-year record.

The crowd turned against their team with venom. Whereas a minute previously they could do little wrong, now they could do nothing right. And as the booing continued, they sank lifelessly to the canvas. Even Gazza, the bloated beached whale, was beginning to get back in the swim. At the final whistle, bottles of water and other debris were hurled on to the running track and the hissing lasted until every Moroccan player had vanished underground. They were buried alive.

Hoddle answered questions from inside a glass-fronted police hut with no light in it. The Wright injury was a hamstring, but it was too early to say if it was torn or bruised and, yes, Michael Owen was 'exceptional'.

Afterwards I came across Dr Crane in the tunnel as the kit was being loaded on to vans. He said Owen had pleaded with him: 'Please let me go on.' Crane had been with England since the 1986 World Cup, when the then doctor Vernon Edwards had a heart attack, and he had been looking after the players at Arsenal since 1970. Before leaving for La Manga I went to see him in his Camberwell home, where a velvet England cap marking 100 appearances takes pride of place on the sitting-room wall. He still works as a GP in the Old Kent Road.

'Hoddle runs a strict regime,' he told me. 'Every day is organised.

A lot of effort goes into planning. Taylor and Robson could be strict too but then they lapsed.' The doc had befriended Gascoigne over the years, and the Cranes were invited to his wedding. Gazza had ordered a long white limo to pick them up.

'Gazza looks a long way from being fit,' I said. And the doctor nodded.

When England scored their goal, a hush had fallen on the stadium, save for a pocket of about a hundred people fifty yards to my left. They were English supporters who had each paid more than £450 for four nights' bed and breakfast, return flights and a coach ride to and from the airport in Casablanca. Tickets were on top of that. Dedication. Matt Woods, from Epping, Nigel Burgess, from Hoddesdon, and Alan Dell, from Dunbar in Scotland, had never met each other before, but they had already formed a small gang. Burgess was a fire and safety officer married to a Jamaican. 'I hate seeing England lose at anything,' he said. 'It doesn't matter if it's football or tiddlywinks, although losing at football is more important than losing at tiddlywinks. It annoys me that the Welsh or Scottish can be fervent about their country and everyone thinks they are patriotic, and I get fervent about my country and people think I may have something to do with the National Front. It's hardly likely, seeing I have a Jamaican wife. I am proud to be here watching England, although I sometimes think I am more proud watching the football than some of those playing. I would like to see the players really singing the National Anthem as if they meant it. I would like their chests to be puffed up and I would like them to want it every time they put on an England shirt. Some of this lot don't seem too bothered.'

Alan Dell, a computer programmer who lives in the Scottish borders but supports Notts County, began travelling to England away games in 1989, after being at Hampden for Scotland–England. He has missed very few internationals since, especially abroad.

'There were 65,000 Scotsmen in the stadium, all wanting to get one over the English, and there were us, a tiny pocket of people who wanted the result to go the other way. We hammered them. It was a great feeling. That was how it all started for me.'

That afternoon, Dell was mugged by a gang of six Moroccans. 'First there was one and then all of a sudden there were half a dozen. They grabbed my bag and ran off. It was our fault really because we had read about not wandering around the backstreets and that was exactly what we did.'

Dell's enthusiasm for a country in which he had just been mugged and where he was paying £7 for a bottle of beer in an undistinguished nightclub had not been damaged.

'It's a bit of a dump but they are very friendly, at least most of them, and they're proud of their country. I like that. The atmosphere in that stadium was amazing.'

Matt Woods met his fiancée in Malmö during the 1992 Euro championships. He was twenty-three at the time. 'We were hanging about in the square where the Swedes had put up beer tents. I saw this girl and she took my eye. She was called Tess. We kept in contact after I got home. I sent her photos and she sent back photos of her and her friends. Then I went out to see her again about three weeks after we got knocked out. She was living with her mother. Things just started moving along really nicely. I was going over every other week and then she came to England to be an au-pair. I wanted to do it properly so I went back to Malmö with her and I proposed in the square where we had met. We were going to get a house together but I wanted to be in Essex and she wanted to be closer to the West End. We started arguing and I went off to watch football and then it all fell apart. You don't go to England games to fall in love, but when it happens it's pretty amazing. I rang her quite recently because I heard her mother was ill with cancer. She wouldn't speak to me and I knew she was living with another guy. I still think of her a lot, but there's nothing I can do about it now.'

Woods is a big man with short hair. He works for the bankers, Robert Fleming, and supports Leyton Orient. 'So, what's going on with the girls around here, then?' he said when we met later. I was wondering that, particularly since the woman sitting at the bar next to me was rubbing her foot up and down the back of my leg. She had olive skin and long dark hair that spilled over her shoulders in thick waves. She told me her name and then put it in writing on the back of a pack of Winston Lights. So I bought her a whisky and fizzy water. At 4 am, she drove me back to my hotel in a little red Renault. She turned down an invitation to inspect my mini bar on the grounds that if the hotel staff saw her there would be big trouble. She gave the sign of her neck being severed from her shoulders.

'But you're with me,' I said.

'That's the problem', said Katy, skipping down the steps, her car-keys dangling from one hand. We should have been starring in one of those moody ads which would have ended with her driving off at speed from the hotel accompanied by the caption, 'Escape With A Renault'.

You don't recover quickly from a hamstring injury, and early next morning it was confirmed that Ian Wright was on his way back to London. How did he take it? So badly that on the Friday morning, when the other players were preparing to leave for Casablanca for the second game against Belgium, he couldn't bring himself to come out of his room. When he finally emerged from the hotel and was driven to the airport he had to sit around for thirteen hours while Spanish air traffic controllers voted on whether to end their strike.

It was now a straight fight between Dublin and Ferdinand for a striker's place along with Shearer, Sheringham and Owen. Ferdinand had nothing much to offer, and then on trotted Dublin for the last ten minutes as a defender.

Gascoigne pulled up with a dead leg after five minutes of the second half, his head already swathed in a bandage from an earlier collision with a Belgium boot, and went off. The dreary game ended 0–0. Nigel Martyn made two or three assured saves and seemed likely to edge out Walker. At the final whistle the players exchanged shirts, only to be told to put them back on because there were going to be penalties. Les Ferdinand needed to score for him to keep England in it, but he hit the ball too comfortably close to the keeper. Shirts were exchanged for a second time. England had been beaten in a penalty shoot-out *again*, but Hoddle dismissed it as 'irrelevant'.

* * *

Hoddle was adamant that the players should be left alone for the next two days. The photographers took issue with this, knowing their picture desks in London were going to be screaming for material for the Sunday and Monday papers. They weren't being paid to sit around the swimming pool all day. It was suggested that Adams might pose up on the tennis court. Better that than nothing, and it might at least lend itself to a banal caption about the big man serving up an ace on behalf of all England. But he wouldn't play ball. Tension was building. The players were to be left alone and yet Beckham had just signed a contract with the *Sun*, Seaman was taking money from the *Mirror*, and Ince was on the books of the *News of the World*. It was like agreeing to marry someone and then refusing to sleep with them.

Two photographers trudged off to play tennis by themselves, and who should they find on a nearby court but Tony Adams?

'Hoddle's a fucking control freak,' said a snapper from the *Mirror*. 'It's never been this bad. If anything it encourages us to start crawling through the undergrowth in search of a picture. No other country operates like this.' Which wasn't strictly true and, anyway, no other country has so many national newspapers – ravenous national papers, all claiming to be the voice of football. Certainly, the Italians operate a more open system, but it doesn't necessarily lead to better stories – or at least not the sort of stories that have become standard fare in England. And it must be said that the FA goes out of its way to have separate briefings for the dailies, the Sundays, television and radio. The Germans and Italians just have one giant session for everyone.

Not that Hoddle's press conferences are particularly illuminating. For the most part they are dreary set-pieces in which, as someone once remarked, the England coach shows that he can speak almost as good English as Franz Beckenbauer. Wherever they are held, they take on a similar pattern. Davies sits beside Hoddle, always on his right. The *Sun*'s Brian Woolnough, the *Express* duo of Martin Samuel and Paul McCarthy, the *Star*'s Lee Clayton, the *Daily Telegraph*'s Henry Winter, the *Times*'s Oliver Holt, the *Mirror*'s John Dillon, PA's Martin Lipton and the *Daily Mail*'s Graham Hunter occupy the centre front row, with David Lacey of the *Guardian*, Nigel Clarke of the *Daily Mail*, Steve Howard of the *Sun*, Glenn Moore of the *Independent* and Harry Harris of the *Mirror* on the flanks. The Sundays bed down with the *Evening Standard* in the rows behind.

Normally the Number Ones will have consulted with each other before the press conference about a particular line of inquiry, but more often than not something will emerge which they will agree on among themselves afterwards, even down to the exact key phrase used by Hoddle. You cover your arse before you cover anything else.

Hoddle disliked these games of ping-pong. Sometimes he hardly bothered to pick up his bat, and when he did there was a tendency to tap the ball listlessly back over the net. There were very few rallies. Terry Venables loved to cut and thrust with the media, feeding them both real stories and total flyers depending on his mood. And you could always pop down to Scribes West, his club underneath Barkers department store in Kensington, buy him a drink and then, if you hung around long enough and were prepared to listen to his appalling friend Eric 'Monster' Hall blathering on, you would usually pick up a story before closing time. Venables had his favourites, and if he took a dislike to someone he would do his best to make that person's life difficult. Hoddle simply had a policy of making everyone's life equally easy – or equally frustrating.

There is a lot of hanging around when you are covering England. And often you're writing utter flam. Before the trip to Casablanca, there was a day when absolutely nothing happened and Hoddle merely went through the motions at his press conference. Every potential avenue of interest came to a dead-end. Then someone asked if he ever felt intimidated by the other World Cup coaches, most of whom were older, and almost all of them more experienced in international management.

'No, I don't,' said Hoddle. This led to banner headlines in some of the tabloids the next morning shouting: 'Hoddle: I'm one of the best in the world.'

'There is still some tension occasionally,' said Winter, when we came across each other in a Turkish bath in Casablanca, 'but I don't believe there is any English football writer out here who is not 100 per cent behind the team. It's a strange life. We spend so much time in each other's company but we are all addicts, which helps.'

They are also sensitive flowers, deeply suspicious of outsiders. The players may be paranoid about the press, but the Groins are just as paranoid when a foreigner invades their patch. At dinner one evening in Casablanca, I was invited to sit at high table with the Number Ones and a few chosen Number Twos and was asked to account for myself.

'I have nothing but contempt for people who feed off others for their own purposes,' said Woolnough, 'and that's my concern about you. I imagine you are here to stitch us up.'

'Exactly,' said Holt. 'Nothing personal, but we've been stung before.' At that moment the music was turned up a couple of notches and out came a belly dancer with a very large, wobbly tummy, who began her routine with gusto at the side of our table.

'Let's say I have had a few drinks and get pissed and start dancing with her, you would love that wouldn't you?' said Holt.

I told him that important as he undoubtedly was, I did not think many people would be particularly interested whether he danced with the belly dancer or not. He didn't, as it happened.

Winter told me later that Woolnough's angst was almost entirely due to his loathing for Harry Harris, who apparently hadn't asked a question in an England press conference for twenty-six years. He told a good story about the day Woolnough suffered the ultimate humiliation at Stamford Bridge. It was shortly after the *Sun* had accused Liverpool supporters of being drunk before the Hillsborough disaster. On seeing Woolnough at half-time, a group of Liverpudlians decided to have a go. They shouted that his paper had lied about Hillsborough. They told him they would never buy it again. They said the *Sun* was scum. Fair enough, thought Woolly. He had no trouble with any of that. But then they started chanting 'You're worse than Harry Harris' and he fled in shame.

On the morning of Sunday 31 May, the Number Ones left messages on the players' mobiles and at the hotel, with little hope that their calls would be returned. Hoddle had told his squad that he did not want anything to leak out before the official announcement at lunchtime next day. He was going to start knocking on players' doors in the morning to tell them the terrible news. He would be taking as much time as was needed with each of them. At least, that was the official plan.

In fact, a private plane had been hired to take out the discarded as soon as they had been informed. Hoddle knew you could not tell the players and then expect it to remain a secret until the next morning. Arrangements to get them out of the country on Sunday night had been put in place months ago. They would fly to Birmingham rather than Luton or Gatwick to avoid the media on arrival. Double would go with them.

Winter announced that he was going to keep in touch with Davies and that he would pass on any relevant information. He enjoyed a close relationship with Davies. Some of his colleagues believed it had been rather too close over the years – that he went out of his way to court favour with the FA. There was a rumour, which Winter enjoyed perpetuating, that he would take over Davies's job after the World Cup, provided Davies could find a suitably elevated position at Lancaster Gate.

For the rest of the day, Sky News, Radio Five Live, the Press Association and a growing pack of football correspondents filed holding stories about who was expected to be in the twenty-two. I felt sorry for the Jeffrey Archer readers sitting around the pool. They had come out for a week's peace and quiet and were treated to an invasion of journalists endlessly shouting down their mobile phones.

''Ello, matey . . . yeah, it's a fucking nightmare here but I'll give you six hundred words of background . . . with an update later after we know what the fuck is going on . . . Okay, put me over to Copy . . .'Ello, darlin', I've got something for Sport, oh, hold on. Shit, my batteries are dying . . . call you back in five. Cheers.'

Sky News had parked its van up the hill from the swimming pool, a tall thin aerial sticking out the back. Every half-hour, Ian Woods went live to report that there was nothing to report. Bored by the sound of his own voice, he resorted to urging journalists to leave their sun-loungers for a few minutes to opine on who was likely to be going to France. There was common agreement. Les Ferdinand was definitely on his way home, along with Ian Walker and Andy Hinchcliffe. Rio Ferdinand would also miss the trip, along with two from Merson, Butt and Phil Neville.

Winter rang Davies at least five times during the day. Finally, it was agreed that the steer would be given, in person, by Davies at 7 pm, in Winter's studio apartment. At 6.45 pm Spanish time, Harry Harris did a live interview with Sky News during which he was asked about Paul Gascoigne. 'Hoddle will take Gascoigne because although he is nothing like what he was during Euro 96, there is still the need for someone to produce some magic in the final third,' he said.

Davies rang Winter at 7.30 pm. There had been a delay. The meeting would be at 8.15 pm and, said Davies, 'you boys can expect to do some rewriting.' I was sharing an apartment with Glenn Moore, of the *Independent*, and Ian Ridley, who at the time was working for the *Independent on Sunday*. Ridley was helping Tony Adams with his autobiography, the final chapter of which had to be turned round within a couple of weeks of the World Cup final. It was going to be a close-run race between Hoddle and Adams to see whose book would be in the shops first. Winter summoned Moore and Ridley and the other Number Ones to his room, but when he telephoned Woolnough and warned him about the impend-ing rewrites, he was told: 'We already have the story, Henry.'

'What is it?' asked Winter.

'I can't say,' said Woolnough.

'Well, give us a steer,' said Winter.

We were in danger of overdoing the steering. Woolnough said he would come over earlier than the others to tell Winter about what to expect. But he never did. Davies arrived in Winter's room shortly after 8 pm, the others following close behind.

'He's left out Gascoigne,' said Davies, adding quickly: 'Purely for fitness reasons.' He then read out the names of the five other deceased: Walker, Butt, Phil Neville, Hinchcliffe and Dublin.

Scramble. The first editions were in the process of being put to bed, but this was massive. This was five pages at the front and six at the back for the tabloids. It was bigger than the earthquake in northern Afghanistan that morning which had killed more than five thousand people. Geri Halliwell had announced earlier in the day that she was quitting the Spice Girls. That was big, but this was bigger. This was football at its maddest, the biggest selection story since Alf Ramsey left out Jimmy Greaves for the 1966 final. More important, this was the dumping of the biggest name in English football. Thrown out like the crumpled wrapping of a greasy kebab and onions.

It had been some steer. Davies had brought along Hoddle's complete list. All thirty original names were on it, with a fading red line through Jamie Redknapp's and a less faded one through Ian Wright's. The blood was still dry over Gascoigne's. Why he didn't summon the whole media bandwagon and give it to everyone at the same time remains a mystery. Martin Lipton, the hard-working Press Association scribe who was transferring to the *Daily Mail* after the World Cup, had filed 3,000 words of fodder during the day that was now bound for the bin. He was incandescent with rage. This was not a steer, this was a full-blown announcement, and the representative of the national news agency had not been privy to it. Mike Ingham, from Radio Five Live, was also seething at what he regarded as a stitch-up between Davies and the prints. Ingham heard it first from a member of his production team who happened to be walking past the Sky News van.

Davies tried to rally a few broadcast people as he walked down the street, but not everyone was in the immediate vicinity. One way or another the news would out. Jonathan Pearce was sitting quietly on his balcony when he heard Harry Harris pacing up and down in the wondrously named Calle de Capa de Ponce below, dictating copy to the *Mirror*. I'll have a bit of that, thought Pearce, and went live on Capital Gold.

It had been a brief conversation between Hoddle and Gazza. A tape of Kenny G was playing when Gascoigne walked in and sat down. 'You're not fit enough. It's nothing to do with anything else,' said Hoddle, which was not strictly true. The coach had been alarmed by Gazza's frame of mind. He had spent hours on the telephone to his wife Sheryl during the trip, sorting out details of their divorce. His focus was elsewhere. When Hoddle broke the news, Gascoigne flew into a rage, kicking a chair with his bare feet and smashing a lamp that sent shards of glass across the room. At one stage, Hoddle thought Gascoigne was about to punch him in the face. Back in room 203, Gascoigne telephoned his wife in Hertfordshire, who rang Rebekah Wade, deputy editor of the *Sun*, who had made it a professional priority to befriend Mrs Gascoigne. Sheryl, on her part, was keen to keep in with the Murdoch empire, having already taken the first steps towards a career as a cable television presenter. A six-figure deal was done.

It was a brave move by Hoddle, possibly the right one, but I still felt sorry for the fat boy. I took a twenty-minute taxi ride to Cartagena, a nearby naval town, and tried to find a bar without a television, but failed dismally, and so I sat drinking the local draught lager and watched the news in Spanish, which featured a piece about the Spanish squad's final warm-up game against Northern Ireland.

Back at Colditz, the inmates were rattling the bars of their cages. The news had even tempted Kenny Dalglish out of his lair. He was holding court at Luigi's, the local pizza palace, and wasn't greatly impressed by Hoddle's squad. He was unfazed by the dethronement of Gascoigne, which he may have half expected after Alan Shearer and Robert Lee had been round at his villa the day before complaining about Gazza's general demeanour.

Gascoigne had let Hoddle down both off the pitch in La Manga and on it in Casablanca. His presence, so often crucial to morale, had begun to cause division. There were England players who were with him and other England players who were against him. Hoddle was somewhere in between. His loyalty had been stretched to near breaking-point when Gazza showed a total lack of contrition over his night out with Evans and company. Then in Morocco he broke down injured after only one and a half games. Even so, it was tempting to believe Gascoigne when he said he would be ready for England's opening first-round game, and if on returning to La

Manga he had made a point of being seen with a glass of water in his hand rather than a bottle of beer when Hoddle allowed the players one evening of revelry, then he might have been spared the axe. But on Saturday night in the Lorca Bar of the hotel, Hoddle and Gorman stared in dismay at the speed with which Gascoigne rendered himself legless. During the karaoke, he was almost too drunk to perform, and you have to be fairly paralytic to fail at karaoke. And then it got back to Hoddle that Gazza had smuggled a couple of cans of beer into his golf-bag the next morning before participating in a foursome.

Seaman was the first player to see him after he had been given the news. 'It was a sight I won't forget in a hurry,' he said. 'Paul was just inconsolable. He was crying his eyes out, and there was nothing either Incey or me could say to make him feel better.'

The *Daily Telegraph* even ran a leader on the subject: 'Whatever one thinks of Paul Gascoigne – peerless artist or Geordie lout – there is a tinge of melancholy in the news that he will not, after all, be playing in the finals of the World Cup. Poor Gazza. His wife, "Shezza", is divorcing him. In the tears of the rejected footballer, we see the anguish of one not now in the first blush of youth . . . What now, when the dolt-genius faces the long declivity of his career? Will he be allowed to stumble downwards, from ill-advised sponsorship deals to the management of some third-rate club, ending as an incoherent after-dinner speaker? Or will Mr [Chris] Evans stretch out a saving hand? The word is that Ginger Spice will find a place somewhere in his empire. Gazza deserves no less. A radio show, perhaps, or TFI Gazza.'

When the chosen twenty-two arrived at the training ground next morning it was 88 degrees in the shade. There was an intensity on the pitch such as had not been seen all week. No jokes. No jolly japes – no Ian Wright, no Paul Gascoigne. Gary Neville tackled his friend Paul Scholes with such ferocity that he would have been sent off if it had been for real, and Graeme Le Saux hit the ball again and again into the back of the net with steely intent. Among the watching crowd, some shook their heads in disbelief at the absence of Gascoigne, while others muttered grudging approval.

At the end of the session, the players got straight back on their bus. No autographs, not even a wave to the crowd, many of whom had sat in the sizzling heat for nearly three hours. The FA went to extraordinary lengths to ship unwanted players away from the public gaze when it suited them, but when it came to giving something back to the supporters they couldn't be bothered. It would have taken ten minutes and would have made a lot of schoolchildren happy. A small boy in an England shirt with Beckham printed on the back looked on despairingly as the bus left the ground. A girl holding a blue autograph book burst into tears. Her father said: 'It's bloody disgraceful but typical. We've learnt to expect this of modern footballers, although I imagine they were only following orders.'

Hoddle made his official squad announcement on the terrace of the hotel. Journalists were not allowed in until 1 pm – or, rather, they were not allowed in until the coach taking the players to the airport had left. It was a close-run race. The two coaches almost met head-on at a mini roundabout.

'Fucking pathetic,' said ITV's Gary Newbon. 'This us-and-them business is getting out of hand.'

Hoddle sat behind a table draped in the flag of St George, with a large La Manga logo in front of him. Sky and Radio Five Live were going live, and there were ten camera crews positioned in the back row. Jonathan Pearce was preparing to do a phone-in direct from La Manga. A ginger-haired Scotsman acted as Spanish translator for the local networks. Hoddle was sitting with his back to the sun but was wearing dark glasses. Was he concealing a black eye after being walloped by Gascoigne?

'We ran out of time in getting him as fit as was needed,' said Hoddle. 'I'm as disappointed as he is. It was a tough decision but Paul has not got himself fit. You have to be an athlete in today's football. I need twenty-two players who can play ninety minutes. I'm not too worried if people think I'm right or wrong. You can't please everyone in life.'

Did he throw a tantrum?

'Not necessarily,' said Hoddle.

How hard was it?

'It was a terrible day. Afterwards I walked into John Gorman's room and the news was on the television about the earthquake. That made me think a little.'

The Number Ones occupied most of the best seats in the house but never said a word. Afterwards, they got Hoddle on their own.

'We heard he took a swipe at you, Glenn,' was the loosener.

'He didn't.' Hoddle had removed his dark glasses. There didn't appear to be any swelling around his eyes.

How did he react then?

'There were some tears. He was extremely disappointed and upset.'

'What about the cans of beer in his golf-bag?'

'I don't know,' lied Hoddle. 'I didn't play with him.'

Hoddle stressed that Gascoigne had only himself to blame. 'I've gone out on a limb for Paul in the past and done so many things to make him see what is needed in the modern game for a player at thirty-one. Come on, I've protected him. I've helped him, I've done as much as I possibly can.'

Hoddle could have given chapter and verse on Gascoigne's imbibing, but resisted. He knew Gazza would condemn himself once he had taken the Murdoch shilling. He said details of the conversation between him and Gascoigne were 'private'. But there may have been another reason the England coach was, at best, economical with the truth about how Gascoigne had responded. Hoddle had a book to write – with the help of David Davies – for which he had received a handsome advance. His publishers would have loved it if he could hold back some meat until publication day, and there were plans to serialise the book in the very same newspaper that had signed up Gascoigne.

It annoyed Hoddle that every question was about Gazza. 'I feel very sorry for the others who have been left out. Their football world has been turned upside-down too.'

Like Phil Neville. He was so cut up that he couldn't speak. A few days earlier he had been led to believe by Gorman that he had made it. He just shook hands with Hoddle and walked out. Back in his room, he sat on the bed in tears. There was a knock on the door. It was his brother Gary. They sat on the bed together and Gary, who is two years older, put an arm around Phil and said, 'I can't believe it.' Hoddle had talked to each player individually. A list of appointments set at five-minute intervals had been posted on the hotel notice-board.

The media, almost without exception, swung behind Hoddle. The same scribblers who had written only days ago that despite Gazza's shortcomings he still merited a place in the squad were now applauding Hoddle for his courage as if it had been their idea all along. In the House of Commons, Tony Banks said it showed that football was even more merciless than politics. Tony Blair said he was grateful that it wasn't a decision he had to make.

Gazza took the money and hanged himself in the *Sun*, admitting that he was drunk on Saturday night and that he had been drinking on the golf course on Sunday morning. His story was spread over five pages.

I was 100 per cent convinced I was going. Glenn and the team of coaches had given me no indication that my place was in jeopardy. I went into Glenn Roeder's room. I have known him for 16 years. I took one look at his face and I knew something terrible had happened. He looked upset and couldn't meet my eye. He just said, 'The gaffer wants to see you.' I didn't need to ask any more. I walked to Hoddle's room and I felt this rage building up inside me. No one had said anything but I knew what was about to happen. He looked at me and said, 'Paul, I'm sorry but you're not coming to France. You're not fit enough.' I completely lost it. I went mad, berserk. I lost my rag big-time. I was shouting and swearing. I couldn't believe the injustice of it. I was swearing. Everything came out. I let go of all the emotion building up inside me. I was so hurt. I admit I kicked the door, kicked the furniture. I let my frustration go. Glenn must have called Paul Ince and David Seaman because they came into the room and led me back to my bedroom. I gashed my knee as I kicked the door. I was crying and out of control. I didn't want to talk to anybody and I didn't want to listen to what Glenn had to say. There is nothing he could say.

The *Mirror* did its best to match the *Sun* with a front-page picture of Sheryl on the arm of a man described as her 'new friend' – but no one bothered to follow it up.

Gazza's financial adviser, Mel Stein, accused Hoddle of treating his client like a Nazi war criminal and of being brainwashed by the media. But every phone-in, every opinion poll, every debate came out overwhelmingly in favour of Hoddle.

The squad were left to their own devices for four days on returning from La Manga. Hoddle stressed that he still considered them to be on England duty and that he would not take kindly to reading about wild evenings in rowdy nightclubs. They should use the time to rest and prepare for the biggest challenge of their lives. Shearer headed for the golf course. Owen went home to mum and dad. Beckham slipped into a designer sarong for dinner with Posh Spice in the South of France – and Sheringham went to the Algarve and ended up on the front page of the *Sun* with his arm around a twenty-year-old blonde and a cigarette in his mouth. Sheringham insisted that it was all innocent stuff, but there were some tricky details, not least the bit about him following a girl into the ladies' lavatory. His agent said his client would never dream of doing anything to threaten his team place and that he was absolutely not drunk. This was at odds with the testimony of some of the other customers that night in the Babylon Club in Praia Da Rocha, who said they saw the other half of England's strike-force stumbling about at 6.45 am looking an awful lot worse than Paul Gascoigne only two weeks earlier at The Pharmacy.

Sir Bobby Charlton was scathing. 'I hope he feels suitably embarrassed. If the players don't have the common sense to be able to behave themselves then it's absolutely nonsensical to think we have a chance of winning the World Cup. If I was giving advice to the players I would say, you have got to think what's happening. This is the expectation of the whole country and you have to behave.'

Sheringham's agent kept up the good fight. 'He does not smoke. Somebody asked him to put that cigarette into his mouth,' he said, without addressing the issue as to why Sheringham had not turned down the request.

Hoddle was livid but said nothing. Nor did Sheringham as reporters camped outside his home in Buckhurst Hill, near Loughton. Gordon Taylor, chief executive of the Professional Footballers' Association, naturally sided with Sheringham with a reprehensible and barely comprehensible justification of the incident. 'They're young men, they've been in strict training. They have got three days' holiday and, basically, different people let their hair down in different ways,' he said, without a passing reference to Hoddle's instruction that the players should consider that they were still in training mode during their three-day break.

The FA damage-limitation department went into overdrive. It was decided that Sheringham would make a public apology as soon as he had spoken to the manager after joining up with the rest of the squad at Burnham Beeches. Hoddle spoke at length to Sheringham on the Friday evening, but gave no indication as to what action he might take. Let him toss and turn. The only person to get Teddy Sheringham out of this mess was Teddy Sheringham. By grovelling. Which he did on Saturday morning, reading a statement written for him by David Davies and edited by Hoddle.

'I want to apologise for the problems my actions have caused to my team mates, to the England coach and his staff, to my parents and to my son,' said Sheringham. No mention, of course, of the ticketless punter already making his way to Marseille in a van needing to be filled with oil every thirty miles, no reference to the kids with their Three Lions duvet and England tooth-mugs. It must have been the final straw for Coventry supporters already struggling to accept Sheringham's selection over that of their own Dion Dublin. He would have to play out of his skin now.

Sheringham continued: 'I would also like to apologise for not taking Glenn Hoddle's advice in every detail on how I acted over the period I was in Portugal. I accept there was a lack of professionalism by me in not realising how my actions were likely to be interpreted. I care about what I do and I want to continue playing for England. I have explained what happened in Portugal to Glenn Hoddle. I now want to put this matter behind me and the England team as quickly as possible. I intend to learn from the experience.'

Hoddle wasn't entirely placated. 'It was a massive disappointment. He's got to start from square one again. It was the hours Teddy was up to more than the amount he drank. He says he hopes to learn from the experience and I hope he does. It doesn't matter what age you are, you can learn from mistakes, but I think Ted might have learned his lesson off the back of Hong Kong and the dentist's chair two years ago. At the end of the day he let himself down, me and a few other people as well.'

Sky News sent a reporter to Manchester to get a Sheringham weather report. It was a grim forecast. 'So many people would give anything in the world to be in his position, and he goes and sticks two fingers up at it,' said a man wearing a United strip. 'He should be thrown out just like Gazza was and Hoddle should play Owen alongside Shearer from the start.' And this was from a Manchester United supporter.

Hoddle made a distinction between the unfit Gascoigne who admitted he was plastered and the fit Sheringham who didn't. 'There are no double standards. Gazza was left out purely because of his fitness, not because of his drinking, while Teddy's fitness wasn't in doubt.'

Sheringham's co-revellers waded in. The pictures told the story, but Martin Bellamy, one of Sheringham's best friends, was keen to explain the details. 'Teddy has a friend who owns a private jet and we paid £5,000 to charter it to take us to Portugal. When we arrived we went straight to our hotel and to bed. Everyone made a big joke of us checking under the name of Horne, but that was because Teddy's pal Brian Horne, a former Millwall goalkeeper, was with us.' Bellamy said Sheringham was up at 9 am each morning to play golf and that he only drank Diet Coke during the day and shandy at night, and that the whole business was a set-up.

Chapter 7

France at Last

My car and sleeping-bag came to France with me. At Dover, it was obvious by the number of camper vans and cars with England or Scottish flags trailing out the windows that many others had the same idea. Driving off the ferry in Calais I felt a wave of expectation roll over me that was almost overwhelming. No job. Second mortgage. But a month of football. I was twelve years old again, heading up to the village for a summer evening's kick-about. There had been expectation, then. The thrill of not knowing what would happen, the chance to pretend the occasion was bigger than it was. That a football match was in some way going to change everything. And the discovery of mannerisms that would last a lifetime. George Best holding the cuffs of his sleeve, Leeds' Alan Clarke with his arms in the air, the wrists flopped forward after scoring, Tommy Smith throwing the ball down in mock anger when a decision went against him. Sometimes I used to forget who I was pretending to be.

About an hour out of Calais I saw a sign for Lens with a football beside it, and within twenty-five minutes I was sitting in the Stade Félix-Bollaert just above the two dugouts. The grass was being trimmed and a man was painting the white lines, not definitively, more of a foundation before applying the gloss in a few days' time. Two men were cleaning the windows of the executive boxes, and a student with a beard was pacing up and down on the touchline scribbling in a notebook. England would be here in ten days and we would know by then exactly what was needed. I went and sat where I thought Hoddle would be. Then I wandered down the tunnel and into a cavernous modern hallway and found a door with

'Changing Room B' inscribed on it, next to the Doping Centre. The door opened into a large room where ten chairs were set around a big rectangular table. Three smaller rooms led off the main one. The first had a huge jacuzzi and several showers; the second was a kitchen of sorts, with a fridge, a sink and an electric kettle. The third was the treatment room, with the loos leading off it.

At that very moment Hoddle was giving his final oration on English soil before crossing the Channel: 'We go to France with no fear,' he declared. 'Plenty of respect but no fear, because when there is fear in the camp, you are already on a downward spiral. As an England player, I know previous squads have gone into the World Cup with a feeling of "Well, we don't know how this is going to go." That gives you a situation of starting in neutral rather than starting in first and driving up through the gears. That's absolutely not the case with this squad. There's a positive vibe in the camp. We are going into the World Cup simply thinking about seven games, nothing more, nothing less. We have to believe that we're going to the final. I wouldn't be sitting here if I didn't think we could actually win it. And that's what the players believe. No team, even Brazil, can say they are definitely going to win it. I think I'm a strong leader. I know what I want and what I want the players to achieve. I believe we are prepared better than any other England team has ever been.'

When I walked back into the Lens Press Centre, I saw a familiar face on the television screens dotted around the hall. It was Stuart Pearce walking towards the penalty spot, about to miss against the Germans eight years earlier. Penalties. God help us if we had to endure another night like that.

The centre of Lens is only a couple of hundred yards from the stadium. I stopped for a beer in the main square, where the barman explained the affinity he felt with the English. 'I like the way your teams play,' he said. 'They are strong and never give up.' I tried explaining that Lens was meant to have characteristics in common with some of England's tougher Northern towns, and that its slag-heaps struck a chord of familiarity that might well end in contempt when the English supporters arrived on 26 June. 'I will be supporting England,' he said. 'I don't think things will turn nasty. The English will feel at home here.'

The Scots were mingling with the Parisians in the capital, living up to their reputation as the harmless clowns brought in to entertain the crowds until the real stars steal the show. I sat on the south side of the Pont Saint-Michel and watched as the kilts filed past. There was a poster on the pavement opposite that announced 'The World Cup is a celebration and sometimes a trial,' over which some-one had written: 'Not if you're Scottish. Win or lose we never get the blues.'

I thought I had found a place to stay, but couldn't locate the street on any map. At 2 am I began wandering around the Latin Quarter until I realised I was lost – but I knew where my car and sleeping-bag were parked. There was no rush. In the Rue Saint André des Arts I found an after-hours hostelry quaking with Scots, three of whom were playing the bagpipes. The leader of the group, with florid cheeks and greying beard, was standing on a table per-suading one of the waitresses to join him in a jig. I found myself in conversation with a huge man wearing a Scotland football shirt and a blonde wig. 'I just want to say that I hope – and I mean this – that you get something from the game with Brazil on Wednesday,' I said. He shook my hand warmly and shouted: 'And I hope you lot get fucking dumped in the first round, you bastard.'

After posing for a group photograph in their Paul Smith beige lightweight suits and matching ties, at Heathrow the England squad boarded a specially chartered BA Boeing 737 called Chelsea Rose, with 'England' painted on the fuselage, and flew to Caen, a Nor-mandy port which had been asked to assemble a football team for an extraordinary match to which only a few VIPs were invited. Caen were a French second division outfit, but they managed to hold the England national side until late in the second half, when Paul Scholes, the popular choice to replace Gascoigne as the main man in midfield, scored after a move involving Michael Owen and Steve McManaman. Beckham had an indifferent game.

No one was meant to know this. The F A had requested government help in maintaining security, and got it. Nearly 200 local gendarmes backed up by 60 military police and a pack of growling Alsatians stood guard. Caen FC had to sign a confidentiality agreement. It must have made the players feel they were taking part in a remake of *Escape to Victory*. Hoddle appeared not to have quite got over the Sheringham shenanigans. He played Owen alongside Shearer from the start. What did this mean? Was Owen now Shearer's permanent partner, or was Sheringham being rested because he was always going to be Shearer's partner? What it meant was that Hoddle was still determined not to reveal his hand (if indeed he knew what hand he was going to play). But it was naive to think that details of the game against Caen wouldn't be made public. By the time the players had got back on the plane for the short hop to St Nazaire airport near La Baule, it was running on Ceefax that Rio Ferdinand played left-back because Le Saux had flu and that Sol Campbell played no part because of his dead leg. Hoddle didn't seem to mind what people thought.

'I cannae just stand here with that gooin on, mon. I'm gooin over and I'm goona give it some muscle mon' – and with that the Scot crossed the Champs-Elysées and lobbed a bottle of beer in the direction of the French national police. He wasn't the only one. A group of more than fifty French students joined in, and within minutes France's most famous street was raining glass. Bang! I thought it was teargas but it turned out to be a giant firecracker. The police charged at the French students and then a line of sixteen police vans passed slowly up the avenue in a dramatic show of strength. There were arrests – not many, but enough to suggest that the World Cup had become a monster in danger of devouring itself. I kept thinking what would have happened that night if it had been England rather than Scotland in action the next day at the Stade de France. Sepp Blatter, the newly elected FIFA President, would have found some way of rearranging the draw. But there was at least one transparently violent Englishman in town that night – Stan Collymore. He hadn't had the best of seasons with

Aston Villa, but found the target in the Auld Alliance Bar in the Les Halles district in front of a packed house. Unfortunately the target was his girlfriend, Ulrika Jonsson. Collymore quickly issued a Sheringham-type apology saying he was 'beside himself with remorse', but not before Ulrika had released a statement of her own confirming that her 'relationship with Stan Collymore was now over'.

The Tartan Army's roots are tangled. It was so named in the 1970s when a Scottish terrorist group called the Tartan Army began bombing oil pipelines as an antidote to the invasion of Scotland by American, Dutch and English conglomerates. The IRA was at its peak at the time and the Tartan Army enjoyed a loose connection to the Scottish National Liberation Army. Membership was entirely male and working-class. During France 98, buoyed by the 'Yes' vote for a Scottish Assembly, the Army welcomed women, children and the professional classes to its ranks with open arms and bare bottoms.

Half an hour before the opening ceremony I walked round the outside of the stadium, where a Brazilian and Scottish fancy dress parade was in full flow. One Scot carried a huge placard: 'You can take our wives but you can never take our freedom.' Some wore Brazilian shirts with McRonaldo written on the back.

At the VIP gate I saw the French Prime Minister Lionel Jospin arrive. He stopped and signed a couple of footballs as he made his way along the red carpet. The Scotland squad walked out onto the pitch in their blue jackets, kilts and white socks. Craig Brown led them over to the corner where the main bulk of Scottish supporters were seated. A few minutes later Brown was practically in the stands himself, chatting to people in the front row and signing autographs.

I had invited myself to breakfast with Brown a few weeks earlier, but he had made it seem as if he had invited me. 'I used to be a raving lunatic,' he said, sprinkling white sugar over his grapefruit segments. 'Everyone was my enemy – the referee, the linesman, the opposing coach, even our own fans sometimes. I still get angry inside but I keep it in, partly because the players can't take it any more. I remember telling a player recently that he was a wee fat lazy footballer and he turned round and said: "I'm a wee fat lazy millionaire, actually."'

Not many people thought Brown was up to the job when he took over from Andy Roxburgh. In a newspaper poll at the time, he only gained 8 per cent support. 'The truth is that I wanted Alex Ferguson or Kenny Dalglish to do the job, because I genuinely thought that they would be better at it than me, but I'm pleased the way things have worked out.' The facts show that Brown's record as Scottish coach is second to none.

'What do the players call you?'

'They call me Craig, from the youngest to the most senior. I prefer it that way. In return, they know how I expect them to behave. Even when it comes to the national anthems I make it clear that I don't want to see them shaking their head or scratching themselves. I try to look after them because deep down I respect what they do. The Scottish players have a modesty about them. They do a lot to help others. I enjoy being with them and I believe they are far more intelligent than people think. Most of them, that is. We were in Athens once and I said to the players that they should go and see the Acropolis and one of them piped up: "I didn't think the disco was open in the afternoon."'

'I think you're going to get to the second round.'

'I'll tell you a wee story. I went to an official dinner the other night and the organisers had produced a fantasy place mat, charting Scotland's progress in France. We played England in the semi-final and won 2–0 and then we met Brazil in the final and beat them by the same margin. I watched people reading the mats, and when they had finished many of them had water in their eyes. I did as well. But, really, my position is a great one to be in. Everything from here is a bonus. I keep reminding myself that 172 countries started out on this adventure and now there are only 32 left and we are one of them. It's amazing.'

The theme for the fifteen-minute show in the Stade de France centred on what the pitch might be thinking about it all, with hundreds of creepy-crawlies rushing around while assembling a billowing lawn fertilised with balloons of pollen, from which sprang five gigantic flowers containing enormous footballs. Professional abseilers disguised as insects and carrying a selection of percussion instruments descended from the elliptical roof to unveil the flags of the competing countries.

Prince Philip, seventy-seven that day, and his grandson Peter Phillips were there, along with all the usual Scottish suspects – Sean Connery, Ewan McGregor, Rod Stewart, Jackie Stewart. Youssou N'Dour and Axelle Red belted out the official FIFA World Cup France 98 anthem. The teams were announced. Massive cheer for Ronaldo. Havelange read out some solemn words, followed by a couple of sentences from Jacques Chirac, and then a little girl recited the 'Footballers' Charter' which included: 'Never behave violently and always keep your self-control,' and 'Give everything you've got, then accept defeat gracefully.'

After the national anthems the players shook hands. Colin Hendry and Dunga swapped pennants. A coin was tossed, pictures taken, and finally, at 5.30 pm local time, Gordon Durie rolled the ball gently forward.

Cesar Sampaio scored from a corner after four minutes, and then Hendry went within inches of heading into his own net. They played music after the goal and told everyone in case they missed it: 'Goal to Brazil.' Ronaldo was looking for a rout. He danced around Hendry, Boyd and Jackson before shooting low to Jim Leighton's right, and from then on there was a collective intake of breath whenever Ronaldo touched it. He was flicking it, dummying it, backheeling it, dragging it back just like he did in the Nike advert at Nice airport. No wonder those legs were insured for £20 million.

'The World Cup is my chance to become the greatest player in the world,' he said before the game. He already was the greatest player in the world in most people's books, but this was the biggest stage in the world. Could he handle it? It had been an odd life. He joined São Cristovão when he was thirteen, leaving school less than a year later. Then he went off to Cruzeiro, then PSV, then Barcelona and then on to Inter Milan, stopping briefly on the way to mimic the Christ statue above Rio de Janeiro for a tyre company advert and scoop up his beautiful girlfriend Suzana Werner. He was twenty-one. 'I have a sense of predestination. That this is my profession, my role in life: to play football and entertain others,' he had said.

Scotland were playing well. The Brazilians looked uneasy in each other's company, with the unsmiling Dunga berating his players for not doing what he expected them to do. You got the impression that there were eleven men in yellow all wondering who was going to emerge as the man of the tournament.

Then just before half-time, the Scots were given a penalty. It was never a penalty but it heralded a defining moment in Scotland's football firmament. John Collins put the ball on the spot and looked at it for what seemed an age. He took a short, angled run-up. And scored.

Brown had told me about his half-time routine. It was always the same. 'They come in and take a drink and sit down and no one speaks for five minutes. I expect eye contact, but not a word. Then I start speaking. I start with a debit and then end up stressing where I think we are in credit. We try to go out on a high.'

Brown was standing up more and more as the second half progressed. The Brazilians were moving the ball back and forth along the Scots penalty area when Dunga sent Cafu scurrying down the right wing. He crossed. Leighton got it away, but back it came off Boyd and into the net.

At the end, Ronaldo entered into negotiations with Hendry to exchange shirts. Brown had a microphone shoved under his chin. Of course there was always Norway and Morocco to come, but to have held Brazil in the opening game would have been special. They may have been world champions but they didn't look invincible, especially at the back. For Scotland it was an opportunity missed.

Brown was gracious in defeat. 'There is no denying Brazil were the better team and deserved to win,' said the Scottish coach. 'Regrettably, it was an own goal which beat us, but Brazil were better and we wish them well in the rest of the tournament.'

Mario Zagallo, the Brazilian coach, offered this: 'I don't care what happens to Scotland. We've beaten them and that's all that matters to me.'

It was raining as the Tartan Army shuffled out of the stadium, but by the time they had boarded the train back into the centre of Paris many had regained their spirit and took comfort from the thought that England might do no better on Monday.

'You know what?' shouted a Scot at the start of what was a well-worked double act.

'What?' said his friend.

'Collins scoring that penalty was the second-best moment of my life.'

'And what was the first, then?'

'Southgate missing his.'

Paris to La Baule in three hours is irresponsible, but Hoddle was making his first and last public appearance at the seaside before heading down to Marseille. The rendezvous was the Escoublac Salle des Sports, opposite a cemetery on the outskirts of the town. There was no question of holding court at the team hotel. That had been hermetically sealed days ago, with two police cars at the entrance and another two at the end of the road leading down to it. The Norwegians were in a similar golf-themed establishment opposite England's base camp, which explained why the flag of St George and the Norwegian flag fluttered from lamp-posts along the main streets of this Breton retirement home.

Despite the presence of two World Cup national sides, there was little interest in the football. A woman in the Tourist Office said it got 'quite lively' in summer. This wasn't exactly the dead of winter, but that's what it felt like: even its three-mile beach, which trades on being the 'most beautiful' in Europe, was virtually deserted. La Baule doesn't even get a mention in the Lonely Planet guide to France, but its soporific qualities were probably just what Hoddle ordered. Certainly the England coach looked more relaxed than he had for weeks as he took his seat in the sterile, blue-carpeted hall. Large mounted photographs of players were nailed to the walls. There was Ince in his blood-stained shirt, Sheringham celebrating a goal from many months ago, Seaman smiling broadly, Campbell on the warpath.

'We feel at home here,' said Hoddle. 'Some of the players are even staying in the same rooms as last summer during the Tournoi. We've got a spring in our step and we're pretty focused.'

The players had individual rooms, linked by an adjoining kitchen. Adams and Merson were next-door neighbours. They got together every morning to read from a book of meditations to bolster their recovery from alcoholism. Roger Narbett, the chef who was once on Aston Villa's books, was happily installed with his pots and pans. Baked beans and tabloid newspapers were off the menu. Hoddle, a vegetarian, was keen that his squad should eat their greens and have plenty of pasta. Eileen Drewery was not in residence, but Tina Westfallen had been appointed welfare officer. Her duties included making sure no one's birthday was forgotten.

I asked Hoddle if he knew what his team would be on Monday.

'I know my eleven, barring injuries,' he said.

Would Owen start? No one knew, and Hoddle encouraged the uncertainty.

'He's got a temperament way beyond his age. What he lacks is experience. He is someone who can start and he's someone who can come on and give us something extra because he is so diverse, unlike anyone else we have in the squad. He's fresh, he's alive.'

The accompanying press pack who had bought into the official England media tour – at £13,500 a throw – seemed to have accepted their isolation from the team, taking solace in the comfort of the four-star Hermitage hotel where President Mitterrand used to spend weekends when his wife wasn't looking. Green Flag had set up a big screen on the first floor and were piping in BBC and ITV. Carlsberg were supplying free beer. The pool was heated, the wine chilled, and the time-difference with London afforded an extra hour in the sun before deadline.

A Russian journalist cleared his throat. 'What do you think about your players having sex during the World Cup?'

'Not with each other, presumably, Glenn,' said the *Telegraph*'s Henry Winter.

The Russian repeated himself, and this time the *Mirror*'s John Dillon came to the rescue. 'Hopefully the sex is behind closed doors, Glenn.'

Hoddle finally produced a line thick with innuendo. 'At the end of the day it's not a major problem for us. If the wives and girlfriends come over it will be at a time when the players need to be given a lift.'

Owen walked in and sat down underneath the photograph of Sheringham. 'I'm ready,' he said. 'I feel very comfortable beside Alan Shearer. If you are intelligent enough you only need play with someone once to know his game. Of course I would prefer to start the match, but the team that begins the World Cup won't be the team that finishes it. I'm not fearful. I'm going in believing that I can cause anyone problems.'

'Is there anything your family would say you are bad at?'

'Losing,' he said.

'When did you last get upset about losing?'

'About an hour ago against Rio on one of those video driving machines.'

Owen was already the golf champion of the squad, playing off an 8 handicap. Only Ince came close with a 10.

'Er, what about snooker, Michael?'

'I had a fifty-six break once,' he said.

Every other time Owen had been brought before the media he had an FA official sitting next to him. Now he was on his own, and looking a lot more secure with it.

'Is the atmosphere tense between you and Teddy, Michael?'

'I get on fine with Teddy. He's a great bloke. We're playing golf with each other tomorrow.'

'With each other or against each other?'

'Against each other.'

Tony Adams replaced Owen behind the table. His hair looked like it had been bleached blond. He could have charged for his media set-pieces.

'Are you still on a high from winning the double, Tony?'

'Who said I was ever on a high? I might have been that afternoon, but it's gone. Forgotten. I move on. I live for every day. When I won the double I had a good day at the office. Now I have to do a good job against Tunisia. That's how I get my self-esteem – by focusing solely on Tunisia. Because the proof is in the . . . oh, no, I can't believe I was about to say that. I can't believe I still use clichés.'

'Are you having the best time of your life?'

'What, here in this press conference? No, I'm sorry, I didn't mean to say that. The answer to your question is that this is an exciting time of my life. I feel physically very, very strong. I am true to myself nowadays. I've got rid of the guilt and the shame, which is why I can talk like this. You guys haven't got anything on me any more. I'm free. I don't have any ghosts stashed away in the cupboard.'

Before leaving La Baule I called in on the Norwegian camp to see what all the grumbling was about among the English press corps. It was certainly different, but to compare the two is to miss the point. There were no more than thirty journalists in attendance, and of those the majority were Scottish, looking for preview material for the Scotland–Norway game. The few Norwegian hacks were happy to sit in the sun and admire the view. From time to time, Egil Olsen, the coach, would wander over to talk. He had been in charge for eight years, and there was speculation that he might take over at Celtic.

'Will you?' I inquired.

'Ask me after the World Cup.'

The paradox about Olsen was that as a player he loved the ball. He loved having it at his feet. He loved dribbling with it. Now he tells his largely English Premier League-based team to get rid of it, preferably with a hoof into the opponents' area for Chelsea's Tore-Andre Flo to chase.

'We are more direct than teams in Britain now,' he said, not with pride but as a matter of fact. 'You could say that we are the most predictable team in the World Cup.'

At the end of the training session the Norwegian players gather behind one of the goals to talk to journalists, but not all of them.

One day it's those whose squad number is even, the next it's the odd numbers.

'This would never work with our lot,' said a visiting BBC reporter.

Why not?

'Because they wouldn't know the difference between an odd and even number.'

The French hadn't got it. Many of them just didn't see the point of it at all. The *Coupe du Monde*? Big expense. Big hassle. Big deal. I had telephoned French friends living near Paris, and they said they might watch the final on television, but only if France was in it. In the immortal words of Willie Whitelaw, the French TV coverage was stirring up apathy. It was awful. Their answer to Des Lynam was a cardboard cut-out smoothie who winked every time the ads were about to come on. The hosts looked as if they were bored rigid by their own party. Of course there were pockets of resistance to this Gallic indifference, but you had to go out of your way to find them.

On the way to Marseille – in an attempt to keep up the promise to myself of watching every single moment of every single game of France 98 – I stopped at a bar in Niort, just off the motorway to the north of Bordeaux. There was a television perched high above one corner, but it was turned off. Paraguay and Bulgaria were about to get down to business on Channel 3.

'Can you put the television on, please?' I asked the barman in my strangulated French.

'*Pourquoi?*' he replied.

'The *Coupe du Monde*,' I said. 'Paraguay–Bulgaria.'

He threw his arms in the air and jerked his head back as if I was asking him to run naked round the block singing '*J'aime les anglais*'. But he finally did flick the switch, and even produced a toasted ham sandwich at the second time of asking.

Les Bleus would be in action later in the day against World Cup new boys, South Africa. I decided to drive as far as I could in the direction of Provence, and would pull off the road fifteen minutes before kick-off, find a cheap hotel and look for a television screen.

I got as far as Carcassonne, which is not a bad place to find yourself just as the light is turning apricot behind the Cévennes mountains, with the snowcapped peaks of the Pyrenees visible in the opposite direction. They'd be up for it here. Even the toll-booths had notices pinned to the windows announcing that the cashiers were on strike. I imagined they were only off for twenty-four hours, so they could watch the game. I found a hotel, put on my 1966 England shirt and headed for the centre of town.

Carcassonne sits on the old trade route between Bordeaux and Rome, which meant that it was forever being taken over by someone or other. Strong fortifications were built. Today, the walled old city is a formidable sight from a distance and a tourist trap close up, as it cashes in on its complicated past. During the Second World War it became a German headquarters. Every single local inhabitant moved out.

This was one of the biggest nights in French sporting history. *L'Equipe*, the sports daily, had talked that morning about the 'whole country holding its breath' as Aimé Jacquet's team prepared for its opening match in what was France's first World Cup finals for twelve years. But no one seemed to be holding his breath in Carcassonne. They have a history of heresy here. In the late twelfth and early thirteenth centuries, the whole area came under the spell of the Cathars, who believed that the universe had been created by two powers, one for good and one for evil. God reigned over the mind, Satan controlled the body. Fanatics used to starve their satanic bodies to ensure eternal spiritual life. The Roman Catholic Church under Pope Innocent III launched a bloody crusade against the Cathars, slaughtering some 20,000 of them in one year alone.

Several bars and restaurants had set up mini marquees on the pavement, with big televisions parked at one end. But the diners were more interested in what was on their plates than on the screens. The strike at the toll-booths had nothing to do with the football. Then a man with a strong West Country accent whispered in my ear: 'With a shirt like that I think we'd better buy you a beer.' I turned and saw a tall man who bore an unnerving resemblance to Fabrizio Ravanelli, the Italian striker who survived a season in Middlesbrough before moving on to Marseille.

'I'm Mark,' he said, 'and this is Pete.'

'I'm Mark, too. A Beck's would be great.'

Mark Hunns and Pete Balsdon, both from Plymouth and both thirty-three, had been saving for this trip for two years. They had come over in Pete's Ford Escort XR3I, bought specially for the occasion because of its soft top, and were making their way slowly south. There was some concern that the car might not go the distance, but fortunately Mark's uncle had a holiday home near Carcassonne where they were going to dump the car and pick it up again on the way back.

Mark worked as a customer services manager for an insurance company. Pete was an electrical fitter at the Plymouth naval docks. This was Mark's first experience of following England abroad. Pete had been to Euro 88 in Germany. They were both ticketless.

It was nearly 9 pm, and I suggested we look for somewhere with more atmosphere. So we wandered off until we heard the French National Anthem blaring from the upstairs window of something called Le Club. On entering we were shown into a large first-floor room where 150 men and three women were standing in rows, their right hands covering their left breasts, eyes forward in the direction of a big screen near a snooker table. We stood at the back and I folded my arms over my England shirt. The game kicked off, and every time a Frenchman touched the ball the room erupted, with a vicious stamping of feet whenever the action came near to the South African penalty area. When France scored, they rose as one and shouted '*Vive la France*' and then sat down and lit up cigarettes. At half-time the lights came on and the men formed a line outside the Gents. They looked like they were men of the fields, their sinewy faces not so much tanned as permanently weathered. I got the impression that this was a major excursion into town, like a school outing. At the end, they filed out, one or two of the older ones settling bills at the bar.

'Weird,' said Pete. We ordered some beers, and quickly the conversation turned to the Teddy Sheringham versus Michael Owen question. Mark and Pete were in no doubt that Owen should start the game but were equally sure that Hoddle would stick with Sheringham. I took up the defence for Hoddle, rehashing his argument that if Owen didn't produce the full works in the first game it could destroy his confidence, and that it was good to have some ammunition in reserve if you were thinking about seven games rather than just three. But I couldn't convince myself.

'That's a load of crap,' said Mark. 'We have to play our strongest team from the start, and Sheringham is just not in the same class as Owen. I mean who would you rather defend against, Sheringham or Owen? It's not hard is it?'

Pete wanted to give a nightclub across the River Aude a go. 'It's Friday night. The top totty should be out and about,' he said. So we got into the soft-top and headed over the river. We almost got there, running out of petrol a few yards from the entrance. Mark produced a can from the back. This was not the first time they had ground to a halt and it wouldn't be the last.

The nightclub was asleep. Four or five men in tight T-shirts stood admiring themselves in the mirrors behind the bar, and that was about it. The dance floor was empty.

'Weird,' said Pete.

Chapter 8

You Could Have Walked Away

I gave Mark and Pete a lift to Marseille. Mark was married, with two children aged seven and four, but was separated from his wife. He lived off and on with his parents, sometimes in a small flat of his own and sometimes with his Spanish girlfriend and her daughter from a previous relationship. Pete was also married and had a two-year-old daughter. He and Mark were best friends who grew up together and will grow old together.

Pete sat in the back, Mark in the front.

'So what makes football so special?' I said. This was a question I had been asking everyone from John Gorman to Craig Brown to Paul Ince to the minicab drivers at Clapham Junction for months. Mark and Pete answered in the same way as all the others.

'It's the passion, I suppose,' said Pete. Precisely. But from where does that passion arise? And why?

'Can I explain my theory?' I asked, as the Autoroute des Deux Mers stretched out ahead of us in the direction of Béziers.

On one level the passion of football is obvious. It comes as a result of two teams of eleven men each wanting desperately to defeat the other. You try anything at your disposal to penetrate the goal of your opponents while fighting with every fibre of your being to stop your opponents from penetrating you. The best way of doing this is for the individual parts to gel as one single unit. It's possible to change two or three of those parts as you go along, but by and large the game develops a momentum of its own. Sometimes it can spiral out of control. Calamities happen. Watching that unit in full flow is like observing a bulging sea as it gathers itself several miles from land. There are all manner of undercurrents hidden beneath the swell. Occasionally the surface is broken with flecks of white, which can be frightening or beautiful or just plain ordinary, depending on the day. The huge sea sways back and forth and sideways in order to move forward. It spills itself out on to the shore, often sweeping up anything in its path. And then it does it again.

The passion is real because it has at its heart both pain and joy. To love football is to experience first-hand several of the Oxford Dictionary's meaning of the word: 'strong emotion', 'an outburst of anger', 'great enthusiasm for something', 'the sufferings of Christ on the cross'. And that passion is increased because it is shared – between the players, between the supporters, between the players and the supporters, and sometimes, in big games, between those in the stadium and millions of people watching at home on television.

A football stadium adds intensity to the passion. Of course more women go to games now than in the past, but it still remains one of only a few places where grown men gather in such huge numbers, sharing a bond that can lead to total strangers embracing each other. There is even a grudging respect for the opposing fans: both sets of supporters are operating under similar constraints, and there is a primary union before the divisions begin, because at the very least you are in agreement about the rules of the game. A fellow Reading supporter, Barry Richards, who is head of the Department of Human Relations at the University of East London, has given considerable thought to this in his book about popular culture, *Disciplines of Delight*. He thinks the acceptance of the rules provides an 'abstract authority' which he thinks evokes an 'awe of civilisation'. As he puts it: 'The passion for football stems in part from the game's representing to us the extraordinary and powerful fact of community.'

'We've got a toll-booth coming up,' said Mark. 'I think I had better take care of it. Don't want to bugger up your concentration. You seem to be really into this.'

Games like football – particularly if you have played it as a boy, tasted the highs and lows on the pitch and can still smell the grass

– allow us to experience pain and loss without the full weight of human trauma. The game becomes an outlet for the dramatisation of life. It presents us with the world in small doses. Mood-swings are not attractive in relationships, which is why we try to keep them under wraps, but in a single football match you can have a dozen violent mood-swings and it's perfectly acceptable. Most football supporters hate what they see in their local stadium on a Saturday afternoon, but they come back for more next week, and the week after that. One in three marriages in Britain ends in divorce, but I would bet that less than one in three marriages between a football supporter and his team results in permanent estrangement. They may go from time to time through periods of separation but divorce is rare.

'It will be one hell of a trauma if we go out again on penalties,' said Mark. 'My mood could swing out of control big-time.'

Despite its growing popularity in the first two decades of the twentieth century, neither Freud nor Jung ever mentioned football. Pity. Freud would have noticed the ease with which football supporters hand over responsibility for their actions to their team out on the pitch. It is no different to our tendency to form groups. Freud said we do this because it is easier than tolerating internal conflicts between our antisocial impulses on the one hand and our need for social relationships on the other. When we are freed from this internal conflict – or think we are – we behave in a group in ways we would not contemplate as individuals.

'Another toll-booth,' said Mark. 'You get this one, Pete. I don't think he's finished.'

Freud would have made much of the sexual dimension to football, not least the effort involved to 'score' a goal by shooting into a sacred orifice. But the sexiest ingredient in football is the fact that you are forbidden to touch the ball with your hands. It is the great taboo. Men spend hours dreaming of 'getting their hands on' some beautiful woman, but in football that desire is sublimated entirely. What other game is there where the hands are not an essential part of the action? In football, ten out of the eleven players are bound by this rule, and even during throw-ins or when the goalkeeper has

129

the ball in his hands the game is strangely suspended for a few seconds. Rather than use his hands the footballer relies primarily on his feet, those appendages of the body more normally associated with aggressive rather than creative movements – hence the term 'put the boot in'. The feet have to do extraordinary things with the ball. Sometimes they stroke it, sometimes they flick it and sometimes they whack the hell of it, but whatever they do the ball never changes shape, the perfect sphere is never deflated by what is inflicted on it.

The relationship between the ball and the player is perhaps the most complex one on the pitch. You want to get it but you also want to get rid of it. At times you play with it as if it was a tiny, delicate baby and at others you treat it with a deep loathing. The ball is the object of desire, the focal point of the crowd. Where it goes and what it does decides the outcome of the match.

The Hand of God goal against England in 1986 was a sin because not only did Maradona break the great taboo but he then had the audacity to claim that it was God who gave him the authority to do it. It was the devil at play.

'Are you still with us, Pete?' said Mark.

'I am,' he said, 'and I've got a comment, which is that if football is a substitute for sex then that explains why so many Plymouth fans are crap at picking up girls.'

'You're getting there,' said Mark. 'Now how much more of this is there?'

We were well past Montpellier now and steaming towards Marseille, the Mediterranean shimmering to our right.

'I'm finished except for a quote from Professor Richards. "the passion for association football is inseparable from the passion for association".'

'Fair enough,' said Pete. 'Now, let's put on Three Lions and open the windows.'

The first person we saw in Marseille was Melinda Messenger, and she had her top on. She had been flown out by the *Sun*, along with hundreds of horrible red and white plastic hats with the names of

Murdoch's money-making papers written on them. Many were already floating in the port beside the millionaires' yachts. Local African craftsmen were selling wooden elephants on the *quai*, as they always did on Saturdays. Gypsy women wandered around with babies in their pouches and outstretched palms. Shops were crowded and the dozens of bars and restaurants around the Vieux Port were doing a roaring trade as the roaring English poured in.

'Magic,' said Pete. 'This is just what we'd imagined. Absolute magic.'

Mark and Pete went straight to the Tourist Office, where despite the grim warnings about there being nowhere to stay – let alone there being no tickets – they were offered a room with a rather too cosy double bed and en suite bathroom for £50 just around the corner. I had booked myself into a small hotel near Cassis, not far from the only decent camp-site in the area, which became home to hundreds of English over the next couple of days. Tickets were on offer on street corners and in bars and on the end of mobile phones all over town, but there was no need to rush into it. The asking price on Saturday afternoon, forty-eight hours before kick-off, was upwards of £200 for a seat originally costing £14. Mark and Pete had budgeted to pay £60, possibly going as high as £80. I thought they were being optimistic.

Marseille was always going to be a big story. Most of the news reporters, known affectionately as 'The Rotters', had been in situ since Thursday or Friday with not a lot to write about. Everyone knew that tickets would be readily available, but that didn't stop the *Mirror* boasting about its 'probe exposing the farce of tickets'. Some probe. All it required was the handing over of £200. The *Sun* launched a half-hearted campaign to persuade companies back home to give their employees the day off on Monday to watch the game.

Nigeria were terrifying Spain in Nantes, completing the demolition with a 30-yard winner from Sunday Oliseh. The Spanish squad's cook put the defeat down to the lack of quality vegetables available in France. It was the game of the tournament so far, but not many of the English seemed interested, which wasn't a good

131

precedent, and with each hour the numbers were growing as trains, planes, cars and, in one or two cases, bicycles brought in more and more supporters. It was thought that 20,000 could be in the stadium on Monday, most of whom would be in and out of France in a day, since there were only 5,263 hotel rooms available in France's oldest town.

I joined the Rotters for dinner on Saturday evening with the FA's Steve Double, who was celebrating his birthday, at a restaurant overlooking the coast about six miles from Marseille. Everyone agreed that the atmosphere in town was tense and that it wouldn't be long before it went off, which rather begged the question as to why they were six miles away. Back in London, the red-tops were still hoping to lead their papers on Monday with an upbeat 'Come On England' and not the usual 'Disgraceful', accompanied by a picture of a drunken English fan hurling a chair across a bar. There is always a dilemma on these occasions. Papers have overreacted late at night in the past after watching TV news showing pictures of a couple of fans being led away by police.

'Why haven't we got that?' the night editor asks the news desk.

'We have,' comes the reply. 'It's in the fifth paragraph.' Which is not high enough when the TV pictures are so dramatic, even though the arrest of the fans may have been an isolated incident in an otherwise raucous but largely peaceful evening.

My telephone rang. It was Mark to say that 'things were getting rather lively' around the port and that the options for having a beer later on in the evening were narrowing. Frightened barmen were closing early.

The police had cleared the area outside La Mercure hotel and many of the side roads were sealed off. Fighting had broken out between English and Tunisian supporters after someone clambered onto a car waiting at traffic lights and began stamping on the roof. A chorus of ''Ere we go, 'ere we go' rang out, followed by the war cry of 'No Surrender to the IRA'. The driver of the car did not appreciate having his car roof used as a disco floor and began jerking back and forth until his vehicular assailant fell to the ground, cutting his head and leg as he hit the concrete verge. Bottles began flying. The scene was set.

The police might well have gone in there and then with their teargas and batons. They could have closed every bar and restaurant in the centre of town and not allowed them to open again until the English were well on their way to Toulouse. With so many disaffected North Africans anxious to express their frustration towards French society at large, it became clear that something had to give. They could have dismantled the big screens on the beaches. They could have done all of this and more, but, then again, why not believe all the hype about the close liaison between the French and British police intelligence agencies? There had been so much tough talk about stopping known hooligans from travelling abroad. The Home Secretary had endlessly announced this or that initiative, giving the impression that all was under reasonable control. The FA had hired Sir Brian Hayes, a former deputy commissioner of the Met, to act as its adviser on security matters, for which he was being paid £100,000 for a year's contract. He must have done his homework.

French newspapers the next morning were restrained. 'The English offer us a long weekend,' said *La Provence*, the Sunday broadsheet for the region. There were plenty of pictures of fat, shirtless Englishmen, but they were mostly taken before the alcohol kicked in and were accompanied by dismissive captions such as: 'The English came to Marseille yesterday and seemed happy to stand around drinking and singing their jolly good fellows.' The road-sweepers and rubbish trucks had removed all evidence of the previous night's ugliness by next morning. It was as if the authorities were prepared to give the English another start, a clean street.

The England squad arrived at the Stade Vélodrome later that afternoon for their last training session. They were greeted by a crowd of about a hundred supporters at the main gate. Moments like these don't come often. The next World Cup will be in Asia and the one after that could easily be in Africa, despite the knighthood earlier in the week of Geoff Hurst in what was a tawdry ploy to give

England's 2006 bid extra credibility. Rogan Taylor, who runs a football research department at Liverpool University, was one of those waiting outside the stadium.

'Do you think the hard core, the nutters, have been sufficiently infiltrated by the new breed of football supporter to bring about a civilising influence?' he asked. I said that on the evidence of the previous night, quite the reverse was the case. Because of the middle-class influx the hard core were even more determined to exert themselves. There was more to kick against.

Rumours were circulating that Beckham wasn't going to be in the starting line-up despite playing a part in every qualifying game. Anderton, rapidly becoming known as the teacher's pet, was going to play in the right wing-back position and Batty and Ince would both start, with Scholes just ahead of them in the creative role vacated by Gascoigne. Beckham wouldn't like that. It didn't look good for Owen either. Hoddle seemed determined to stick with Sheringham.

'Substitutes are going to be very important in this World Cup,' Hoddle said, and everyone knew what he meant. The coach was relaxed. As ever, he talked up the opposition to make his task look sterner than it was. 'I don't think it's an ideal situation at all to be playing Tunisia. This is their big moment. They are a very good side and we respect them.'

Tunisia were in fact in some disarray, with their Polish coach Henryk Kasperczak and the captain Sami Trabelsi at odds over tactics, the coach favouring a more direct, long-ball style of play, the captain determined to rely on neat, short little passes and all-round technique.

Hoddle was asked to clarify his remark that Shearer was a better player than Ronaldo. I noticed how Hoddle was forever being asked to clear up some earlier statement. Perhaps if he stopped deploying so many riddles, stopped firing off blanks and stopped imagining he was in charge of some secret service outfit on a mission that not even the men under his command knew about, there might not be such a need to rewind the tapes.

'Yes, I would like to get this clear. When I said that I meant that

Shearer is the best player for England and that if Ronaldo played for England he might find it difficult. But let's get this straight, I think Ronaldo is the best player in the world.'

I couldn't grasp why if you are the best player in the world you would find it difficult to perform for England, but it made me wonder if even Ronaldo would persuade Hoddle to part company with Sheringham if the Brazilian had been born English.

'You may have heard that there has been some trouble this afternoon in the centre of the city,' said a man from BBC radio. 'Do you have any comment?'

'We will have to see what happened. It is too early to comment. There are two sides to every story.'

Not always. This one had at least three sides to it, and three stories. There was the English fans' 'Everyone hates us, we did nothing wrong, they started it.' There was the police's 'Disgraceful drunken violent thugs started it.' And there was the middle-of-the-road 'The English started it but the North Africans were longing to get involved.' I fancied the third option.

The teargas started at 4 pm on Sunday and continued every fifteen minutes or so until 4 am on Monday – twelve hours of uninterrupted horror at the end of which there had been more than 100 arrests, and 30 people taken to hospital. There were four stabbings, dozens of assaults, theft on a grand scale, and nails galore hammered into the coffin of England's bid to host the World Cup in 2006. A man in a 1966 England shirt with 6 on the back – the number worn by Bobby Moore in the final – kicked a Tunisian senseless as his mates cheered him on. Four Englishmen smashed the windows of a van parked near a bus-stop amid much sneering about the 'fucking French bastards', and women and children screamed in terror as bottles smashed all around them. It was some *Fête de Football*.

I parked my car to the west of Place du Général de Gaulle and walked into the Canebière, the main street running down to the marina. Ahead of me a skirmish line of riot police were banging the inside of their shields and firing teargas in all directions. They looked like a platoon of Darth Vaders. I turned round. A huge group of

135

English supporters were fifty yards up the street. I ran into a nearby hotel lobby. On and on it went. All the bars and restaurants were closed. Ambulances and police vans raced through the streets. A car had been overturned at the far end of the Quai de Rive Neuve. At one point I found myself outside the restaurant where I had had dinner after the draw six months ago. It stood abandoned. Its customers had been sent reeling from their tables, coughing and spluttering in a cloud of teargas that wafted through the narrow streets. I was terrified. The Rotters were out in force, and many of them didn't look too comfortable either. The thugs had singled out the media for special punishment. A photographer had already been taken to hospital after coming under bottle fire and an *Evening Standard* reporter was shortly to be kicked unconscious. I came across a former colleague who had covered wars and riots in the Falklands and Brixton, Prague and Toxteth. He said this was as bad as anything he had experienced.

Sir Brian Hayes and Pat Smith, the F A's deputy Chief Executive, were on the scene. So too was Steve Double. Smith's face was white. There was pandemonium. The media wanted a statement. What had gone wrong? Who was to blame? What happened to the intelligence liaison? Had the French police blown it? Should England think about pulling out of the World Cup?

Sir Brian said he needed ten minutes to assess the situation. But in ten minutes' time the situation would need to be reassessed. It looked suspiciously as if the F A's highly paid security adviser had only just finished his dinner and was playing catch-up.

'Look, just give us ten minutes and we'll come back with a statement. We'll do it here on this corner,' said Double.

'If this corner has been neutralised,' added Sir Brian.

So off they went to make feverish telephone calls and survey the grisly spectacle. More riot police spilled out of vans. Another car was turned over and set on fire. A flare was let off on the other side of the marina. Sir Brian returned, but before he could open his mouth the jeering began from behind him.

'Blame it on us, as usual, you bastard,' said an Englishman with tattoos across his knuckles.

'You had four years to get this right,' barked another.

'If the French wankers had given us enough tickets this would never have happened,' said a third.

'I'm not taking excuses like that from anyone,' said Sir Brian. 'This is all about drunken hooliganism and I condemn it absolutely. I believe the French police have done a good job after coming under severe intimidation from about four hundred people determined to cause trouble.'

'The Tunisians started throwing bottles first,' shouted an Englishman, who failed to mention that the public burning of a Tunisian flag might not have helped.

'I don't believe that,' said Sir Brian, 'and even if it were true you could have walked away.'

Then it was the fault of the media. 'You lot wanted this to happen. You helped get it going,' said a man in a T-shirt two sizes too small for him. 'You report what you want to report, not what you see, and you're probably getting overtime for this. You're nothing but fucking scum.'

Sir Brian was asked if there was a case for pulling England out of the World Cup. 'That is absolute rubbish. The team is here to play a football match. They have been training hard for it. We will play a game of football tomorrow.'

But England's bid to stage the 2006 finals wasn't looking promising.

So what can be done to stop this sort of thing, Sir Brian?

'I don't want to get into that now,' he said, as a group of England fans closed in.

'Get on the fucking planet, you bastard.' Sir Brian walked off.

I headed back towards my car, but couldn't get to it because the road was blocked. 'You from England?' asked a man carrying a Tunisian flag with a cut on the bridge of his nose. 'Italy,' I said, and he moved on.

Another splintering of broken glass rang out, but it wasn't beer bottles. It was the front of a clothes shop. Two men, neither of them English, were ramming the window with pieces of wood the size of a policeman's baton. Then they squeezed inside and rummaged for a few seconds before coming back out with dresses, belts and handbags. The same was happening in shops further to the north of the port, where the Africans were running amok. One man was carrying off a television from a looted department store. The further north you went the more evident it became that the police were engaged in running battles not with English football supporters but with disenfranchised North Africans. The papers made little mention of this.

Mark and Pete had spent the night in their hotel room arguing about whether to have the window open or closed. Keeping it closed kept out the teargas but made it impossible to sleep because of the heat. Keeping it open kept the temperature down but made it impossible to sleep because of the teargas.

On the day of the game, every street corner near the stadium was occupied by the CRS and there was an unseemly tension at the turnstiles. It was Mark's birthday. In the end, he and Pete had splashed out £100 each for tickets. They were 'well pleased', as Mark put it, but there was always a nagging doubt that the tickets were fakes or that they would have to prove that their names were the same as the French ones printed on the front. No chance. The chaos at the entrances to the stadium ensured that no such checks were made. Jack Straw might just as well have dumped £1 million in the North Sea for all that his ad had achieved. Mark was desperate to take his mobile phone into the ground but feared it might be regarded as an offensive weapon. So with the help of his phrase-book he prepared a note in French to show security guards. It said: 'Mobile phone needed. Wife is having a baby in two days' time.'

It was a hot afternoon, but not oppressively so. The 60,000-seater stadium was three-quarters occupied by the English. A giant Tunisian flag moved up and down the stand behind one of the goals. 'All You Need Is Love' blared out from the sound system. Graham Kelly was sitting with Ray Stubbs in the BBC's makeshift studio high in the main stand. 'It's absolutely disgusting what happened last night,' said Kelly. 'Four hundred people came here to cause problems.' The recurring four hundred. Sir Brian Hayes had fished out the same number.

Chris Waddle, a local hero after playing for Marseille, was waiting to go live with Gary Lineker. Finally a trapdoor opened at one end and the two teams emerged. Anderton was there. So was Sheringham. Beckham and Owen were on the bench. Southgate sang the National Anthem and looked as if he was going to burst a blood vessel. Batty gave a little Gazza-style wave as the camera panned down the line. Sheringham stood in silence.

Tunisia had a great chance after five minutes but then began bedding down in their own half. It was soon obvious that they had no intention of trying to win the game. The goalkeeper, Chokri El Ouaer, laboured over his kicks and there was lots of rolling round whenever a player was tackled. Marking at corners came down to grabbing a player's shirt and holding on to it for dear life. They looked the weakest side in the tournament. How had they got this far? Campbell came storming forward and gave the ball to Scholes, who should have scored. Sheringham hardly touched it for the first thirty minutes but then unleashed a beauty that the goalkeeper palmed on to the bar. England were beginning to settle. The supporters were magnificent. No others had come close in terms of noise and numbers, and the English noticed every nuance as if they were on the pitch themselves. The Brazilian supporters may look pretty as they sway back and forth, but they have nothing like the same intensity about them as the English. The English are involved. The Italians? Depends on the weather. The French? Silent, so far.

Adams went down on his knees clutching his head. Scholes missed another good chance. I wondered if Gazza was watching in Florida. Tunisia had ground to a halt towards the end of the first half. In the forty-second minute, England won a free kick on the edge of the penalty area. Anderton and Le Saux, who seemed to specialise in double-dummies at set-pieces, performed a single one this time which ended with Le Saux lofting the ball towards Shearer just where he likes it. One nil to England. Shearer ran to the far touchline, his right hand raised, palm open. This was England's first goal in a World Cup final series for eight years.

During half-time the word went out that there had been more stabbings, more teargas and more arrests at the Plage du Prado, where a big screen had attracted thousands of ticketless supporters from both countries. But there was no trouble in the stadium, none whatsoever.

It wasn't until twenty minutes into the second half that Tunisia won their first corner. Every England player wanted a piece of the action now. This game was there for the taking. Tunisia made three changes. Riadh Jelassi had only been on for ten seconds when he got his head on the end of Sheringham's boot, and then ten seconds later he was booked for chopping down Ince.

Tension on the touchline came to a head over the water-bottles. When the Tunisian captain Trabelsi went down injured, Alan Smith, one of the England physios, grabbed a bottle that was standing just outside the Tunisian bench's allotted space. The Tunisian coach didn't like that and tried to grab it back, but Smith wouldn't let go. Then Ince came up and nicked another bottle.

'We want Owen,' the English supporters were chanting. Owen was warming up behind the Tunisian goal, and in the eighty-third minute the youngest player in the tournament, and the third youngest ever to play in a World Cup, went on, welcomed by such an eruption of noise that you felt a bit sorry for Sheringham. Campbell picked up a yellow card which could easily have been red. Ince was suddenly jinking his way into the Tunisian penalty area and the ball was played on to Scholes, who had his back to goal. He ran with it for a couple of paces and then turned just enough to catch sight of the top left corner. He lashed at the ball and in it flew. There was only a minute on the watch – a full minute for uninterrupted sightseeing. At the final whistle, Hoddle turned to the crowd and stuck up a thumb.

'It was magic,' said Pete. 'We got the mobile in and called people in England at half-time. Magic signal. Great Scholes goal. We were directly in line with the ball when he hit it. Sheringham did nothing and I didn't fancy Anderton much, but you can't argue with the result.'

'Talking of results,' said the birthday boy, 'have we told you about Pete's possible date tomorrow night with Isabelle?'

They hadn't. Isabelle was the maid in their hotel, who spoke not a word of English. She had two children but no husband and lived miles out of Marseille. Pete described her as 'lovely' and thought he had noticed her casting a favourable eye in his direction while emptying the wastepaper bin. I feared he might have taken to heart the reference to the Vieux Port area of Marseille in his European Football Rough Guide book, which said 'more than just a bed' could be found in hotels like theirs. The phrase-book had come in handy again. Pete had written on a card: '*Bonjour, Je m'appelle Peter. Est-ce que vous pouvez venir prendre un verre demain?*' She would give her answer in the morning.

Chapter 9

Scoring

Isabelle said 'Yes.' Pete was 'well pleased'. So after a scrub and a polish, and with the phrase-book in his back pocket, he headed across the road to meet her at the agreed venue, which was McDonald's.

It didn't go badly, thanks mainly to the young Frenchman collecting the dirty trays, who had a little English.

'Why did you choose me?' asked Isabelle.

'Because of your beautiful laugh,' said Pete, opening up another pack of tomato ketchup.

Mark, meanwhile, had been stopped twice in the street by bemused young boys who had mistaken him for Fabrizio Ravanelli. The Italian striker had pulled out of the Italian squad at the eleventh hour with a virus, and so it was feasible, just, that he might be wandering around the streets of Marseille admiring the views, but then Mark decided to go one step further by buying a Marseille football shirt and saying '*Ciao, ragazzi*' to total strangers – and the autographs dried up.

While Pete was with Isabelle in McDonald's and Mark was passing himself off as a £5 million Italian striker, I went to O'Malley's, the Irish pub that had been in the thick of the action on Saturday and Sunday nights. Now, more than twenty-four hours after the game, a weary calm had descended on the place, enlivened only by an exhilarating Brazilian performance on the TV against Morocco. Hoddle and his squad had stepped out of the compound to watch the match in Nantes. By demolishing the Moroccans 3–0, Brazil had done Scotland a favour. The Jocks, after a spirited fightback against Norway earlier in the day – a game they deserved to win –

would find themselves in the second round if they could beat Morocco in their last match. It seemed too good to be true.

Several of the day's English newspapers were doing the rounds – to mixed reviews. 'They're just sensationalising it all, aren't they?' said a man from the north-east. 'I've been here for the last three days and don't recognise any of this,' said a Fulham supporter. Others flipped through the pages of the tabloids and shook their heads. 'You can't excuse that,' said a big, bald man in shorts and Hackett ('essential kit' for the English gentleman, as the ad in the *Spectator* puts it). 'It's disgraceful that is. I don't care what anyone says, it's out of order.'

But there was another group poring over copies of the *Sun* and *Mirror* like newlyweds inspecting the contact sheets from their wedding pictures. They appeared to know many of the people photographed and seemed proud of it. I hoped they weren't best mates with James Shayler, the so-called 'Pig of Marseille', who was reported to have launched the first missile. Pictures of the shaven-headed, bare-chested Shayler with a flag of St George tattooed on his belly and a pair of expensive sunglasses covering his eyes being led away by French police made almost all the front pages. The papers had moved with formidable speed, identifying many of those arrested and revealing full details of their professions. There were several members of the armed forces, an antiques dealer, a couple of postal workers, the son of a probation officer, a hospital electrician, a water company accounts manager.

The *Independent*, under yet another new editor anxious to make waves, called for England to pull out. After running around in pursuit of 'these cocksure young adolescents', the editorial concluded: 'The sad truth is that we have tried almost everything to stop hooliganism and have failed. Travel bans, ticket restrictions, even dedicated police squads have all had some effect. But there is something so fundamentally untrustworthy about the behaviour of young English fans abroad that it is now time to impose the ultimate sanction: we should withdraw from the World Cup and spare France any more violence and the nation any more shame.'

La Provence was conducting its own post-mortem, which included a long interview with Marseille police chief Michel Sappin, who defended himself against criticism that more could have been done to stop the carnage and said the TV coverage was so spectacular that it misconstrued events.

'On Sunday we were confronted by a group of drunkards, and as they were not really that violent and due to the fact that they continued to drink, we decided after much debate that we would leave them to drink themselves into a stupor. It wouldn't have been wise at that point to send in the CRS. We did not want to start crushing a few insects and put in danger the ordinary men and women in the street.'

In fact, most ordinary men and women had spent the day cowering in their homes. Sappin went on to say that there had been virtually no looting except from one jewellery shop, and that the culprit had been quickly arrested. Which didn't exactly marry with what I saw: men running down the road cradling television sets.

On Wednesday morning, as I was putting very dirty clothes at one end of the bag and quite dirty but perfectly wearable clothes at the other, Mark rang. 'Are we still on for that lift to Montpellier?' he said, sounding chirpy.

'Of course. We're leaving at 4 pm.'

'Would you feel comfortable if this girl I met comes along too?' said Mark.

I said it wouldn't affect my comfort in the slightest, but it might be a bit cramped in the back seat with all the luggage. Still, perhaps in the circumstances that wouldn't worry him.

The girl was an Australian called Marilyn. Mark had met her that morning on a bus on the way back from the Basilique Notre Dame de la Garde, the enormous Romano-Byzantine basilica that stands 162 metres above sea-level just south of the old city. Marilyn was doing the usual Aussie world tour (loosely based in London's Earls Court, European Student Rail Card, back home by Christmas) and happened to be in Marseille because a friend owned a boat moored in the harbour. She had spent the previous night on board, but I got the impression she hadn't stayed for breakfast. When I arrived at Mark and Pete's hotel I wondered if Marilyn realised that Montpellier was nearly 200 kilometres away and that we were not coming back. Apart from the thin cotton dress she was wearing she only had with her a multi-coloured string bag of the kind that was all the rage in 1974.

I also wondered if she knew we were going to watch the Italy–Cameroon game. I wasn't sure if she even knew the World Cup was going on at all. Mark clarified the position. 'Marilyn has never been to a football match', he said, 'but she's really looking forward to it, aren't you, Marilyn?'

Marilyn was grinning. From the vantage point of the rear-view mirror, she seemed perfectly at home in the back with Mark, her head resting on his shoulder. Pete was in charge of the music but couldn't find anything he liked except 'Three Lions' and the Mavericks' 'Dance the Night Away'. We stopped just outside Montpellier, where free shuttle-buses were on hand to take people either direct to the stadium or to the city centre. I went to the stadium; they went to the Tourist Office to sort out a hotel. The French organisation was good. What they lost in certain areas – there was an appalling lack of signs to the stadia, for example – they gained in others, particularly the willingness of the green-uniformed volunteers to help solve problems and answer silly questions. Apparently more than 23,000 had applied to help out.

I didn't have a ticket to the Italy–Cameroon match, but one of the volunteers was only too happy to give me one when I pitched up at the stadium. Mark, Marilyn and Pete were expecting to pay £40 or £50 for theirs. Group B was wide open, with three draws in three games, Italy being given a lucky penalty late on against Chile. That afternoon, the South Americans had missed out again when Austria came back from the dead in the ninetieth minute. The pressure was now on Italy to sweep aside Cameroon. Cesare Maldini had a Sheringham/Owen dilemma, not knowing who to play between the tried and tested Roberto Baggio and the white-booted pin-up Alessandro del Piero. Debate raged in Italy. The actress Claudia Cardinale was a Baggio man, while Sophia Loren wanted del Piero to lead the line. Romano Prodi, the Prime Minister, thought Maldini should play them both.

It was a hot night, but the football failed to catch fire. On paper the Italian team read like a list of blue-chip companies listed on the Footsie 100 Share Index, but there was little substance to their play. No one seemed to be in charge. The Cameroons went into their huddle before the kick-off, but from then on they were in different worlds. Kalla was sent off for an assassination attempt on Di Biagio and Njanka should have been dismissed for chopping down Baggio. They were fortunate only to be one down at half-time. It felt good not having to care about the result. There was time to look at some of the side-shows.

The Cameroon TV commentators provided the best entertainment of the evening. With binoculars and team scarf around their necks, and wearing African head-gear in the national colours, they were truly fans with microphones. They kept banging the table in front of them and pointing threateningly at the referee when he gave a contentious kick to the Italians. They didn't have a lot to cheer, but when the Cameroons won a penalty late in the second half they greeted it with squeals of delight. Del Piero came on for Baggio and by the end Italy had scored three. Pleasant night, pleasant ground, but the Italian supporters seemed more interested in perfecting the Mexican wave than scrutinising the deficiencies of their midfield. Afterwards, the Cameroons coach, who was a Frenchman, Claude Le Roy, was chatting away merrily in the mixed zone. He used to be a television commentator. His style of management was diametrically opposed to that of Hoddle. 'If you want to protect your players, it's either because you're afraid or not confident enough in the quality of your work. It's a great game, eh? The pressure is such that some coaches would love it if there were no matches,' he said.

I had an inkling that Pete, Mark and Marilyn never saw the game. It seemed a safe bet that Mark and Marilyn had been detained at the hotel while Pete was sent to buy postcards. Not a bit of it. They hadn't made it to the stadium, but they watched on the big screen in Montpellier's Place de la Comédie.

'It was magic,' said Pete, as usual. It was looking spectacular when I got there shortly before midnight, with the opera house lit up just enough for a kick-about with crumpled beer cans. Italians, French, Cameroons, Scots, Dutch and English mingled merrily into the early hours. My last sighting of Mark and Marilyn was of the happy couple pressed up against a wall near the station. Pete was tactfully keeping his distance and was preparing to do the same in the hotel. 'I've got no problems sleeping on the floor', he said. 'He's my best mate and it looks like he's pulled at last. I reckon if he doesn't score tonight he's a homosexual.'

They were going back to Carcassonne in the morning to collect their car. I was planning a diversion to Cahors to see the family I stayed with as a schoolboy sent out to learn French more than thirty years ago. But first I drove down to Le Cap d'Agde, where England supporters were camping before converging on Toulouse. Many had fled there from Marseille directly after the game.

'It's beautiful here,' said Dave Sturridge, a builder originally from Doncaster, now living in Sydney, Australia. The camp-site was called La Clappe. 'We plan on staying until Monday and we'll just try to buy tickets on the day in Toulouse. But there won't be much trouble this time. A lot of the hard core have run out of money. There was about five of them in Marseille. Big blokes. They were having a great time stirring it up. Wankers.'

There are the good guys and the bad guys and there are the non-complainers and the whingers. The bad guys tend to be the whingers. They whinge about the price of beer while pouring it down their throats; they whinge about police brutality while throwing cans and bottles at them; they whinge about the lack of tickets while never bothering to become members of the England Travel Club; they whinge about the opposition fans while burning their flags; they whinge about the lack of attention from local women while belching at them; they whinge about the FA, about Glenn Hoddle, about the price of a ham sandwich.

Sturridge was one of the good guys. After saving up for this trip for three years, he and 750 Brits living in Australia had bought a

World Cup package through Global Tours, which included flights and tickets, and accommodation if you wanted it. But when they arrived in France there were no tickets. Vanished.

They weren't the only ones to suffer. FIFA had already admitted that a special investigation had been launched to look into claims that an employee of ISL France, one of FIFA's corporate partners, had sold thousands of tickets that never existed. It had affected not only England and Scotland fans but supporters from Japan, Holland, Germany and Brazil.

'Bit of a mess,' said Sturridge. 'We're going to sue the company. It's all down in writing what we were meant to get. I reckon we're looking at a free holiday at the very least. But we'll deal with that later. We're having the time of our lives. Despite everything that's happened the French have been brilliant.'

I had two abiding memories of Cahors from that student exchange over thirty years ago. One was the unrelenting heat in a valley enclosed by hills and mountains, the other was standing on a platform at the train station waiting for the then Princess Margrethe of Denmark to arrive. Henri de Laborde de Montpezat had recently proposed to the princess and she had accepted. It was thought she was marrying beneath her. I was staying with Henri's sister and her husband and their three boys, one of whom was my age. This was the princess's first official visit to Henri's home town, and the locals were excited. Photographers jostled for position. Men with notepads looked at their watches. I was more conscious of my raging acne than the impending arrival of Margrethe, but I remember going for lunch at Henri's parents' house, when we sat down to eat at 5 pm. His mother and father had a mystique about them. His father died shortly before the World Cup at the age of ninety. There was an obituary in the *Daily Telegraph* which alluded to some complicated details of his life. His widow, now ninety-one, still lived in the same house, and so I went and saw her the day after France had walloped Saudi Arabia 4–0. She couldn't see me; her tiny eyes were only able to pick up the shadow of someone standing in front of her.

'So you are here for the *Coupe du Monde*,' she said, with a smile that sent ripples across her fragile skin. 'I always have it on the television. I can't see anything but I like the excitement in the commentators' voices. Such little things make them so excited.'

I noticed that the countryside was more verdant, less harsh, more welcoming than I had remembered it. I wondered why.

Madame de Laborde de Montpezat's mother was a dominating woman, but not dominating enough to stop her daughter running off and marrying a priest while she was still a teenager. They ran and ran, ending up in French Indo-China, where they stayed three years. During that time she met Monsieur de Laborde de Montpezat, whose father had made a fortune in the Far East as a farmer and owner of a newspaper. He persuaded her to leave the priest and return to Cahors with him. She went on to have nine children, only six of whom survived into adulthood.

'I have lived a full life,' she said, her eyes beginning to close, 'but now like most people I am alone. That is why it is good to learn how to be alone when you are young.'

Despite the blazing heat outside, it was dark and cool inside the house. Nothing in the room had changed from when I had last been there, but the view from the window had altered dramatically.

'The countryside seems so much greener now,' I said. 'It used to be quite barren.'

'The reason is simple,' she said. 'When you were here there were goats all over the place who had eaten everything up. It is only now that the fields and the woods have recovered. But it shows how many things in life get better not worse.' And then her eyes closed again, more heavily this time.

Chapter 10

Salsa in Toulouse

David Beckham had taken it badly. And Hoddle was prepared to let the glamour boy talk about it, which made things worse. The Groins, sitting by the pool in La Baule, were lapping it up.

'I was devastated when the manager told me. He announced it in front of the rest of the team and I was really hurt. I had this feeling coming up in my stomach, my insides were turning over and over so many times. It was an unbelievable sensation. I tried hard to hide my feelings because it happened in front of everybody, but it wasn't easy. Then we went straight into an afternoon training session and I had to carry on. It isn't easy because I can't really figure out what went wrong. I know the manager picks his final eleven and sticks with it, and there is nothing I can do or say about it because it's his choice. Standing there by the bench and listening as the team sang the National Anthem was just as hard as when I was told I was not in the squad. It's so difficult not to be involved. It's particularly upsetting because I played in every game leading up to the World Cup finals.'

Beckham and Hoddle had spoken about it. 'The things discussed are private. But, put it this way, he didn't turn around and say that you're not playing again, thank God. He said: "You're going to get your chance." But I want to start. I don't just want to come on for the last twenty-five minutes.'

Adidas, his boot sponsors, must have been upset as well. And Posh Spice and all those parents who had bought their children England shirts with his name on the back. Hoddle had given the impression that he thought Beckham's feet were not always on the

150

ground, that he was not always able to control himself when under pressure.

'I get a lot of publicity,' said Beckham. 'People surround me whenever I go out, taking pictures. But just because I have a famous girlfriend doesn't mean I am up in the clouds.'

It seemed unlikely that Hoddle would alter the team, even though Romania were expected to provide sterner opposition than Tunisia. Those calling for Beckham and Owen to be included stressed the importance of winning so that England would end up top of the group and face the second-place finishers from Group H in the next round, which were likely to be Croatia. Otherwise, Argentina would be parked on England's lawn.

My car almost arrived in Toulouse before me. At the toll-booth about 20 km from town, I handed in a ticket and was told that it was the wrong one and that unless I found the correct one I would have to pay as if I had come from north of Limoges rather than south of Cahors. It was a big difference. But the ticket was nowhere to be found. I paid the full whack. The cashier seemed to take pity on me and suggested I pull up about 50 yards past the *péage* and conduct a more thorough search. If I was to find the little stub she would reimburse me. I found it and returned to the glass box. She was just about to give me the money back when I glanced down the motorway and saw the car disappearing.

'That's my car,' I said.

'Ten, twenty, thirty,' she said, handing over the notes.

'My car. That's my car driving down the road without me.' I ran after it but it was picking up speed. No one was in it. It was being driven by the wind because I hadn't put on the handbrake and the windows were open. A group of Germans went past in a BMW with their jaws on the dashboard. Other cars began sounding their horns. I caught up with it, opened the door and jumped in Wild West style.

Toulouse was sweltering – 35 degrees in town. The main influx of English was still twenty-four hours away, but the city was bracing itself. All bars would have to close by 11 pm. Anyone breaking this law would be fined £1,500 on the spot and a further £1,500 if still serving alcohol after midnight. The *Fête de Musique*, which was planned for that weekend and usually attracted as many as 100,000 people, was postponed. No giant screens would be showing the game as they were in Marseille. A children's theatre festival, a rowing competition, a jousting tournament and a fancy dress parade were all cancelled – although a rather different sort of fancy dress parade lasting more than two days was about to begin. A cartoon in the local paper showed two French intellectuals talking. 'So the English are coming to neutralise 600,000 inhabitants in three days . . .' said one and the other replied: 'Well, of course, how do you think they colonised India?'

Le Dépêche du Midi ran an editorial in English saying: Welcome to Toulouse. It stressed how everyone in the town wanted to make the supporters' stay as memorable as possible and urged them to 'stroll around the streets before or after the match' and take in the 'unique architecture dominated by the red-brick hue whose colours change almost miraculously on each successive day'. Some people thought it was going to be a miracle if the city was still standing by Monday evening.

At the station, members of the Football Supporters Association were handing out *Total Football*'s free *Fan's Guide to France* booklets. 'A group of about 150 English supporters has just come through', said one of the FSA volunteers, 'and there must have been almost as many police here to meet them. What sort of message does that send out?'

In the Place du Capitole there was hardly a policeman in sight, and everyone was behaving themselves. It was hard to work out what the police strategy was, which may explain why it was so successful. At first it seemed as if the English were being given the cold shoulder. Ignore them. Let the heat sap them of energy. But the police were going out of their way to be helpful, and the locals showed no animosity as their town was slowly decorated red and white.

The Football Supporters Association had been given the elbow by the mayor's office. A request to install their 'Fans Embassy Bus' in the Place du Capitole had gone unanswered, so instead it spent the weekend in a car park near the station across from the brothels along the Canal du Midi.

'Getting an answer from the French about anything is becoming almost impossible,' said Kevin Miles, whose official title was Fans Embassy Coordinator. 'They're all off with their mistresses.'

The FSA had persuaded Mastercard to come up with £50,000 to sponsor its work during the World Cup, out of which Miles, who was also chairman of the Independent Newcastle Supporters Club, was the only person drawing a salary. 'The sacking of the Newcastle directors gave me a crash-course in media relations,' he told me, sitting in one of four club-class airline seats in the back of the Transit van. And then his telephone rang. It was GMTV wanting a word. It rang again. A local radio station in the north-east was keen for a sound-bite criticising the French.

'You are regarded as an apologist for the hooligans,' I said.

'What happened in Marseille wasn't a football issue. It was a turf war between the local youths and the police. Okay, I accept that there were two hundred looking for trouble, but . . .'

'Brian Hayes and the FA keep talking about four hundred. Where do they get these numbers from?'

'They make them up. There were about two hundred looking for trouble, but what happened in the end was much bigger than that. It was the English who were being beaten and robbed. At least a dozen had knife-wounds, but the police showed no interest in protecting the English fans. Hundreds were actually trying to get away from the trouble, but they were being picked off by North Africans. Some of the neutrals knew what was going on. A restaurant owner pulled a couple of us off the street and put the shutters down because he thought we were in danger. In four hours I did not see a single English fan commit one act of violence.'

The sun must have addled my brain, because I'm sure the man in the 1966 shirt kicking the shit out of that Frenchman in a doorway was English.

On the way back from the station, I called in at the Sofitel hotel on Allée Jean Jaurès, where FIFA officials were staying. Sir Brian

Hayes was outside giving a TV interview similar to the ones he gave in Marseille. He hoped everything would pass off peacefully. Liaison with the French police had been 'excellent'. The violence has 'taken us by surprise'. It was a 'complex problem' which we were 'beginning to get on top of'.

No mention of the *Mirror*'s front-page story that morning that asked in its headline: 'Where is Sir Brian?' And then gave the answer, reporting that he had taken a five-day break in Spain after the Marseille business. 'For all the good he is doing, he might as well stay on holiday. For ever. And if he does come back, the FA should sack him. We need a tough guy in that job, not a man who prefers topping up his suntan to sorting out the thugs,' the paper sneered.

He did look nicely tanned, but few other papers touched the story because it was thought that Sir Brian had taken his wife to Spain because she was dangerously ill, which may have been what he meant when he said he was on 'family business'.

There was no mention either of the arrival in Toulouse of Paul Dodd, one of the most notorious Category C merchants, with more than thirty convictions for soccer violence to his name. He was once banned from every ground in the country, but here he was in the pink city having bought a ticket to the game for £200 in a hotel near the Place de Wilson. He was busy offering the sale of his story of how he got into France. He wanted £10,000 for words and pictures. There were no takers so he talked about it anyway, with one eye on publicising a book he had written about soccer hooliganism.

'I couldn't believe the security. It was a joke,' he said. 'I was stopped at the airport but then let go. The French police even pointed the way to the taxi rank and waved goodbye. If you took away the passports of about two hundred bampots like me the trouble would disappear overnight. It would be easy to stop it. I don't know why they didn't. Anyone could see it was going to kick off. The Home Secretary has spent two million quid on security, and what's it achieved? Nothing.'

Dodd was full of admiration for Alan Clark MP, who praised the fans for embodying 'the English martial spirit' overseas. 'He's a top man because he just says what all the other MPs think. They love it when the English fight for England abroad. We have always done it. The war was won by boys like us.'

I wondered how Mark and Pete were getting on. Tickets were scarce. The asking price was £200. Toulouse's stadium was almost half the size of Marseille's, and there were a lot of Brits living in the area who worked for British Aerospace. And when the Japanese had been here they were prepared to pay ridiculous prices, encouraging the touts to reassess their profit margins.

Mark was reclining against an eighteenth-century balustrade in the Place du Capitole, looking bronzed. 'I'm knackered,' he said, 'and Pete's got blisters all over his feet. We've been walking round town all day but can't find a ticket anywhere, so we've stopped for today and decided to chill out. Beautiful women. Great weather. Great buildings.'

It was nearly 10 pm. Closing time in an hour, so I went off to find something to eat and drink. About half an hour later the mobile phone rang. It was Mark saying they had met a man who said he was a rock singer, and they were about to go with him to a supermarket to stock up on beer.

'He wants to take us to the best nightclub in Toulouse,' said Mark. 'Tell us where you are and we'll come along in about twenty minutes.'

'If you want anything more to drink you must order now,' said the manager of the restaurant, looking at his watch. 'It is stupid this law. We got up a petition signed by most bar and restaurant owners and we handed it in to the prefecture but they didn't listen. They are destroying my livelihood. If there is trouble here I will carry the can for it. They are acting like dictators.'

Mark and Pete and Monsieur Le Rock Star arrived, weaving through the tables with plastic bags bulging with Kronenbourg. Their new friend looked like Swampy. His name was Wilfred.

'You like salsa?' he said. 'You like salsa, we make salsa. All the beautiful girls in Toulouse like salsa. All the beautiful girls want you to make salsa with them tonight.'

155

'I fancy a bit of salsa,' said Pete but he didn't look in the mood for dancing. He seemed ready to lie down.

Wilfred drove us to the salsa bar in his souped-up Volkswagen, mainly down one-way streets in the wrong direction. It looked like a locked-up garage from the outside. Then a Spanish-looking man opened a tiny door and asked for 20 francs each to come in. Wilfred seemed to get away with paying nothing. Inside, the proportion of men to women was at least four to one – that's four men for every one woman – and the men looked big and strong and they seemed to know how to salsa. Mark put Pete in a chair, propped his head against the wall and ordered three beers. And then, suddenly, the place closed. Lights went on. The band folded away their instruments and out we trooped.

'You want to go to the best nightclub in Toulouse?' asked our tour guide.

'I've rather lost it,' I said. 'I would like to go to bed.'

'Don't worry, you will go to bed with one of the most beautiful girls in Toulouse.'

'This beats a Saturday night in Plymouth,' said Pete, recovering slightly.

We got back in the car and drove around in circles for ten minutes, with plenty of screeching of brakes, flashing of lights and tooting of the horn.

'Here we are,' said Wilfred. We walked down a brightly lit passage that led to a door that opened up into a large reception area from where you could hear loud music and see strobe-lights flashing from the dance floor. A man stamped our hands and welcomed us as long-lost friends. He was wearing a white T-shirt with sequins on it that covered only his chest. He had a bare, flat muscular stomach and his belly button was embroidered with a small, sparkling stud in the shape of a heart. Two men were standing by the wall behind him, stroking each other.

The man with the hand-stamper began talking to Wilfred, who turned to Mark and said: 'There is maybe one problem.'

'Only one?' said Mark. 'That's fine.'

'One maybe big problem. Tonight is special homosexual night.'

*　　*　　*

The England squad arrived in Toulouse on Sunday, and checked into the Hotel Palladia on the outskirts of town. Their training session in the stadium was booked for 7 pm – much to the consternation of the groundsman, who was complaining that in addition to the three Group One matches already played, the turf had endured six full-length training sessions and was beginning to show signs of irreparable wear and tear. Rain was needed but there was no chance of that. A decision had to be taken at the highest level. FIFA broke the news in a press release: 'The grass is usually mowed twice a day, but this has been reduced to once a day.'

It was a muggy evening. Hoddle was supervising target practice with Shearer, Beckham, Scholes and Les Ferdinand. Did that mean anything? Shearer and Beckham working together? Why wasn't Anderton in that little quartet? Southgate's ankle injury, which he had picked up in training during the week, meant he spent the whole session sitting behind one of the goals rather like he had in Rome, and so there was no guarantee that he was injured at all. Seaman never did much during these public sessions. While Nigel Martyn and Tim Flowers had balls pinging in at them from all directions, England's number one goalkeeper tended to stroll around with Ray Clemence admiring the view, occasionally catching high balls kicked from the flanks. Practising to save penalties was certainly never part of the routine.

Brian Moore was in his commentary position running down the Romanian team-sheet, hoping that Gheorghe Craioveanu and Liviu Ciobotariu were going to have quiet games. This was Moore's last World Cup. He had done 1966 for radio and every one since then for television. Life without Brian won't be the same. 'And now the familiar sight of Liverpool lifting the League Cup for the first time' and 'After a goalless first half, the score at half-time is 0–0.'

Sitting in a small box of an office high up in the LWT offices on the South Bank a few weeks earlier, Moore had given me his top six players of all time, not just taking into account ability, but the six who had meant the most to him personally. 'Stanley Matthews and then Tommy Lawton. Then Pele, then Cruyff, Maradona and George Best. But the one I admired most was Kevin

Keegan. He was twice European Footballer of the Year and carved out an amazing career for himself with limited skills. He said to me once: "You know Brian, I wish I had a quarter of the skills of Alan Hudson." '

Moore said he saw a lot of Alf Ramsey in Glenn Hoddle, and confessed that he was an unreconstructed David Beckham man. 'I saw him as a schoolboy and I remember Alex Ferguson telling me: "He's the one." I think he's absolutely exceptional. I would play him every time. Who would have thought that Geoff Hurst would become the hero in 1966? Who knows what this World Cup would mean for David Beckham?'

In that morning's *Sunday Times*, Alex Ferguson had entered the Beckham debate with a vengeance. 'What bothers me is the way the upsetting effect of being dropped has been made more painful for the boy by some of the things that have happened since in the England camp. Why was Beckham put forward for a mass interview with the media while he was still reeling from the shock of being left out of the team for the match with Tunisia? He must have been devastated emotionally, and asking him to bare his soul in public was not likely to help anybody but the headline writers. I would never have allowed it.'

Imagine the fall-out if Hoddle had dared interfere with Ferguson's team selection at Manchester United. Think what the Scotsman would say if Hoddle stated publicly that Ryan Giggs was playing out of position or that Roy Keane was a liability. But here was Ferguson comparing the abilities of Anderton and Beckham, and fanning the flames for all they were worth in his lucrative newspaper outlet.

'I felt there was a real question about whether the Tottenham man should even be in the squad after missing so much football because of the injuries he has suffered over the past two years,' wrote Ferguson. 'Why reject Beckham, who is hardly ever injured and has tremendous stamina, in favour of somebody who is still trying to find his top-level game after long spells on the injured list?'

The heat had inspired some curious fashion statements on the touchline. David Davies, wearing tracksuit bottoms and white plim-solls, looked like a member of the cabin crew of the *Queen Mary* in the 1950s, and Steve Double was in a pair of long, baggy shorts and blue suede shoes like David Niven used to wear with a matching cravat while wandering around St Jean Cap Ferrat. Noel White, Chairman of the FA's International Committee (the best committee of the lot apparently), looked out of place in his FA blazer, but his tan was on a par with Sir Brian Hayes's. Even Brian Moore had dressed down. The navy jacket was on but he had dispensed with the tie.

Hoddle was clutching a large cup of Coca-Cola that may or may not have had any Coke in it. 'We're not going for a draw. We're positive. We will try to win the game,' he said. And with that out the way, the decks were cleared for the Ferguson factor.

'How do you respond to the criticism today from Alex Ferguson?'

'I'll give my conclusion about that after the game. I've got more important things to think about at the moment.'

'Were you aware that dropping Beckham would be such a talking-point?'

'I don't need to answer that. I'm just focused on the next game.'

'Do you get fed up with what people sometimes say about you?'

'No, I don't even bother to read a lot of it. It's just a bit dis-appointing that you guys have now asked three questions about it.'

And a fourth. 'How is Beckham's frame of mind?'

'I'll tell you about Darren Anderton's if you like. He's been great since he's been here, and I'm sure David will be the same if he's called upon.'

Mark and Pete had drawn a blank on the ticket front. So had many others. On every street corner there were weary Englishmen holding signs reading '*Cherche de places*' or simply 'I will buy ticket.' And those holding signs always had to ask anyone else holding a sign if he was looking, or selling while pretending to be buying. The prices wouldn't come down either, but Mark and Pete were prepared to wait until the last moment.

The Prefect of the Midi-Pyrénées region, Monsieur Alain Bidou, held a press conference that afternoon in an ornate square room near his office with gold chandeliers hanging from the ceiling. He had assembled eight extremely important people to join him behind a long table with an interpreter standing at one end. Heads of various police forces were there, with a huge map of Toulouse lit up on a projector in one corner. I was hoping there might have been some sandwiches and a cup of coffee thrown in, but this was strictly business.

'We are approaching the England–Romania game in the normal way, but it has long been clear that special arrangements have to be made for this match,' said Bidou in a rasping voice, looking at his Australian translator. Questions went flying in but quickly vanished into the ether as Monsieur Bidou went on, and on.

'We have postponed the music festival because it would not be good for so many people to come into contact with football supporters who may be inebriated.'

A French radio man gave his opinion. 'I think you will cause more problems by not having the big screens. If the English cannot watch the game together they will be very unhappy.'

'We may have made a mistake but I don't think so,' he said, pointing at a chart showing that a total of 1,800 police officers would be on duty in the next twenty-four hours, including 600 men from the rapid force unit.

Bidou may have lacked the charisma of Inspector Morse, but he had done a good job sorting out his policemen. The trick was that you hardly saw them. You knew they were there of course, lined up in buses in streets leading off the main squares and boulevards, but they weren't peering over your shoulder. And because there were hardly any Romanians in town, and with few North African locals straining at the anti-immigration leash, it was easy enough to let the English get on with their pre-match rituals.

There were two gathering-points. The main one was in the Place du Capitole, the other in a bar called the Melting Pot on the Boulevard de Strasbourg. The good guys were mainly in the Place du Capitole while the whingers stewed in the Melting Pot. I watched the first twenty minutes of the USA/Iran peacekeeping rally – which included a game of football – in the Melting Pot.

'Come on you, Yanks,' shouted a shirtless American, but it didn't quite have the ring to it. It was an odd game. Flowers were exchanged at the start, and there was a joint team photograph. President Clinton had gone on television to claim that the match would cement a new relationship between the two countries. What he meant was that it was a chance to bolster the new regime in Iran, and FIFA were only too pleased to go along with it. It was all very timely. Secretary of State Madeleine Albright had just made a speech calling on the Iranian government to help formulate a 'road map' to normal relations with the US, and Iran's deputy Foreign Minister had praised the Clinton administration for its efforts to 'better understand the realities of the Islamic Republic'. Even so, security guards had their work cut out as they rushed around the stadium confiscating banners showing the faces of Massoud and Maryam Rajavi, whom the opposition forces wanted to seize control from the mullahs. A Press Association reporter had his shaving cream and razor removed from his bag in case they might be used as offensive weapons.

I felt a hand slide into the pocket of my shorts and my wallet being removed. It belonged to a Frenchman who looked barely old enough to be drinking in the bar. He began shouting and accusing me of trying to steal from him. This was building into an incident, what Sir Brian Hayes would call a 'flashpoint'. The thief had two friends who supported him. They closed in and began jabbing their fingers into my chest. Time to go. I wondered if I should request the help of the American, but he was so absorbed by the game that it would have been a gross intrusion. I bolted.

The bars around the Place du Capitole began closing well before the 11 pm deadline. Thousands of English fans were in the square, but there were dozens of police spotters as well. The big test came when a car attempted to drive through the crowd and a man carrying a flag leapt on the roof. He was encouraged to stay there by some, but others began grabbing his legs to get him off. And then the first chant of 'Glenn Hoddle's Barmy Army' went up, evoking the harmless imbibing of those who follow England on cricket tours abroad. 'No Surrender to the IRA' was still in the charts, but slipping down a bit. The mood was changing. There was no sign of the so-called Category C 'generals' coordinating mayhem on their mobiles. A stream of cars was now cutting a narrow swathe through the English. An element of self-policing had begun, with two men taking it upon themselves to make sure no car was unduly held up, and when one lunatic jumped on a passing bonnet he was swiftly removed.

Two girls in halter tops were paraded on their boyfriends' shoulders, prompting a rousing rendition of 'Get Your Tits Out for the Lads'. They didn't. 'Let's Go Fuckin' Mental' led into a giant conga around the square, and by 2 am the evening performance was over.

By lunchtime the next day, the square had become a shrine to St George and Three Lions. The authorities could so easily have sparked a horror by ripping down the various flags that had been tied to the 120-metre-long façade of the city hall. Following England is a chance for those who support unfashionable clubs to sniff the big time. There were no flags with Arsenal written on them, or Manchester United, but there was Northampton Town, Welling, King's Lynn, Eltham Town, Newbury, Lincoln, Kettering, Mansfield, the Dog and Dart.

Kevin Miles and his Fans Embassy Bus were finally allowed to park in a corner of the square. Police occasionally strolled through, stepping over the weary and the passed-out. Red wine was a popular tipple – cheaper than beer and it didn't need to be chilled. The procession to the stadium began early, and included Mark and Pete, £300 poorer. They were 'well pleased'.

This was a home match for England. Even the perfectly symmetrical stadium felt like a mini Wembley. It was hard to believe that three thousand Romanians were there. Something extraordinary happened at the end of their National Anthem: the English broke into spontaneous applause. I felt myself being drawn inexorably into the fantasy that I knew should be resisted, the one that had England walking out at the Stade de France on 12 July to contest the final.

Anderton was playing. And so was Sheringham. Gary Neville,

who had been taking creatine and had been given injections to build up his iron levels and reduce a build-up of lactic acid, was in for Southgate. Hoddle had not been swayed by the prevailing winds calling for change – and the stakes had been raised during the afternoon when Colombia beat Tunisia. They would have a real incentive to defeat England in Lens.

Shearer kicked off, and England began chiselling away down the left with Le Saux sprinting back and forth from one penalty area to the other. He wouldn't be able to keep that up for an hour and a half. Romania's Adrian Ilie, known as The Cobra, soon looked the classiest player on the pitch. Old man Hagi, booked for a tackle on Campbell, wasn't happy. He kept shouting at the bench and the bench kept shouting back. Then Sheringham gave the ball away in the centre circle, and Ilie raced off with it and hit the bar.

Something wasn't right. It was Paul Ince. Hagi had chopped him down in the second minute and he was struggling. There was going to be an early substitution. Beckham was going to play in the middle of midfield. In the driving seat. Shearer was in dire need of a decent cross, a ball he could run on to. Romania scored immediately after half-time. Hagi chipped the ball into the box. Adams couldn't reach it but Moldovan could. He chested it down and volleyed past Seaman. There were three thousand Romanians in the stadium now – you couldn't miss them. I had read that one Romanian was spending four hours a day with his head immersed in the bath praying to God that his country would win the World Cup. His wife had said: 'I've come to hate football. I want my husband back the way he was.'

Owen was warming up behind the Romanian goal. 'There's only one Michael Owen, one Michael Ow-en, there's only one Michael Owen.' After twenty-seven minutes of the second half, he took off his green bib. Sheringham looked up and began walking to the touchline even before the FIFA official had put up his sign. Hagi retired at much the same time. Suddenly there were only ten minutes left. Beckham pressed up and gave the ball to Shearer who whipped it into Scholes, and there was Owen, the man described by the coach as 'not a natural goalscorer'. 1–1. England were off the hook. But not for long. Dan Petrescu was being chased by his Chelsea team-mate Le Saux. They were shoulder to shoulder. Seaman came out and hesitated in no-man's land. Le Saux seemed to make out that he was being fouled. He wasn't watching the ball and then Petrescu somehow got a foot to the ball and it went through Seaman's legs. The Romanians went berserk. Owen hadn't quite finished. He received the ball just inside the opposition's half and ran with it before hitting the post. It was almost the last kick of the game.

At the whistle, the Romanians prostrated themselves in front of their supporters and coach Anghel Iordanescu said: 'Tonight we have made a lot of people happy in Romania. It was a victory that came from the bottom of our hearts.'

In the mixed zone, Hoddle blamed the defeat on the giving away of 'two dreadful, ridiculous goals'. But apart from that he seemed reasonably content with the performance. John Gorman said the atmosphere in the dressing room afterwards had not been too funereal.

'What happened tonight should never have happened but we will be okay. We know exactly what we have to do now', he said.

The mixed zones in France were usually set up between the dressing rooms and where the players' buses parked. So you had to walk past a few hundred journalists to get out of the place. But there was no rule about talking to anyone. Apart from the coaches, who were bound by FIFA law to say a few words, anyone else could walk through and remain silent. Sheringham had good reason to keep his thoughts to himself, but he stopped and chatted, and was brutally honest.

'It does hurt me when I hear the fans chanting for Michael, but I wasn't pleased with my performance. I don't know why. I guess it was just one of those things. But I'm not stupid. Michael did very well when he came on. He's a great talent and I realise there is going to be a huge demand for him to be in the starting line-up.'

Batty said England had 'showed Romania too much respect' and that 'perhaps we should have got more stuck in – to use a crude term.'

A man from Saudi Arabia asked for a lift back into the centre of town. He wanted to talk. I didn't. He said he spoke fluent French and was looking for a job as an interpreter. Then he asked: 'Do you have a friend?' I was feeling distinctly friendless, but in no mood to make a new one, and there was something about him that reminded me of that nightclub Wilfred had taken us to on Saturday. 'Would you like that I become your friend?' he said. I dropped him at the next corner, picked up three sandwiches and made my way to Pete and Mark's hotel, which was above a sex shop. When I walked into the room, they were lying on the bed watching a recording of the game, their face-paint blotched. Pete had a flag of St George on each cheek. Mark's face was one large flag, his nose the crossroads of red. I took out the sandwiches and they produced some cans of warm beer.

'You can't demand victory,' said Pete. 'You have to earn it, and we didn't earn it tonight. But there was one highlight. I was interviewed by BBC News. They asked me what I'd paid for my ticket and I told them – more or less.'

If their car was up to it, Pete and Mark were driving north in the morning to catch an overnight ferry back to Plymouth. They had been away just over two weeks.

'We'll still qualify,' said Mark, 'and if we get through to the quarter-finals I know I'll be back.'

'I won't,' said Pete. 'That's it for me. But I wouldn't have missed it for anything. It's been absolutely bloody magic.'

11

We're in the Race Now, Aren't We?

'I have a problem,' said Paul Durkin. 'Of course I want England to go all the way, but the further they get the less likely it is that I'll feature in the latter stages. For me to make it to the final would be the greatest thing ever. If it happens I would probably retire and join the after-dinner speaking circuit.'

We were sitting in Durkin's Portland home, drinking tea and eating chocolate cake made by his wife. He was about to leave for a final FIFA fitness test before moving on to France. This was his first and last chance at a World Cup. You retire from international football officialdom at forty-four. He was forty-two.

Durkin was in charge of the Italy–Austria game the day after Romania defeated England. It was in the Stade de France, which might have been a good sign. Let him soak up the atmosphere before handing him one of the semi-finals. But Durkin had been quoted as contradicting Sepp Blatter's edict that referees should crack down on tackles from behind. Blatter thought players were getting off lightly in the opening games. It wasn't the tackles from behind that were the problem, it was the shirt-pulling and the rolling around in mock agony that needed to be stamped out. But what Blatter says, goes – and twenty-four hours later five players were sent off in two games.

Durkin was getting £15,000 for making it this far. At home, he picks up £375 for each Premier League match, with petrol and accommodation on top. And a cup of tea at half-time.

'All my mates said I was mad when I gave up playing so young, but I said to them: I'll get to Wembley before you – and I was right.'

Another reason he gave up was that his own disciplinary record was so poor. 'I was aggressive, no question about it, and I gave the ref a lot of lip. I was often suspended, but I also realised early on that I was never going to be good enough to go all the way – unlike my father, who played for Aldershot, Bradford City and Weymouth. Refereeing was the one chance for me to make it to the top flight.'

Durkin, a short, ginger-haired man who runs with a steel rod down his back, works for a housing association in Dorchester. I asked him if he had ever considered becoming a policeman.

'Why, because I'm strict?' he said.

'Not strict,' said his wife, '*very* strict.'

His big break came during Euro 96, when Dermot Gallagher was carried off injured during the France–Bulgaria game at St James' Park. On went Durkin and played a blinder, gaining top marks from the official adjudicator in the stands.

'Many managers don't really know the rules,' he said. 'They think they do but they don't, and nor do a lot of the players. Having said that, I don't like the way FIFA keeps changing things. This no tackling from behind business is going to be a nightmare. Steve Bould might as well retire right now.'

During any match, Durkin has about his person two plastic Fox 40 Classic whistles, one of which is tied to his wrist, the other placed in the right-hand pocket of his shorts. He carries three pens, one in the back of his shorts, one in the side pocket, one in his chest pocket. He puts a notebook in his chest pocket along with two yellow cards and two red cards. He wears two watches, one of which incorporates two stopwatches. He spins an Australian 1988 fifty-cent piece to decide the toss.

'You have to concentrate hard, but I can still appreciate the quality of the football. Sometimes I say to the players "Great shot" or "Unlucky, son." Once I was in charge of a game when Gary McAllister split the opposition defence with an absolute beauty and I said to him: "Great pass, Gary," and he replied: "What the fuck do you know about football?"'

He seemed to be doing a good enough job in the Stade de France, whipping out yellow cards every now and then. He showed five in total but couldn't muster a red one. And then it looked as if he missed a foul before Baggio's goal, and he turned down Vastic's claims for a penalty after a heavy challenge from Maldini. He was on the plane home shortly afterwards.

Passing through Bordeaux on the way back to La Baule, I stopped at the thirteenth-century cathedral. There was a picture of Maradona holding the World Cup trophy near the door with '1 Corinthians 24' written under it: 'Do you know that in a race all the runners compete, but only one receives the prize? So run that you may obtain it.' The next verse says: 'Every athlete exercises self-control in all things.'

'I reckon Gascoigne would have taken control of the situation,' said Barry, a Charlton supporter, as we watched the Brazil–Norway game on television in La Rochelle. 'He might not have been completely fit but he would have fired them up. No one seemed to be in charge.'

It was almost the first time Gascoigne's name had been mentioned. Barry had a point about the leadership issue. Shearer was the captain, but Adams always seemed like the commander-in-chief. Hoddle's thinking was that Shearer led the team by example, but when they fell behind to Romania it needed someone to *say* something. Adams should have been Hoddle's captain. He had the grit and the discipline, and he was inspired after winning his fight with drink. He was reading Superman Christopher Reeves's musings on life since his riding accident, and had just finished Jean-Dominique Bauby's extraordinary book *The Diving-Bell and the Butterfly*, written after he suffered a stroke that left him speechless and paralysed apart from one muscle in his eye.

La Rochelle, on the Atlantic coast between Bordeaux and Nantes, was the last town in France to be liberated by the allies in the Second World War. The German navy had submarines there and was reluctant to give it up, despite repeated bombings. Today it has an air of middle-class respectability about it, attracting hundreds of tourists in summer. There are several camp-sites on the nearby Île de Ré, which is approached across one of the longest bridges in the world. Several Chelsea supporters were in town, rallying behind their man Tore Andre Flo as Norway hammered Brazil into submission.

Canal+, the French cable company, kept switching back and forth between Norway–Brazil and Morocco–Scotland. At times they were showing pictures of one game and commentary from the other. Scotland were two down by the forty-sixth minute, and then Craig Burley, who dyed his hair specially for the occasion, was sent off. When the Norwegian bench heard what was going on in St-Etienne, the order was given to increase the aerial bombardment.

'Go on you Chelse', shouted the London contingent every time Flo touched it. But it was Brazil who scored first. Then Flo received a superb pass from Liverpool's Bjornebye and equalised. Ronaldo seemed out of sorts. In the eighty-eighth minute, Flo was awarded a dubious penalty and Rekdal scored. Norway were in the second round.

Morocco went three up, but it didn't mean anything. They were out. The coach, Henri Michel, looked like he had peered over a wall and witnessed some colossal human tragedy. Canal+ switched to Marseille, where Egil Olsen was on his knees offering thanks. Back to St-Etienne, and Michel kicked his plastic seat and drew on a cigarette. Craig Brown shook his hand warmly. The Moroccans, now wearing Scotland shirts, were given a rousing reception by the Tartan Army as they wandered around the stadium in a daze. A huge Moroccan flag was spread out on the pitch. They had scored five goals in their three opening games and still not qualified.

It was going to be close between the Scots and the postcards. Brown was apologetic. 'I am so sorry for our wonderful supporters who have been here with us. We gave our all but we weren't quite good enough.'

John Gorman was tidying up after Hoddle in La Baule but making heavy weather of it. Twenty-four hours earlier, the coach had said: 'David Beckham was not focused coming into the tournament.

Maybe his club needs to look at that further. He was not focused, he was vague.' Asked to elaborate, Gorman said: 'I didn't hear him say that. I always felt he was fine. I don't think Glenn meant that in any disrespect to David.'

'Why has it taken this long to get to the truth about Beckham?'

'With respect,' said Gorman, 'why should we tell you everything?'

With respect, no one wanted to talk to Gorman. A request had been put in for Owen to make an appearance, but it was turned down. Woolnough was seething. 'Quite honestly, John,' he said to Gorman, 'we wanted Owen to be here this morning. We wanted to do a really uplifting piece, which would have been good PR for the team.'

Davies rescued Gorman. 'I understand that, but this was a decision Glenn took and it's one that I share.' Afterwards, Davies told me it was Owen who was reluctant to 'parade himself again'. I didn't believe him.

Gorman's presence encouraged a new line of questioning. 'Is there a danger that the England camp is becoming blinkered? Are you aware of what people are saying in the pubs at home about Owen and Beckham?'

'We're not blinkered. We talk to our families at home. We watch Sky and some rooms pick up the BBC and ITV. We know what people are saying.'

Steve McManaman wandered in with his wrong-way-round base-ball hat. He hadn't played a minute of proper football so far. 'It's a bit frustrating but I'm right behind the lads. There's a good spirit. We have a good time, enjoy a good laugh.'

Did it rankle that the debate about who should play in the right wing-back position was always between Anderton and Beckham? There was never a mention of him. 'Not really, because I've never played in that role for anyone.' Except for England. 'If I am going to play, I would want to be in the centre of midfield.'

The conversation switched – as it was in the habit of doing – to the eminence of Owen. 'He can only get better and better,' said his Liverpool team-mate. 'I think pace is the most dangerous thing for a defender. Frankly, I've seen a lot of average players look good because of their pace. Michael can also read the game brilliantly. He gets on with everyone, too.'

England's defeat prompted the *Sun* to launch a 'For Hod's Sake Pick Owen' campaign, with a coupon to fill in which would be sent to Hoddle. The *Daily Mail* accused Hoddle of refusing to listen to his back-room staff and reported on the odds released by William Hill about a successor being in place by August. The paper also called up a 'behavioural expert' who had observed Hoddle following the Romania game and concluded that 'the way he fiddled with his hair' proved there is 'some doubt creeping in'.

Woolnough used to ghost a column for Hoddle and has written an unauthorised biography of him. But he still hardly knew the man. 'He's changed a lot since getting the job he really wanted. He's become more introverted. None of us can say we are close to him. Bobby Robson took a hell of a lot of criticism from us lot, but there was something we loved about him.'

A couple of days later, Woolnough dished out to Hoddle the sort of treatment that was served up every day to Robson and Taylor. 'Of all the sides in France,' he wrote, 'England are the most unhelpful. I have supported Glenn Hoddle down the line, but not once has he said thank you. That support will run out if he gets it wrong and England go out. For England not to qualify provides only one conclusion. That his job is too big for him. He'd have to go.' Hoddle would reply in due course. His diary was coming on nicely.

Spain were next into the torture chamber. They put six past Bulgaria, but Paraguay were beating the Group D leaders Nigeria to grab the second-place spot. At the end, a television camera kept returning to a blond-haired Spaniard standing in the emptying stadium sobbing like a baby.

It was sudden death for England now. Lose to Colombia and the castle of hopes and prophecies would collapse, burying Hoddle beneath it. France, meanwhile, moved into the second round with maximum points, and there was just a flicker of interest registering across the country.

Whatever the result, Lens was never going to be a laughing matter.

Long before England arrived, the violence perpetrated by German extremists had cast a long shadow over this already depressed town where unemployment was higher than almost anywhere in France. Daniel Nivel, a forty-three-year-old policeman, married with two children, was lying in a coma after being beaten senseless by a group of Germans wielding iron bars. There were eighty-six arrests. The German neo-Nazis weren't fuelled by drink. But the English would be given half a chance – so the mayor ordered a twenty-four-hour ban on the sale of alcohol from 8 am on the day of the game. This was extended all the way to Calais, creating a forty-mile booze-free corridor. The mayor was a popular figure. He was widely credited with keeping Racing Club de Lens alive in the 1960s when the fossil fuels business crashed. The council bought the club from the coal company for one franc and the slow fight back began. Last season, they had won the French Championship. The stadium seats 41,000, more than the entire population of the town.

'We would like to send all our thoughts and prayers to the family of Monsieur Nivel,' announced Davies at the stadium on Thursday evening, 'and we wish him a very speedy recovery.'

A Canadian lightened the mood when he asked Hoddle, 'If Teddy Sheringham is the Rolling Stones and Michael Owen is the Beatles, whose tune will you be whistling in the shower tomorrow morning?' Hoddle said he would be singing neither. 'I've always been more of a Beach Boys fan.' Then it got serious. 'It's a bigger game than Rome because it's the next one. If we lose we're packing our bags, but the bigger the game the more England players have responded,' said Hoddle. His hackles rose when someone 'presumed' that Owen would start the game.

'You are talking as if I've announced the line-up, which I haven't, so I won't answer whatever your question is,' he said. 'All I will say is that there is no fear in the camp.'

Unlike on the streets outside. It was both ghostly and ghastly the night before the match. Police in thick black helmets stood in the square, waiting for a second wave of terror to hit an already trauma- tised town. Buses with grilles over the windows moved slowly up and down the main roads, their sliding doors open to reveal rows of armed men perched on the edge of their seats. As many as 40,000 English were estimated to be on their way, the biggest influx of people into northern France since D-Day. Prince Charles and Prince Harry would be among them.

'I would have moved from here years ago', said Jean-Luc, sitting in front of a big screen at the end of a bar near the station. 'But I stayed because of the football team. And now that we are champions of France I have to stay another year to see what happens.'

The Germany–Iran game was on television. Germany looked, well, German. Tough, focused, methodical, but creaking, past their best. There was no score in the first half. Jean-Luc offered to buy me a draught Leffe, which arrived in a tall glass with a picture of a Belgian castle on it. Bierhoff scored early in the second half and then Klinsmann made it two a few minutes later. Germany qualified as group leaders, meaning they would avoid Holland in the second round. Winning your group was important.

It was my round. I took our two empty glasses to the bar and ordered two more. The barman looked at me, quickly removed the glasses and reached for the pile of plastic cups standing next to the Carlsberg pump.

Less than 30 km away in Arras, it was possible to get a drink *and* have it served in a glass. With its cobbled streets and seventeenth- and eighteenth-century Flemish-style buildings, it's a pretty town – and a town in fear on the morning of the game. 'We don't know what to think,' said the owner of a café just off the Place des Héros. 'For us, this is good business, so we will stay open for as long as we can. The ban does not affect us here. We come under a different authority.'

For those either not wanting to pay £150 for a ticket or not prepared to hang around in Lens for twelve hours on the off-chance of coming across one, Arras was a good alternative. I was feeling pleased with myself for finding such an agreeable place to spend the day, but by mid-afternoon the English began arriving in big numbers. Arras was not a secret. Then Steve Double suddenly appeared round a corner and told me the FA was using the town as one of its bases. He was clutching a thick wodge of clippings from that morning's English newspapers. On the back pages, every paper confirmed that Owen and Beckham would both be in the starting line-up – and every paper claimed it as an 'exclusive'.

The *Sun*'s front page had a picture of Des Lynam kneeling on a 'hallowed turf mat' praying for England. 'All you have to do is take up a position in front of the telly, follow the turf mat's easy instructions and yell: "Give us a win, for Hod's sake!" The mat had indicated where to put your knees, and there was a round circle in the top right corner where you should place your beer glass.

The news from Lille, to the north of Lens, was not as bad as had been expected. There had been ten arrests overnight after fighting broke out in the town centre. German police were expected to be patrolling in force along the border with France following a warning from the British Consul General in Lille that German gangs were planning an excursion to Lens. Cologne was only a three-hour drive away.

But Paul Dodd's book tour had come to an end in Calais when he and four members of the neo-Nazi group Combat 18 were detained and then deported.

A group from Nottingham had taken over a small bar in Arras called Le Flush. Their leader – at least the one who had drunk the most – had 'Glasgow Celtic' tattooed across his chest. He was carrying a copy of the *Daily Mail* which had the headline 'Alcohol Ban 50 Miles Long' on the front. 'But only two miles wide,' said Glasgow Celtic, picking up a chair and banging it on the ground. The owner ran out and said in poor English that he would call the police if the man did not sit down and shut up.

'Piss offo,' said the man. There was a small boy with the Nottingham group wearing the now deleted grey England shirt. He looked bored.

In another bar, the Argentina–Croatia game was on television. The chances were that England would play the winners. Hoddle had said Croatia represented just as big a threat as Argentina, but nothing during the game supported this. Argentina won 1–0. Ariel Ortega was again in menacing form and the Argentines were yet to concede a goal.

174

The police stopped me on the motorway just outside Lens. I had been driving well above the speed limit for the last three weeks. One of the wing mirrors was dangling from an electric cable. The exhaust was loose and rattling like machine-gun fire. But all of that went unnoticed. The problem, they said, was that one of the back wheels was wobbling. It was unsafe to continue, and the game was going to start in an hour's time. I asked one of the policemen if I could get a lift to Lens with them. The answer was 'NON.' I would have to wait until a tow-truck came along. They said they would call a garage for me and order one. I thanked them for their help and waited until they were out of sight before proceeding to Lens.

The CRS outside the stadium had two yellow strips around their helmets. They couldn't have fitted any more accessories to the belt around their waists. There was a gun, walkie-talkie, baton, whistle, handcuffs and four small black pouches, contents unknown. Dogs barked and a helicopter circled above. All roads within 100 yards of the stadium were sealed off by portable fences. No one without a ticket could breach the thick black line of police leading to the entrances. Then you showed your ticket again, which got you into the park near the ground. And at the turnstiles you produced it a third time. The alcohol ban made for a macabre atmosphere. Half an hour before kick-off, tickets were changing hands for £200.

A swell of people gathered at one entrance. It was taking longer than expected to check tickets. Someone threw a Coke can. At the same time a coach carrying corporate clients of FIFA arrived. It would be impossible to stop hundreds of English fans getting through the security check if it was allowed in. There were only ten minutes to go, and Prince Charles and Prince Harry were still to arrive. I walked to another entrance.

The stadium was 90 per cent England, the noise, as ever, spectacular. Unlike the symmetrical 'petit Wembley' in Toulouse, this comprised four detached stands, each banked steeply. The distance between the pitch and the first row of the stalls was less than 10 ft.

Leider Preciado, Colombia's answer to Michael Owen, who scored their winner against Tunisia but had only been used as a substitute in four previous internationals, was going to play from the start. He was twenty-one. Carlos Valderrama was thirty-six. There was no Faustino Asprilla. He was back in Medellin after his expulsion from the squad for speaking out of turn.

England wore red, Hoddle was in white. The inclusion of Owen and Beckham led to some people calling it The People's Team. Southgate's injury had not fully responded to treatment so Neville kept his place. Charles and Harry took their seats. After the National Anthems Adams went along the Colombian line shaking hands and nodding his head fiercely. The referee, the Mexican Arturo Brizio Carter, was the same man who had sent Zinedine Zidane off a week ago. Ince put a reassuring arm round Owen, but as the eighteen-year-old waited for Shearer to tap the ball to him at the kick-off, he looked the most assured player on the pitch.

Colombia began knocking it about, short and neat. England were going in hard and fast but couldn't get the ball. It was what the South Americans did four years earlier in America, but it got them nowhere. Beckham and Anderton were meant to be rivals for a place in the team but they began combining perfectly. England's right flank looked awesome. In the twentieth minute, Owen crossed to the near post. The clearance was half-hearted. Anderton was there. The ball was rising but somehow he got on top of it and it zinged into the roof of the net. Beckham was the first to congratulate him. Anderton who'd taken all the flak, who'd hardly played all season.

It would be good to be in St-Etienne. Back to the sunshine and a chance to move forward to the quarter-finals. Argentina. They would have to be special to beat this England side. Then Preciado fouled Ince and England had a free kick 25 yards out. A Beckham free kick. He had never scored for England. Scholes was in the wall and then he wasn't. Beckham hit it with power and movement. It dipped a little, swerved a little and ended up sailing past the keeper. Beckham ran behind the goal and thrust his pelvis in the direction of the England fans. The man working the electronic scoreboard was so mesmerised that he put up Colombia 1 England 0 before coming to his senses.

A group of English fans started a conga round the stadium. There was leadership in all departments now. Ince was shouting. Adams was pointing. Campbell was telling Le Saux to hold his position. Shearer looked liberated because there was someone alongside him who seemed to terrify the opposition every time the ball was played over his head for him to run at. Valderrama was yesterday's man. And the news was good from the Stade de France where Romania – now all blonds – weren't having much fun against Tunisia. They were one down.

I phoned home at half-time. His teachers had said he hadn't looked happy all term, but he was smiling now.

Colombia made three changes in the second half, but they couldn't contain Owen. England should have scored at least three more. McManaman was finally parted from his baseball hat and came on for Scholes. Rob Lee was given an outing in place of Anderton, who had been booed at Wembley three weeks before. Not now. Shearer was booked for taking a free kick too quickly. The Colombian keeper was having a great second half. It would have been a landslide without him.

The England fans were singing 'God Save the Queen' at the end and Prince Harry was wearing an England scarf. Valderrama exchanged shirts with Beckham. Romania had equalised late on in their match. There was no escaping Argentina. Hoddle looked exhausted. 'We're not going to go overboard,' he said. 'We don't go overboard when we lose – unlike some people – so we won't go overboard now. We had always marked out Owen and Beckham for this game. We were looking for pace and that was what we got. It was a conclusive performance. They all get eight out of ten, plus.'

And he couldn't help justifying his policy towards Beckham. 'Without a doubt what happened with David helped against Colombia. Whether the boy would agree with me or not I don't know, but I am experienced at this sort of thing.'

Before getting on the bus, Beckham said he knew the ball was going in the second it left his foot. And then he took a swipe at Hoddle. 'Nothing has ever got in the way of my football. Nothing. I have always been able to keep football apart from anything else in my life.'

Sir Bobby Charlton was surrounded by a group of Colombian

journalists outside the stadium. They wanted to know what he had made of the South Americans. 'This may not be the best period for them at the moment but they have some talented players,' he said, politely.

'And what about England?'

His eyes lit up. 'Well, we're in the race now, aren't we?'

Arsène Wenger had several microphones in front of him. 'England were dynamic,' he said. 'The real score was five or six nil. This was the performance they needed. But it is unfortunate that they have to play Argentina.'

The green-uniformed volunteers were excited. In the mixed zone one of them said: 'We have had a lot of teams in Lens but the English supporters are the best in the world. I have never experienced an atmosphere like it.'

Chapter 12

A Chance to Put Things Right

There was nothing wrong with the car. The Vauxhall dealer said the reason the police might have thought it had a wobbly wheel was because the tyres on the back had different treads, creating some sort of optical illusion. He suggested the real fault was the English number-plate.

The players went straight to a château near St-Omer for a night with their wives and girlfriends. I went to Paris hoping to find a ticket for the second-round game between Brazil and Chile at the Parc des Princes. The last time these teams met in a World Cup was in Rio de Janeiro nine years ago, when a firecracker landed near Roberto Rojas, the Chilean goalkeeper, and his team-mates walked off. FIFA later ruled that Rojas had feigned injury and banned him for life.

A Frenchman standing in a bus shelter to avoid the rain outside the stadium offered me a ticket for 1,000 francs. It would have to be an intoxicating game to justify spending that sort of money. This was only the second round. I told him I wanted ten minutes to think about it. Perhaps I could persuade one of the volunteers in the media centre to slip me a ticket. No chance. They were under siege from hundreds of ticketless journalists claiming to be indispensable to the future of South American football. There was jostling at the ticket counter.

'Gone, gone, gone. Can't you see? Gone,' said a flustered official, holding up two empty boxes and banging them together. But they didn't believe him. A security guard had to be called to restore order. I returned to the bus shelter. The Frenchman was smoking a small cigar. A Brazilian in a little tweedy hat walked up and entered the negotiations. Suddenly he pulled out a wad of notes and began counting. The ticket was his.

'*Merci, monsieur*,' the Frenchman said to me with an impish grin as he stepped out into the drizzle.

It turned out to be a one-sided game. Chile pushed forward for the first ten minutes but were never in it after that. Brazil looked as if they could turn up the heat at will. And with Denilson, their £22 million sub, perched on a plastic seat beside the pitch, they were giving new meaning to the idea of 'strength in depth'. Ronaldo, after a poor first half, scored twice but could have had a hat-trick when he crashed the ball against the crossbar after an archetypal Brazilian move involving Dunga and Roberto Carlos. Towards the end, Ronaldo was playing for Ronaldo only, which was amplified by more and more frequent television shots of his girlfriend watching in the stands. Every time he got the ball he set off in pursuit of the record books, to the obvious irritation of Rivaldo. Afterwards he said: 'I have to help the team but the team must also help me.' Dunga kept shouting at his team. Something was bothering him – and it wasn't Marcelo Salas or Ivan Zamorano. When Cesar Sampaio scored Brazil's second, Dunga eschewed the celebrations and pulled Ronaldo to one side for a private word. Perhaps not even the managing director of Nike knew what was going on between Dunga, the captain, and Zagallo, the coach, as the two men snarled at each other. Brazil won 4–1. They were picking up steam but they weren't a happy ship.

I couldn't face another drive from Paris to La Baule and wasn't sure the car could either. So I jumped on a train hoping to arrive in time for Hoddle's Sunday sermon. One or two Argentinians were in the congregation – or so the taxi-driver told me on the way from the station. He had picked them up the night before. He said they were worried about England. I asked him who he thought would win.

'Argentina,' he said, looking in the mirror to gauge my reaction. 'Why?'

'Why? Because it's what I hope will happen. Having England here has done nothing for the town. If anything it has kept people away. All the taxi-drivers here will be cheering for Argentina on Tuesday.'

Then he charged me £15 for the two-mile ride. 'That's a lot,' I said. He pointed to a list of charges written on a piece of plastic stuck to the glove compartment. Double fare on Sundays, it said, and I assumed he had added a further supplement for single occupancy in cloudy weather.

Hoddle was warming to his theme. We should avoid thinking in terms of revenge. 'This game gives us a chance to redress the balance,' he said, his voice still impaired by the exertions of Friday night. 'I hate the word revenge. It's ugly. I like to think about turning things around, getting something out of our system. Life is like that sometimes. You get a chance to put things right.'

England would have stood a far better chance of getting things right if they were playing Croatia rather than Argentina, but Hoddle could not bring himself to admit it. He fooled no one. He even dared suggest that he had intended to come second in the group from the start, and that losing to Romania might prove to have been 'no bad thing'. He pointed out that Brazil had lost a first-round match but failed to mention that the world champions had already qualified for the second phase by the time they played Norway.

'We spoke about this amongst the staff and agreed that we wanted Argentina. We are better when we play against a big football country, better against a team like Argentina. We wanted it to be them rather than Croatia. The people back home would expect us to beat countries like Croatia.'

Hoddle had a personal motive for 'redressing the balance'. He was playing on the day Maradona handed Argentina victory in Mexico City on 22 June 1986.

'It took me three or four days to accept what had happened, but I never had negative feelings towards Maradona about it. No one in our camp blamed him. He was allowed to get away with it by the referee. It was a blatant hand-ball and it stopped us in our tracks. That second goal would never have been scored if it was

0–0. We were still in shock when he began his run – even though it was a very good goal. After the game Terry Butcher and myself were in the drugs room with Maradona and I shook his hand. Despite what happened that day he was the greatest player I've ever seen – better than Pele. The world will never see another player like him. Pele might have been a better team player, but Maradona was the best individual of all time.'

'Argentina would claim that 1986 was making amends for 1966,' said the *Guardian*'s David Lacey, the veteran among the Number Ones. This was his ninth World Cup and it entitled him to make statements rather than ask questions. Geoff Hurst had scored the decisive goal that day after the Argentinian captain Antonio Rattin was sent off for dissent. Alf Ramsey had called the Argentinians 'animals' and told his players not to swap shirts.

'I feel pretty spot-on with my plans,' Hoddle concluded. 'We've got really positive vibes in the camp and the team is relishing the idea of playing Argentina.' It was put to him that he had yielded to pressure in his team selection against Colombia. 'That's garbage,' he said.

Shearer was on holiday in the Algarve when Maradona was playing volleyball with Peter Shilton in 1986. Owen had just completed his first year at primary school. 'I felt like everyone else,' said the captain, sitting with his arms folded across his chest. 'I don't know if revenge is the right word. The right result is the important thing. Our confidence is sky-high. There was an aura the other night that said we weren't going to be beaten. I told the manager before we went out on the pitch that there was a feel-good factor. I don't believe Argentina have been tested yet. They'll be saying to themselves: "We would prefer to play Romania."'

All Englishmen except Hoddle were saying to themselves: 'We would prefer to be playing Croatia.'

Just as Tony Adams had made no secret of his preferance for the traditional four-man defence rather than Hoddle's three defenders and two wing-back system, Shearer was crawling out of the closet over Michael Owen. 'Michael always gives you another option,' he said. 'You can knock it over him and eight out of ten times he'll end up getting it. I'm not sure what the manager will do, whether he'll play an attacking side again or whether he'll be more defensive, but it will be hard for him to change it now.'

Shearer said England were so desperate to do well that they weren't afraid to argue with each other in the pursuit of excellence. He and Ince had had a difference of opinion during the Colombia game when Ince began complaining that neither of the strikers was dropping back to cover. 'I told him Owen was already doing that. Incey looked about and saw that I was right but he still wanted to have the argument.'

Shearer's assessment of England's abilities was more realistic, more straightforward, more honest and a lot more believable than those of his coach. 'Technically, we are not as good as the Brazilians, but we've got big hearts. We come out fighting when we need to.'

I had read an interview a couple of days earlier with Emmanuel Petit in *Le Soir*. After a season of Premiership football with Arsenal the Frenchman was asked to explain the differences between English and French football. He said the abiding tenet in England was that if you are 2–0 down with six minutes left, you don't give up, whereas in France, 'you stop if you are 2–0 down with sixty minutes left.'

Several French journalists were listening to Shearer. They were scribbling down every word, most likely weaving in the Malvinas, Margaret Thatcher and Galtieri. Then the word went out that the Shearer material was to be held for forty-eight hours. 'Why?' protested the French. Because their English counterparts said so, that's why. The French surrounded David Davies and began shouting.

Erik Bielderman, one of only two foreign journalists on the official media package with England – Giancarlo Gavarotti was the other – was asked to make his French colleagues play the game in the proper spirit, but his heart wasn't in it.

'The English have been able to organise the news amongst themselves, but from here on they cannot expect to have such control,' he said. I asked Bielderman about Hoddle. Was he impressed? 'He makes you think he knows where he's going. A good professional coach is a good liar, so I don't know if what he says is true and I don't know how much the English media trust him. I think they have come to respect him but I wouldn't say they like him much.' Bielderman said the tabloids' interest in the players' private lives had come as a shock. 'In France if someone has a drink problem we may refer to it but we don't have the sort of papers that would actually pay for pictures of a player looking drunk in a nightclub. In France, we treat the players more like human beings. How would you like it if someone wrote that you enjoyed sex at six in the morning with the hotel maid?'

There were about twenty English supporters at the end of the road leading to the training centre. One family, who were camping nearby, had organised tickets for the second-round match in Bordeaux, after assuming that England would end up top of the group. 'The idea of watching Romania and Croatia is not exactly what we had in mind,' said the father, who was wearing the England home strip. The plan was to swap tickets with some Romanians who might have made the same presumption – although there weren't many Romanians wandering around La Baule waiting to be propositioned. But this was a fortunate family. They had turned up in Lens without tickets but ended up finding seats for a tenner, along with some 150 others, courtesy of a Mancunian sting that involved bribing one of the turnstile officials. The only snag came when the rightful ticket-holders turned up. 'Luckily there were one or two empty seats around and about so we moved off there. Don't ask me how it all happened. We were just told to follow these guys ahead of us and that was it.'

Back in Paris, I headed straight for the Place de l'Hôtel de Ville to watch France's second-round game against Paraguay on the big screen. If you are going to show football on big screens you need the commentary and sounds from the stadium to go with it, other-wise you can never hide the fact that you are standing outside Dixons with your nose squashed against the window-pane. The square, with Notre Dame peering over it from across the river, was packed.

France were making heavy weather of it. The weight of expec-tation was holding them back. And they were suffering from the lack of a great striker. Ronaldo, Christian Vieri, Davor Suker, Dennis Bergkamp, Jurgen Klinsmann, Gabriel Batistuta – these are the men whose names were in the headlines more than any others. They might not always shine, but they had reputations that sent a tremor through opposition defences. The striker is the first violinist in the orchestra. This gaping hole was made to look worse by frequent sightings of the suspended Zinedine Zidane sitting on the French bench. By the beginning of extra time France were parked permanently in Paraguay's half. The Paraguayans were hanging by a thread, and their inspirational goalkeeper Jose Luis Chilavert knew it. He had known it since the eighteenth minute, when he was booked for time-wasting. Petit was substituted in the second half, prompting groans behind me. They may have been Arsenal supporters, for whom the solution to France's lack of firepower, Nicolas Anelka, wasn't even in the squad.

In the 113th minute Pires crossed the ball, David Trézéguet knocked it down, and Blanc scored the first golden goal ever to decide a World Cup-tie. It was the moment France began to get dressed for the party, the moment many of those who considered themselves above it all succumbed to the allure of Le Foot. It was the day Paris reverberated to the sound of blaring horns and the National Front's grasp of the Tricolour slipped.

That evening in the Métro I spotted a familiar face standing at the end of the platform. It was René Simoes, the Jamaican coach, with his wife and daughters. There was no chauffeur-driven car now, no men in black with walkie-talkies, no Channel 4 fly-on-thewall camera crew. 'Was the whole experience harder than you had expected?' I asked. The Reggae Boyz had lost 3–1 to Croatia, 5–0 to Argentina, before belatedly beating Japan.

'No,' said Simoes. 'Our problem had nothing to do with football. It was the documentary which went out the day before our first match that did the damage. It destroyed all the spirit I had spent months building up. It caused terrible divisions between the Jamaicans and British-based players. It was a disaster.'

It was good telly. Simoes had allowed the cameras into every nook and cranny.

'In what way did the programme distort the facts?' I asked him.

'In every way,' he said. 'It made out we only had one bathroom in our training camp when actually we had four. The crazy thing was that we invited the cameras in.' The train began filling up with Danes on their way to the Stade de France for their second-round match against Nigeria. 'We encouraged the disaster. I remember saying that we should consult a lawyer about watching it first, but nothing happened. This was Jamaica's great moment to show the world and it came to nothing.'

Nigeria lost to Denmark 4–1. Everyone expected the Africans to produce slick, attacking football. They were the big outside bet. Everything about them seemed fresh – except their coach, Bora Milutinovic, who four years earlier had been in charge of the USA team. Before that he had coached Mexico and Costa Rica. He was the Ron Atkinson of national team management, on and off the carousel. You'll find him employed by some other country in 2002. Nigeria were one down with only three minutes on the clock, and conceded another nine minutes later. The defending at free kicks was unorthodox. Their wall had almost as many holes in it as an Irish jail.

I got back to my hotel shortly before midnight. It would soon be England's turn. I telephoned a friend in London. Chris had been captain of our school team when we were twelve years old. I told him this match required a special effort, and that he should catch the 6.18 am Eurostar from Waterloo, I'd pick him up at the Gare du Nord, and we'd drive to St-Etienne. I was confident he would pick up a ticket on the street for about £200. Not many people can drop everything for an overseas football match, particularly not if, like Chris, you have recently got married, just started your own business, just moved into a new house, your wife is pregnant, and you have tickets to the theatre on Monday evening.

'Give me ten minutes to sort it out,' said Chris. Five minutes later he called back to say he would be arriving in Paris at 10.30 am. By lunchtime we were in St-Etienne.

Chapter 13

Bottle

The Rotters had fallen out. Three weeks of hooli-watch were always going to be fraught, and no one was surprised when the miscreant turned out to be The Animal. Colin 'The Animal' Adamson, of the *Evening Standard*, had committed the heinous crime of reneging on an agreement among the blunts (journalists) to share a line about how much the policing of English fans was eating into the French security budget. Adamson got wind of the story and proudly announced that he had phoned the figures over just in time to make the *Standard*'s last edition on Monday – when the plan had been for the dailies to have it to themselves on Tuesday.

'Classic, typical Animal behaviour,' said Shekhar Bhatia, the *Express*'s newsman, as he patrolled St-Etienne. 'We've decided not to talk to him for twenty-four hours. He'll have to hunt on his own for a bit.'

Adamson seemed perfectly happy hunting on his own. When I came across him he was sitting on a park bench near the Place Jean-Jaurès next to a tall plastic beaker of chilled lager. It had been a short walk to the office. Adamson's room was overlooking the square, giving him a grandstand view of the previous evening's largely peaceful revelries.

'I've finally got rid of my photographer,' he said. 'He's run off to the hospital in search of an exclusive picture of a woman who doesn't exist. Poor sod.' The Animal knew how to drink but had never learned to drive, which meant that on assignments like these he was reliant on whichever photographer he was working with to ferry him around. He found this stifling. To give himself some breathing space, he had told the photographer that in the small hours of Monday morning a pregnant English woman had been involved in a fight with French youths and been rushed to hospital by ambulance, where she gave birth prematurely to a boy and was naming him Alan Shearer. The snapper scarpered.

The FA's ticket allocation for the game was 2,049 in a stadium with an overall capacity of 36,600. As many as 25,000 England supporters were expected to turn up, creating what David Mellor described as 'one of the biggest black markets since the trade in nylons in the Second World War'. The FA had appealed for more tickets and were granted an extra 30. On Monday evening, Chris was offered a seat for £400 by a Frenchman and £350 by an Argentinian. He wasn't interested.

The Loire Valley police chief said he was determined that St-Etienne would not become a 'dead town' like Lens. 'Banning alcohol would be difficult to enforce,' he said. 'It would stop police dealing with more serious problems and we want everyone to enjoy the festivities. Louts are only a tiny minority and many of them have already been sent home.' Even so, at least 1,500 police were on duty, nearly double the number deployed for the previous five matches in town. It was decided that the game would not be shown on the big screen and that the bars would close at 11 pm.

England trained in the heat of the late afternoon sun in the Stade Geoffrey Guichard. David Beckham and Rob Lee played little part in the proceedings, which presumably was Hoddle's smokescreen for the day. There was a long wait for the England coach in the sweaty mixed zone afterwards. The number of camera crews had doubled, reporters had doubled, uniformed officials had doubled. The stakes had doubled. On various TV monitors around the room you could see Germany riding their luck against Mexico, coming back from a goal down to win 2–1. Luis Hernandez missed a sitter in the second half which would have sent the Germans home, but in the end Klinsmann and his not so merry men maintained their country's extraordinary sixty-year record of reaching the quarter-finals in every World Cup.

They were joined in the last eight a few hours later by Holland, who finally got the better of Yugoslavia with an injury-time goal from Edgar Davids. Bergkamp distinguished himself by stamping on a Yugoslavian defender right under the nose of a linesman who never got a whiff of it. He walked away without even a wag of the referee's finger. So it was Brazil, France, Holland, Italy, Denmark and Germany in the next round, to be joined by the winners of England against Argentina and Croatia against Romania. Hoddle's preference for playing Argentina would mean meeting the Dutch in the quarters and most likely Brazil in the semis. A snip.

'We don't feel we're underdogs to anyone,' said Hoddle. 'They've got extremely good players but so have we. For every question I get asked about Argentina I'm sure Passarella gets asked about Shearer, Owen, Beckham and Adams.' Hoddle was dressed all in blue. He seemed composed, unlike David Davies, who stood in the background looking to be in considerable discomfort. His usual place on the podium had been taken by a blazered FIFA official who was a dead ringer for Tom Selleck. The Hawaiian floral shirt was missing, but he would have one in his car ready to put on when his time came to perform in the piano bar at the local Novotel hotel later that evening. He had a Des Lynam moustache and his suntan was perfect. This was his show, and there was nothing Davies could do except grimace and bear it. To prolong the agony, every question and answer had to be translated first into French and then into Spanish. Argentinians held their tape recorders up to the speakers whenever the word revenge was uttered, but Hoddle stuck by his 'redressing the balance' formula. Then came a game of Chinese whisper. Hoddle was asked if England would play in red shirts, as they had done to good effect against Colombia. There had been calls to stick with red, not least because more and more English fans in France were wearing the red 1966 long-sleeved cotton shirts. Hoddle said England would wear white socks, white shorts and white shirts, just like they did against Argentina thirty-two years ago at Wembley. But by the time this had been passed down the line, Hoddle's answer had all the makings of a major diplomatic row between London and Buenos Aires. 'England will not swap shirts with Argentina at the end of the match' was how the Spanish interpreter reported it. Great story. But then multilingual Gavarotti began flapping his arms in the air.

'No, no, no,' he said. And war in the South Pacific was averted.

Almost the last question was about penalties. 'We've been working on it for some time, and I'm confident that we'll be all right if it comes to them on the night,' said Hoddle.

We stayed in Lyon that night, partly because there were no rooms left in St-Etienne, but mainly because Chris was looking for a gastronomic blow-out with almost as much energy as he was hunting for a ticket to the game. We asked the waiter if he knew anyone who had a ticket for sale. He said he would talk to his manager. The manager made several telephone calls and then handed us a piece of paper with the name of a St-Etienne restaurant called Le Grillon written on it. Next morning, after coffee and Paracetamol, we booked a table for lunch at Le Grillon, where the owner, a languidly dapper man called Jean-Jacques, welcomed us as if we were a couple of inspectors from the Michelin Guide. We explained our need for a ticket, and then Chris added that we had nowhere to stay that night and any suggestions would be gladly received. Jean-Jacques took out his mobile phone and pressed some buttons. 'The mayor would like you to be his guests this evening in one of our best hotels near the station,' he said, 'and at 6 pm he is hosting a reception at the town hall to which you are most welcome.'

Towards the end of lunch Jean-Jacques and his staff rearranged the tables at the front of the restaurant and a curious assortment of people began filing in. There were two women in wheelchairs, an old man wearing a denim jacket over a shirt and tie, several pony-tailed students, and a young woman with curly black hair who sat holding hands with a woman with a stud in her nose. Then Rogan Taylor walked in, followed by Mark Perryman, who runs Philosophy Football, the trendy T-shirt company. He and his girlfriend were moving about France on bicycles.

'This is a *fête du livre*,' said Jean-Jacques. 'Usually we hold it in October, but we've brought it forward. We want to make people feel that there is more going on today than just a football match.'

Some of the readings were in French, others – for the benefit of passing Argentinians – were in Spanish. It was hard to decipher the French, apart from some Gallic agonising which asked: 'Who am I? And what does it matter when I know who I am?' A man with an accordion played a long piece, during which one of the organisers spread himself out on a banquette at the back of the room and passed out. Chris was looking at his watch, knowing that time was running out and that soon he would be wandering around St-Etienne like dozens of others with a piece of cardboard hanging from his neck inscribed with the words '*Je Cherche les Billets*'.

William Shakespeare made an appearance with a passage from *The Tempest*. It was the epilogue spoken by Prospero, the relevance of which was not immediately clear. But I hadn't heard it since A-levels.

> Gentle breath of yours my sails
> Must fill, or else my project fails,
> Which was to please. Now I want
> Spirits to enforce, art to enchant,
> And my ending is despair,
> Unless I be relieved by prayer,
> Which pierces so that it assaults
> Mercy itself and frees all faults.
> As you from crimes would pardon'd be,
> Let your indulgence set me free.

The introduction of Prospero led to another series of phonecalls by Jean-Jacques. 'The rooms are booked but I cannot help with the ticket,' he said. 'And whatever happens in the game – win or lose – you must come back here afterwards and we will talk about it.'

The final readings were from a book by François de Cornière, the last of which was called 'The Penalty' and was read in English:

The penalty makes you hot or cold. Hot when called in favour of your team. Cold when it is the other way round. In both cases

I always watch the player responsible for shooting. The way he puts the ball on the strategic spot is vital. You can never stress enough how the ball, too, feels these things.

There was a lot of embracing at the end of the performance, and we thanked Jean-Jacques as profusely as our French allowed.

Back in the centre of town the decision not to ban alcohol appeared to be working. The English were mainly congregated in the Place Jean-Jaurès, which was about half the size of a football field. There must have been grass in the square at some stage. Now there was just dust. Trees lined it on three sides, and there was a stage next to the large screen which was showing the Croatia–Romania game. Suker had just scored from a disputed penalty and it remained 1–0. A rock band was about to entertain the troops.

The Argentinians were gathered 100 yards up the street in the distinctly prettier Place de l'Hôtel de Ville. They were kept amused by jugglers. Between the English and Argentinian settlements stood the mayor's office, where I was expected for drinks half an hour ago. I left Chris sitting outside a sunny bar with Dave Sturridge, the man I had met in the camp-site near Montpellier, who had been ripped off by a tour company in Australia. Chris ended up sharing Dave's cardboard sign pleading for tickets, which he propped up at the side of the road on a music stand. Chris was drinking brandy and getting anxious.

I found a pair of trousers in the back of the car and set off to meet Michel Théollière, who had been mayor for four years. Girls in short yellow skirts with matching sashes ushered guests into a tented courtyard, bedecked with greenery and small stone statues. St-Etienne may not have the sophistication of Lyon, but every local we met was unfailingly friendly, and as a glass of champagne was thrust into my hand I concluded that it was a great little town. The French railway system was born here. More recently it had seen the dramatic decline of its armaments industry, and its football team, which once employed Michel Platini before he moved on to Juventus, had seen better days.

Over a huge plate of canapés I spotted Jean-Jacques chatting to a woman wearing a floral turban. He waved. I introduced myself to Monsieur Théollière. He had taught English in London for a year before deciding to move into local politics. On Saturday afternoons he used to stand behind the goal at White Hart Lane and watch Glenn Hoddle.

'I used to see some fighting too,' he said, 'and I know what the difference is between hooligans and real fans. I've asked the people of St-Etienne to show no provocation. Considering the number of English there are here we have had very little trouble, and I have to say there is something immensely moving about the English support.'

I asked what would happen if the game went into extra time. Would the bars still close at 11 pm?

'I don't think it would be wise to do that, do you?' he said.

There were speeches, during which the secretary-general of Interpol appeared to be representing the British government. The Argentinian Ambassador in London was there. He said: 'The English are a proud nation and it is right that they should show their passion . . . and I think they have forgiven Maradona for what he did.'

Chris had closed the deal. He paid £120 after half an hour of traumatic trading which ended down a backstreet outside an abandoned church. An absolute bargain. Pete would have called it 'bloody magic'. Thousands of others were less successful, and for the first time in four games there were more opposition supporters in the stadium than English. Almost double the number, and when England came out for their warm-up the jeering from the Argentinians came as a shock. The stadium, known locally as The Cauldron, was the smallest England had played in so far. Rival banners competed for air space. One flag had Las Malvinas written on it, but only one.

Argentina were wearing dark blue. They looked relaxed during the playing of their National Anthem. Hoddle put out the same team that had taken Colombia apart. Adams, with several days' growth on his face, was standing to attention and finding it difficult

193

to make himself heard above the hissing during 'God Save the Queen'. The woman in question was at Holyrood Palace, entertaining the Lord Provost of Edinburgh. She had ordered dinner to start an hour early, and asked for a larger than usual television screen to be wheeled in.

The referee was Kim Milton Nielsen, a towering thirty-eight-year-old Dane who already knew that he had no chance of going any further in this World Cup because Denmark were into the last eight. He had nothing to lose.

Argentina kicked off. The first ten minutes would be crucial. Within seconds Darren Anderton was off the pitch putting in his contact lenses. Argentina were first to attack, once in the air, once on the ground, but both times Sol Campbell dealt with it. England and Argentina fans sat next to each other uneasily.

Owen's first run ended with him performing a somersault just outside the Argentinian penalty area. The ball rolled back to Graeme Le Saux, who let fly. He missed, but Shearer was within a couple of feet of getting a toe to it at the far post.

Then Ariel Ortega played the ball over the England backline for Diego Simeone to run on to. Seaman rushed out to smother it and Simeone lodged a foot between his knees. He kept it there for as long as he could before falling to the ground. The referee gave Argentina a penalty and booked Seaman. It was the worst possible start. The sight of Batistuta picking up the ball and placing it on the penalty spot was horrible. He struck it to the right of Seaman, who got a hand to it, but the ball was moving too fast. Argentina were one up after only five minutes. Gaps began opening up in the crowd behind the England goal. Fists were clenched, punches thrown.

Within a few minutes Owen was running with the ball again. This time he went across Roberto Ayala and went down when he knew the ball was out of reach. The referee pointed to the spot. We were playing penalties already. During the Argentinian deliberations with Nielsen, Ince added a word or two of his own and was shown a yellow card. Alan Shearer put the ball down and smashed it into the roof of the net. Even the hand of God would have struggled with that one. The gaps in the crowd quickly filled in. 1–1, and only ten minutes gone.

Five minutes later, Beckham floated the ball to Owen on the halfway line, who brought it under control with the deftest of touches, using the outside of his foot. And he was away, scorching upfield in an acre of space, with no one fast enough to catch him. When he came across José Chamot he put his foot on the accelerator and you thought he was bound to spin out of control, but he just kept going. Ayala was his next obstacle, but not for long. One swerve, another surge, and he was beaten. Now there was only the goalkeeper left. Suddenly Scholes was running in over Owen's right shoulder, and for a second it seemed that he was better placed to shoot, but Owen wouldn't let him near it. He swung his leg and the ball went screaming into the top corner. Argentina had not conceded a goal for eight matches and all of a sudden they had let in two in quarter of an hour. Owen's was the best goal of the World Cup so far, and he was only eighteen and he was English.

Mark and Pete had telephoned earlier in the day to say they would be in the Millbridge pub in Plymouth. 'See you in Marseille,' had been Mark's last words before hanging up. And Chris had been going on all afternoon that England would win by two clear goals. It should have been 3–1 when Scholes met a Shearer header three yards out. It was on his left foot, but that was no excuse for the ball rolling past the post with the goalkeeper beaten. Juan Veron hacked down Owen in the forty-third minute and was booked. Batistuta was being kept under control by Campbell and Le Saux appeared unaffected by what had happened to him in Toulouse.

Argentina were given a free kick in injury time of the first half. England had five in the wall plus an Argentinian. Zanetti hung about behind the line, minding his own business. As Veron stepped up to the ball Javier Zanetti strolled into an empty space. The ball was played neatly to his feet. He swivelled and hit it firmly with his left foot past Seaman. The Argentinian coach Passarella and his assistants rushed to the touchline in their suits and ties as Zanetti fell to the ground in front of them and rolled around in ecstasy. The Argentinian fans celebrated throughout half-time, banging drums and waving their shirts in the air. One long banner said simply: 'Diego.'

Beckham hadn't touched the ball in the second half when Simeone crashed into him. He was spread-eagled on the ground. Simeone patted him on the head for the benefit of the referee, who was standing four yards away. Suddenly, Beckham jerked his right foot up and his heel struck Simeone behind his knee. It was as if his leg was on a pulley being operated by some sinister character hidden deep within the stadium. The kick wasn't hard – from that position it couldn't be – and it didn't hurt Simeone, but the Argentinian captain went down clutching at various parts of his leg as if amputation was imminent. The Argentinians crowded round Nielsen, who put his hand in his pocket and began fishing for a card. Shearer feared the worst and waved the meddling Argentinians away. The referee called Beckham towards him and showed him a yellow one, but then his hand went back into the pocket and came back out with red. Beckham looked back only once, briefly, as he walked off. By the time he reached the touchline he had untucked his shirt and his eyes were watering up. He didn't look at Hoddle and Hoddle didn't look at him. But Batistuta smiled.

What chance now? Hoddle was right all along about Beckham. Or was it more the case that he had wound him up so much that something like that was bound to happen? It may have been a harsh decision but it wasn't the wrong one. It's there in Law 12 of the game: 'A player is sent off and shown the red card if he is guilty of violent conduct.' Nielsen had been lenient with Beckham on their one previous encounter during Manchester United's European Cup quarter-final against Porto. Beckham had got himself involved in an off-the-ball scrap and Nielsen let him off.

Behind Seaman the ten-strong band, which was sponsored by one of the tabloids and had attended every game, began playing 'The Great Escape' and didn't stop for the next seventy-five minutes. Ray Clemence and John Gorman were slumped in their seats, arms crossed. Alan Smith, the physio, shook his head. Doc Crane was looking his age. How could Beckham have done that? What was in his mind? Something must have been going on, because he had time to think about what he did.

England were being pinned back now. Seaman just got a finger to a shot from Lopez and then Shearer, playing at right-back, cleared the ball almost off his own line. Argentina made a double substitution. Batistuta and Lopez came off. The England fans sang 'Rule Britannia' and 'God Save the Queen'. Shearer and Owen were taking turns as the sole man up front. It would be heroic if they could hold on and take the game to penalties. Hoddle began pointing out something to Southgate on a piece of paper before sending him on in place of Le Saux. In the seventy-fourth minute Owen finally got to run, with the ball ending up in an almost identical position to when he scored in the first half, but this time it was on his left foot. He lifted it high over the bar. Adams handled the ball in his own area but got away with it. Neville made a two-footed tackle and got away with that too. Shearer was taking the free kicks in place of Beckham. Adams was playing with a flat back four now – at last – but he could never have imagined he would get his way in such circumstances. Merson came on for Scholes in the eightieth minute. An eeriness descended on the stadium.

Into the last ten minutes, and Shearer took a free kick just outside the penalty area and won a corner. Anderton took it. Shearer and the goalkeeper went up together but both missed the ball. Campbell got his head to it and scored. The music came on as Campbell and Ince went off the pitch to celebrate. Then the goal was disallowed and Veron was back down the other end with the ball. It was at this point that the Queen reportedly shouted at her television and retired to her private room.

I was working my way through a brand-new packet of unfiltered Gitanes. There were four left after eighty-five minutes. Someone must have spiked Merson's water. He was falling over every time he got the ball. 'The prat's wearing fucking plimsolls,' yelled Martin Samuel, from the *Express*.

The band played on. I wondered if Elmer Bernstein, who wrote the theme music to *The Great Escape* in the 1960s, was still alive.

I hoped the band's seventy-three-year-old saxophonist was still with us.

At the end of normal time the entire England squad went on to the pitch. Hoddle did the rounds like a consultant at a busy hospital's Accident and Emergency department. If they had survived forty-five minutes they could hold on for another thirty. The 'big hearts' that Shearer had talked about in La Baule were keeping the blood pumping fiercely. This was a rear-guard action of a different kind.

Simeone was substituted at the start of extra time and gave the captain's armband to Veron. Shearer and Chamot went up for a header and Chamot punched the ball with his hand. It was more of a penalty than the two that had been given. Hoddle could make one more substitution. He had three experienced penalty-takers on the pitch – Shearer, Owen and Merson. Presumably Anderton would take the fourth. But then Anderton came off, to be replaced by David Batty. Argentina had at least six recognised penalty men out there.

Ince seemed to get stronger as the game wore on. He barged his way past three Argentinians and shot just wide in the tenth minute of extra time. Doc Crane was on his feet now in the dugout. He had seen some tense games in his twelve years as team doctor, but none so terrifying as this. Hoddle and Gorman rushed on with water-bottles as the teams changed ends. Passarella was complaining to the fourth official about the intervention of the English bench. Then Batistuta and a FIFA man squared up to each other. On the pitch, Ortega was still in business. He tried to sell Adams a couple of dummies, but Adams refused to buy either. This was one of Adams's greatest performances. Penalties were two minutes away.

When Nielsen blew, Hoddle went first to Owen. He was eighteen years old and he was about to take a penalty for his country in front of a television audience of more than 24 million in England alone. Owen went to talk to Shearer. Seaman gulped from a plastic bottle and shook Adams by the hand. Ince paced up and down, joking nervously with his friend McManaman. Campbell was having his calves massaged. Overall, England looked the more confident. The Argentinians were flopped on the ground, shattered. A list was handed to the referee with the names of the first five penalty-takers and the order in which they would be taken.

The goalkeepers shook hands and walked towards the end occupied entirely by Argentinians. Sergio Berti went with them. He put the ball down and hit it firmly past Seaman. 1–0. Shearer came forward. You could tie yourself in knots thinking about it. Shearer had already taken one penalty. Should he put it in the same place? It might be sensible to aim for a different spot, but then the goalkeeper would have worked that out and so why not go for the same place after all? But then the goalkeeper knew that Shearer knew what the goalkeeper knew. The best thing would be to strike it so that even if he dived the right way he could never get near it. Which is what Shearer did. 1–1.

Hernan Crespo walked towards Seaman. One of the substitutes. Only twenty-two years old. Seaman dived to his left and saved it. The England fans let out a roar. For the first time since Beckham was sent off, England were in front. Surely, one more save from Seaman would clinch it and then on to Marseille for a second time. Owen would be next. But Owen wasn't next. Nor was Merson. It was Paul Ince. 'What the fuck's going on?' shouted Samuel. 'Fucking hell,' said his *Express* colleague Rob Shepherd, 'I don't believe this.' But then Shepherd, who got on well with Ince, rallied. 'Go on, Incey. Stick it in the fucking net and let's get out of here.' Ince bounced the ball twice on his way to the penalty area, and as he put it down his eyes darted about like they had done four months earlier in his car outside Liverpool's training ground. 'If it means going to take a penalty, then I will have to take one,' he had said. He hit it with the inside of his right foot and Roa saved.

Then Veron scored. You knew he would. It was Merson's turn. Roa was off his line, but when the referee told him to get back he began complaining that the ball wasn't properly on the spot. Merson picked it up and bounced it a few times while the referee showed Roa a yellow card. But it didn't put Merson off. He stayed on his plimsolls and scored. It was 2–2 with two to go. Marcelo Gallardo, another substitute, scored his, and then came Owen. Six months ago he was turning up at England training sessions for work experience and was too young to buy a drink in a pub. He hardly looked at the goal. He just thumped the ball and it hit the inside of the post before ricocheting into the net. Owen turned round and rubbed his hands together.

Seaman would have to save the next one. But Ayala's penalty was too good. Advantage Argentina. It was down to David Batty to keep England in the World Cup finals. He looked confident enough, but he had never taken a penalty in his life, never scored a goal of any kind for England. People used to joke that Batty didn't even know how to play a forward pass. Beckham was watching from inside the tunnel. Behind me and to the left, Brian Moore was asking Kevin Keegan whether Batty would do it. 'Yes or no?' said Moore. 'Yes,' said Keegan. Batty missed. England had lost in France.

Argentinian players, coaches, doctors, physios and whoever else was hanging around their bench ran on to the pitch, their arms stretched out in rapture. Southgate, who was to have taken the seventh penalty if it had gone that far, was the first to console Batty, but he didn't seem to want consoling. He would deal with it on his own. Curiously, Hoddle didn't approach Batty. Campbell hobbled towards the England fans in a daze. Owen dropped his head and McManaman put an arm around him as if he was his kid brother. Shearer stood with his arms behind his back. Neville, who would have taken the sixth penalty, was ashen-faced. Ince started to weep and Hoddle looked like he had just witnessed a terrible motorway pile-up. His wife and two youngest children were looking down at the carnage from the main stand.

'We wish you a very good evening,' said an electronic scoreboard at one end of the ground. Hoddle walked to the touchline and told ITV's Gary Newbon: 'I don't know if it's destiny or what. Everything just went against us. It's not a night for excuses, it's a night to be proud for England.'

Thousands of Argentinians remained in the stadium. A few English fans stayed as well, staring into the concrete beneath their seats. It was going to be a long, bleak journey home. Hoddle said later that the England dressing room was silent, that Alan Shearer sat naked on the floor for fifteen minutes. Beckham was there but in a different world. Batty was one of the first into the shower. A FIFA official came in and asked Hoddle to report to the mixed zone for his interview. When he got there, Passarella was still holding court. Hoddle and Davies returned to the dressing room. The FIFA official came in again and asked them to go back. Passarella had finished. But in his place five Argentinians were answering questions under the supervision of the Tom Selleck lookalike. Davies flipped. 'You have insulted our national coach,' he told him. 'Do you understand that? You have insulted our national coach.'

When Hoddle was finally allowed on to the stage, he stopped short of crushing Beckham. 'I'm not here to blame an individual. He will be back in four years' time for another World Cup and he simply has to learn that you cannot do that sort of thing.'

Beckham was first on to the bus. He walked through the mixed zone with his head down, a cap hiding his eyes. Batty said: 'I volunteered and felt good. I had this vision of putting us through.' As the England bus left, the Argentinian players jeered from the comfort of their own coach.

Almost an hour after the end of the game, I walked back into the stadium. A huge Union Jack with 'Everton' on it was the only England flag left behind the goal. Its owner was sitting beside it. Two Argentinians walked up, stopped, shook his hand and helped him fold the flag into a small back-pack.

It was well past midnight. The trams had stopped for the night. I wandered back towards the centre of town, and when a white van stopped at some traffic lights I asked for a lift. Terry Butcher and Radio Five commentator Alan Green were inside. Butcher had experienced it all before in Turin. There had been some trouble in the square, but I found my way to Le Grillon, where Jean-Jacques let me in a side entrance and filled me with wine and Camembert. There was no sign of Chris.

'That was the final,' said Jean-Jacques. 'There will not be a better match.' But it wasn't the final. It was not even the quarter-final. It was the second round. Jean-Jacques opened another bottle.

I saw Chris sitting on a bench behind a line of policemen. He had forgotten where the restaurant was, forgotten where our hotel was, forgotten my mobile phone number. It was 3 am and beginning to rain when we reached the hotel. I was going to get up two hours later, drive to Lyon, catch a plane to Nantes, and find a taxi to La Baule, where Hoddle was to deliver his valedictory address. I told Chris we would meet in Paris in the evening.

At Nantes airport, the *Independent*'s Glenn Moore gave me a lift. His car radio was able to pick up Radio Five's phone-in. There was only one topic. Most callers reflected what had been said in the morning papers – that the English performance was heroic, brave, heart-stopping. Even Jeff Powell had been impressed: 'To come from behind against an Argentine team feared even by Brazil and which had not previously surrendered a goal in these finals was an epic achievement. To Glenn Hoddle, in his unwavering convictions, the credit.' *L'Equipe* ran a picture of Owen with the headline: 'A star is born.' *Le Monde* called Owen the 'Leonardo diCaprio of the tournament'. *AS*, a Spanish daily, said: 'It's not the World Cup of Ronaldo, nor Del Piero, nor Ortega. It is Owen's. But the throne is left without a young king.'

But some callers took no comfort in the notion of yet another gallant England defeat. A man from Gloucester wanted to know why, if Hoddle was such a master of detail – 'there will be no team better prepared in the world' were Hoddle's words – England were so glaringly ill-equipped to take penalties. Another caller said England would never have been playing Argentina if Hoddle had realised Owen's potential earlier. Moore said he was looking forward to asking Hoddle why a man who had never taken a penalty was allowed to take one in such momentous circumstances. And if Hoddle was going to come up with the line that practice is not the key to a successful penalty he was going to ask him why golfers practise short putts over and over again.

There was no police barricade outside the England headquarters in La Baule, no fans waiting for autographs, no French schoolchildren given a lesson off to greet the team. Hoddle seemed to find it good to talk. It was the longest Hoddle press conference I had attended in almost twelve months. He was received sympathetically, and he spoke with feeling.

'The saddest thing is that we will never know that we could have achieved. I really thought we were going from strength to strength and that, who knows, we might have gone on and won the whole thing. But I'm big enough to bounce back. I got a very encouraging phone call from the Prime Minister, which was nice. Even so I don't feel very good. It's a cruel game sometimes. I have an empty feeling inside me.'

He wouldn't admit to mistakes. Not one. He said he was right to 'nurse' Owen into the competition, right to take off Anderton and bring on Batty. He was even right to let Ince and Batty take penalties. And when Moore asked him about practice making perfect on the golf course, he said: 'A golfer can practise a thousand putts on the putting green, but he can then go out on the last day of a tournament when there's 30,000 there and miss it. If it was all down to practice, then it would be a simple scenario. It isn't like that.'

Again and again, he was asked if he had any regrets, if he would have done anything different. He mumbled something about the importance of concentration, and that was about it. He finished by pleading for clemency on Beckham's behalf. The Bible Society followed suit, and by the middle of the afternoon, yet another England player had released a public statement of contrition. 'This is without doubt the worst moment of my career,' it read. 'I will always regret my actions during last night's game. I have apologised to the England players and management and I want every England supporter to know how deeply sorry I am. I only hope that I will have the opportunity in the future to be part of a successful England team in the European Championships and World Cup.'

It fell on deaf eyes at the *Daily Telegraph*, where the editor, Charles Moore, who hates football, watched the game in his office high up in Canary Wharf. Afterwards, he addressed the subject in a leader. 'Beckham's silly little kick at his Argentinian opponent was what's wrong with the national character. This Gaultier-saronged, Posh Spiced, Cooled Britannia, look-at-me, what-a-lad, loadsamoney, sex-and-shopping, fame-schooled, daytime-TV, over-coiffed twerp did not, of course, mean any harm. Like almost everything stupid that makes English life less fun than it should and could be. It was only "messing about". As always, other people have to clear up the mess.'

But Moore was inspired by the efforts of the remaining ten men. 'England showed how moving the idea of a team can be. Why work together like that? Why put your heart so absolutely into that particular 120 minutes of your life? There's money in it, of course, and fame too. But that's not the reason. Love of country has a lot to do with it; the great psychological, moral, religious perception that it is in giving that we receive has even more.'

British Airways laid on Concorde to bring England home. Hoddle and Beckham stood in the middle of the plane and had their first proper talk. Owen was invited into the cockpit for landing. A flag of St George stuck out of the window as it taxied to a halt at Heathrow.

'We tried,' Hoddle said as he stepped onto the tarmac.

Chapter 14

Writing on the Wall

Chris was in Paris, I was in La Baule, the car was in Lyon. Everything suddenly seemed such an effort. Little went right. I lost my credit card, left a notebook on a bus and missed the train to Lyon airport, where the car was parked in the expensive short-stay car park, looking dirty, whereas a few days earlier it was pleasingly weathered. The snazzy CD player had packed up. The weather was so much colder. In a snack-bar near the airport a television was showing the best goals of the tournament, and Michael Owen's was right up there, and so was Paul Scholes's. Across the road, a Mastercard ad showed a goalkeeper saving a penalty with the caption: 'Some Saves You Hold On To Forever'. It was time to leave.

I could pick up Radio Five in northern France. Tim Henman was doing his best at Wimbledon against Pete Sampras. The semi-final. Another glorious defeat. France were up against Italy for a place in the last four – but Calais couldn't have cared less. There were five people watching in what was meant to be one of the busiest bars in town. A group of students playing cards in the corner walked out just before the penalties. Pulling oneself together at Dover wasn't made easy by the huge number of flags still hanging from pubs and shops, and in London the cab-drivers seemed reluctant to remove St George from their aerials.

Argentina lost to Holland, which helped; Croatia crushed Germany, which helped some more. People were still talking about it and others were talked out. An old man in my street said he found the atmosphere strangely similar to the one that gripped the country after Diana's death. Which is absurd. But there had been real angst.

A friend who was a recovering alcoholic said he had to leave his wife and children in the house during extra time while he wandered up and down the street. He said he had never been closer to returning to the bottle. A former colleague telephoned to say that because he had missed the first fifteen minutes after getting back late from work he had convinced himself that he should not watch at all in case it brought England bad luck. They were 2–1 up at the time. He sat reading a novel and didn't turn the television back on until just before the penalties. He wanted to turn it off again but couldn't, and now he blames himself for England's defeat. Mark and Pete almost came to blows outside the Millbridge pub in Plymouth over Hoddle's tactics. Pete thought he got it right, that England were simply unlucky; Mark said that sort of attitude was typical of what was wrong with the country and it was about time someone took responsibility when things go wrong.

France won it. And deservedly so. Zidane atoned for himself by scoring twice, and Petit added a third. Aimé Jacquet, the coach, who had been vilified by sections of the French press right up to the final, was made a member of the Légion d'Honneur. Platini deliberately wore his suit over the French team strip in an acknowledgement that the majority of tickets had ended up in the hands of corporate companies rather than real fans. The stadium appeared strangely muted, but outside there was no holding back. One estimate put the number of people celebrating in the Champs-Elysées at more than two million in what was France's biggest street party since liberation from the Nazis at the end of the Second World War. France's cult of self-flagellation was fleetingly forgotten as Algerian immigrants joined in the singing of the Marseillaise and waved Tricolour flags.

Jacquet's bitterness towards the media remained intact. 'I will never forgive them, never,' he said. 'One day they will pay for what they have done to me and my family.' And Zidane, asked what it all meant to him, answered: 'It means everything and nothing, at the same time.'

The final was overshadowed by the Ronaldo business. Forty-five minutes before kick-off he wasn't on the team-sheet, but no one quite knew why. Edmundo was down to play in his place. Ronaldo was reported to have suffered a convulsive fit in the early hours of Sunday morning and was rushed to hospital. After a series of tests he was released. Nothing was wrong with him. His room-mate Roberto Carlos said the twenty-one-year-old was 'stressed out', and that 'the boy needs a break'. There were rumours that his girlfriend had strayed. Zagallo gave a team-talk at 4 pm, stressing that Brazil had won the World Cup in 1962 without Pele, and there was no reason they couldn't win it this time without Ronaldo. Ronaldo arrived at the stadium in a FIFA car long after his team-mates and pleaded with Zagallo. Ricardo Teixeira, President of the Brazilian Football Confederation, visited the dressing room, and frantic discussions meant the team did not go out for their warm-up. Teixeira denies that his intervention had anything to do with a recently signed ten-year deal between the Confederation and Nike worth £250 million. Ronaldo was reinstated, and was kept on the pitch for the full ninety minutes, but he never got started. Zagallo said afterwards: 'Ronaldo was not fit to play.'

The paper that Hoddle banned his players from reading during the tournament serialised his World Cup memoirs less than a month later. At least five papers had taken part in an auction to acquire the UK rights, but it was the *Sun* that won it. The figure of £250,000 was bandied about.

Sympathy for Hoddle vanished overnight. It was like watching a classroom spat turn into a playground brawl. Hoddle's supporters became his new doubters, his new doubters became his new enemies, and his enemies were turned into willing executioners. Shortly before the World Cup, the *Sun*'s Brian Woolnough wrote of Hoddle: 'He is a caring, deep-thinking man with strong religious beliefs. I have always had the utmost respect for Hoddle, first as a player, then as a manager and friend.' After publication of Hoddle's book, Woolnough concluded: 'You cannot feel sorry for him. His fierce self-belief has engulfed him. He never admits he is wrong and there is no humility about the man. Glenn Hoddle does not deserve a new contract.'

Much was made of Hoddle's account of how Gascoigne reacted to his axing, his determination never to recall Chris Sutton, his admiration for Eileen Drewery, his insistence that it was right to play Sheringham ahead of Owen in the first two games. But we knew much of this already. The mistake was to have written a book at all while the embers of defeat were still smouldering, particularly one that reeked of self-justification. It wasn't so much asking for trouble as crying out for universal damnation. One headline simply said: 'False Profit'.

The fact that David Davies was Hoddle's co-author meant you could take a pop at both of them in one throw – at last. The hacks had resented Hoddle's imperviousness and were tired of Davies's acquiescence. They hated the way the two of them would conceal information. They were fed up with Hoddle's obstinacy, and the pious disdain in which he held the press. This was the chance they had been waiting for, and, as Hoddle himself would put it, you have to take your chances at this level. A lot of the criticism centred on the betrayal of confidences – 'Players need to know that the next time we go to Glenn Hoddle with a problem or for just a chat that it won't end up in a book,' said Paul Ince – but there is a case to be heard on behalf of the defendant, however flimsy. It is that Hoddle actually went out of his way to protect Gascoigne and that it was Gascoigne who squealed first.

'Did Gascoigne have a tantrum?' he was asked in La Manga.

'Not necessarily,' he replied. Not necessarily until Gascoigne chooses to go public about it, at which point I will tell my side of the story because it would be dishonest not to do so.

Graham Kelly, the FA's chief executive, had been approached about the book in the summer of 97. He had no objections. He agreed with Davies that it would be helpful to have it written in-house rather than ghosted by a working journalist whose colleagues would not take kindly to one of their number being given preferential treatment. And it wouldn't be the first time that an England manager had written such a book while still in the job. Bobby Robson was the incumbent coach when his account of the 1986 finals went to press. But Kelly should have asked to see it. He might at least have suggested cutting down on the flagrant abuse of the exclamation mark.

Far more worrying than the 'Drunk Gazza Trashed My Room' headline was Hoddle's insistence that his handling of Beckham and Owen was without fault. 'Events proved me right,' he wrote. What events? England going out in the second round because they failed to win their group? Far more disturbing than his lack of clemency for Sutton were his reasons for not making his players practise penalties morning, day and night. 'You can never recreate on the training ground the circumstances of a real shoot-out . . . Frankly, you've either got it, or you haven't.' Far more perplexing than his trust in Eileen Drewery was his belief that Ince would somehow leave his fear and loathing of the penalty kick in the semicircle before setting off towards the dreaded white spot.

And then Adams went in. Hard. Kelly would have done anything to have toned this one down, given a chance. 'I have to be honest and say that a lot of what Glenn was doing and saying did not particularly impress me,' Adams said in *his* book.

Anything in particular? Everything in general. 'I felt that we were too regimented, treated like kids in fact and expected to do too much in training.' The treatment of Beckham? Adams recalled that when Beckham was struggling to perfect a free-kick routine in training, Hoddle, 'to the disquiet of the boys, said: "Obviously you're not good enough to do that skill."' Relations with the outside world? 'I reminded Glenn at one point that he had told us to be honest, but he replied that there were times when you had to withhold the whole truth and press conferences could be one of these times.' Croatia would have been harder to beat than Argentina? 'Most of us felt the Croats weren't as strong right through the team as the Argentinians.'

And on it went. Adams said Hoddle was wrong to encourage Gascoigne to drink in La Manga; wrong to make Shearer captain; wrong to play a three-man defence. And whereas Hoddle said, 'Of course we put in a certain amount of practice' of penalties, Adams wrote: 'We had not practised penalties in training, except for Alan Shearer, who always likes to . . . I believe that they should have been rehearsed, especially after our Euro 96 experience, but nobody had suggested it at the end of training the previous day.'

It was open season. Merson and Wright sided with Hoddle, Southgate and Seaman with Adams. The players were calling Hoddle Chocolate because he seemed to think he was good enough to eat. And England were about to play Sweden in the first of their qualifying games for Euro 2000. Davies had to spin into action. He brought Hoddle and Adams together for a press conference and up went the same limp excuse about how the serialisation had sensationalised the Adams book just as it had the Hoddle one. Hoddle said all was well in the England camp.

Sweden won 2–1. Ince blew a fuse and was sent off, tugging the hairband of Henrik Larsson, flicking a V-sign at John Gorman and seeming to mouth 'fucking bald wanker' at the referee as he left the pitch. It didn't help that Christian Gross was sacked as Spurs manager just before kick-off and that Hoddle was stalling on signing an extension to his contract, but there was no need to stomp off as soon as the subject came up. Shearer said: 'All the crap that went on before the game did not help . . . the stuff about the books, the things said, the criticism, everything but football, had an effect.' Adams hit back at Shearer, with whom he had never been close. 'No book, article or whatever affects the way I do my job.'

Then the Neville brothers criticised Hoddle for the way he handled the ditching of players not going to France and said it was 'nonsense' to describe Beckham as not being focused at the start of the tournament. Gary Neville wrote in his World Cup diary: 'Penalties had never been mentioned. The regular takers like Alan, Michael and Teddy might practise, but the rest of us never bother. They're not a part of our training sessions and Glenn Hoddle has never told us to practise them in our own time.'

Hoddle said he would talk to me after the World Cup, but when his book was greeted as if he had written *Lolita* and *The Satanic Verses* rolled into one he decided not to discuss anything with anyone. I could fax him through some questions if I wanted. Then, on the day he went before the FA's international committee to present his World Cup report and discuss his contract, the telephone rang. It was Glenn Hoddle.

'How did the meeting go?' I asked.

'It went fine. It's so ridiculous the way it's been blown out of all proportion. It was a routine get-together. It was no big deal.'

Had he read Woolly's piece in the *Sun* that morning, the one saying that 'arrogance is his biggest problem'?

'No,' said Hoddle. 'I don't read that rubbish.' Even though it was the same 'rubbish' that had serialised his diary for a six-figure sum only a few weeks earlier.

So who really caught his eye at the World Cup? Was there one player he wished more than any other had been English?

'Not really. Zidane showed some flashes, but the days of individuals winning the tournament have gone. There will never be a situation like there was with Pele and Maradona. You can build a team up around an individual but they won't win it for you.'

Is that a good thing or a bad thing?

'It's a shame but it's the way of the world. Just look at tennis – the bigger the serve the better your chances. There's less finesse than ever before. You can't do anything about it. Everything in life is faster. We want our faxes to work faster, we want to get through on the telephone faster.' I got the impression he wanted to get through this conversation fairly quickly too.

A lack of finesse. Michael Owen looked well-stocked in the finesse department when he took that ball on the run with the outside of his foot before single-handedly destroying the Argentinian defence. He might have done the same to Romania if he'd had longer on the pitch. I wanted Hoddle to say as much, because he still has the potential to be the coach he thinks he is. I'm not convinced by those who say he shouldn't be given another chance. Chelsea's late Matthew Harding was right when he said of Hoddle: 'He isn't an easy man to get to know. I believe I know him as well as anyone who doesn't know him, if that makes sense.' It's certainly frustrating, but that shouldn't disqualify him from the job. Hoddle had a lot going on off the pitch while in charge of England, and he handled it. Brian Clough said Hoddle was never trusted as a player but he also said it took moral courage to play the way he did. Even Adams said that Hoddle is an 'excellent technical coach' with a 'human, caring' side to his character. He made mistakes in France, but the way he organised England's ten men in St-Etienne was extraordinary. Everyone knew what they were doing. And they *were* fit. And they *were* focused, and they did come agonisingly close to pulling off one of the bravest victories of all time. And how do we know that Roy Hodgson would make a better England manager than Glenn Hoddle? He might be less infuriating, but that's another matter.

'Michael did fantastically well,' Hoddle conceded, 'but he's still very inexperienced at this level.'

Any regrets? 'We lost concentration in the Romania game, but in terms of would I do things differently the answer is that our preparation was spot-on. I think everyone would agree with that, and even the players admit that they were fitter than ever before.'

Davies had warned me that he would not discuss Paul Gascoigne in any shape or form. He had said it all in the book.

'Would you accept, in hindsight, that the book was a mistake?'

'I haven't got any problems with the contents of the book,' said Hoddle.

Perhaps it would have been better not to have written it at all. At least not so soon after the event. 'The timing of it was unfortunate,' he said. Which was an uncharacteristic statement, suggesting as it did that he might have made a small miscalculation, a tiny error of judgement. But then he said: 'It was the one area over which I had no control.'

So if the timing was unfortunate, when would he have chosen to have published it? After qualifying for Euro 2000 perhaps? After retiring as England coach?

'I would have preferred it to have come out in October.'

We were heading for penalties. The more I thought about it, the clearer it became that Ince's miss was the costly one, the one which England would always have struggled to recover, because Ince, for all his stoicism, his longing to succeed for his country, should never have been allowed to take the second penalty. Hoddle said Ince had volunteered and specifically requested to go second. So what? Seaman might have volunteered to have taken the first one. The Queen Mother might have wanted to play in goal. What mattered was who was going to score and who wasn't. And Southgate would have stood a better chance than either Ince or Batty. He missed in 96, but Pearce had missed in 1990 and look what he did six years later at Wembley. There was never a doubt in his mind.

'If Paul had not gone second, the pressure would have built up on him even more,' said Hoddle.

But were those five the best penalty-takers in England shirts still left on the pitch? Wouldn't Adams have relished the chance of kicking the ball through the back of the net with all the confidence of a man who had reclaimed his life from the slavery of drink?

'There are reasons why those five people took the penalties,' he said, and for a glorious second I thought he would put me out of my misery, stop my trying to work out how Ince ever found himself in that position, and why Batty's career as a penalty-taker had to start in St-Etienne against one of the strongest sides in the world.

'There are reasons,' Glenn Hoddle said, 'and those reasons will remain private.'